COMPREHENSIVE GLOSSARY FOR LIBRARY AND INFORMATION SCIENCE

CONCEPTS IN COMMUNICATION INFORMATICS & LIBRARIANSHIP (CICIL)

For a list of titles in this series please see pp. 133-136 at the end of the English-Hindi part of the book

About the Author

Dr. O.P. Gupta (*b.* 1947) is at present working in University Grants Commission. He holds Ph.D. (Hindi) Agra and degree in Master in Library Science from AMU, Aligarh. He began his career as college librarian (1971-73); served at central headquarters, CGWB, Ministry of Agriculture (1974-80) and since December 1980 has been serving the UGC in various capacities.

Dr. Gupta is a scholar, writer and is associated with a number of professional and non-professional bodies and committees. He has been working as member secretary to the panel on LIS education and to the Committee on Curriculum Development of LIS education of UGC. His publications include *Dictionary of Library and Information Science*, *Development of University Libraries in India after Independence*, and *Higher Education in India since Independence*; *UGC and its Approach*.

Concepts in Communication
Informatics & Librarianship-61

General Editor: S.P. Agrawal

Comprehensive Glossary for Library & Information Science

English-Hindi : Hindi-English

O.P. GUPTA
University Grants Commission
New Delhi

CONCEPT PUBLISHING COMPANY, NEW DELHI - 110059

ISBN 81-7022-528-0

First Published 1994

Published and Printed by
Ashok Kumar Mittal
Concept Publishing Company
A/15-16, Commercial Block, Mohan Garden
NEW DELHI 110059 (India)

GENERAL EDITOR'S INTRODUCTION

Almost all major disciplines, be they within Humanities, Social Sciences or Sciences, have built up their own concepts and vocabulary, and it would be difficult to comprehend fully and clearly the indepth ideas and perceptions of these disciplines without understanding the terminology accompanying them. Everyday we find some new technical terms on a particular subject coming up in the course of research and investigation and even the specialists of that particular discipline, who are not familiar with the new ones, will not be able to understand the new findings in their field of study. Moreover, one of the factors that determine the status of a subject is as to how much comprehensive it has developed its own vocabulary and to what extent it has absorbed the technical terms of other disciplines which are related to it.

Not very long ago, the claim of the Library and Information Science (LIS) as a scientific discipline was questioned. Even the scholars and book lovers, who made extensive use of libraries, were not inclined to recognise LIS as a full-fledged science. But within three decades or so, through the untiring efforts of LIS stalwarts and the intellectuals supporting the library cause of this country and abroad, LIS made a rapid and phenomenal progress. In recent times the communication technologies, such as computers and storage media, have revolutionised its entire system. Like any other discipline, LIS too has developed its own terminology which is quite impressive. Since the LIS professionals were expected not only to know the varied aspects of the book production and library services but also to understand new developments of other related non-library fields, it was natural that a large number of technical terms of other disciplines got included in LIS terminology. With this fruitful seeding of technical terms of non-library fields, LIS glossary became very rich.

We have had a good number of publications on LIS terminology brought out by professionals/specialists in developed countries as well as in our own country. Dr. S.R. Ranganathan made significant contribution in this direction, so much so that no librarian of standing even in the West can match in this regard.

The present glossary in CICIL series is basically Indian in its scope, and is, to some extent, different from other such works, inasmuch as that apart from defining the terms, a brief explanation has also been given for the benefit of users particularly Indian LIS professionals. Hindi equivalent of English terms and *vice-versa* has also been provided.

It is hoped that this LIS glossary in CICIL series will prove useful to LIS professionals and educators in their work, as also meet the requirements of the present-day LIS students.

S.P. Agrawal

PREFACE

Fast advancing technology has revolutionised Library and Information Science (LIS) education and services throughout the world. New subject areas such as information science, management techniques, communication studies and computer application are accepted as LIS eduction, as a result new dimensions of studies have emerged. The present-day LIS education in India is more or less on the principles framed by the West. The promoter or initiator of modern Indian LIS education and services, Dr. S.R. Ranganathan, first realised the gravity of the language need to strengthen LIS education. As an evidence his works include a glossary since then. In government efforts ISI has brought out publications for standard terms from time to time, on various LIS branches such as classification, cataloguing etc. The efforts are being continued by individuals in the form of dictionaries, encyclopaedias in LIS in the past four decades.

Now the LIS is an established branch of knowledge, which is in use to develop the scientific process of dissemination of information in the society. The increasing quantum and complexity of information organization has opened new areas for study. Modern education systems like distance education, media education have direct concern with library and information services.

Medium of instruction for LIS education in almost all the Indian institutions is English. But some of the institutions are reviewing the practice and promoting either link language that is Hindi or regional language to make the discipline more useful. The LIS is a professional discipline, therefore, to extend efficient service and also to know the subject in its totality, language has a very vital role.

In literature survey, it has been found that most of the terms are converted to simple Indian English and process of translation was taken up. The present effort is to group the selected terms as these are used by the various LIS specialists.

In recent developments in the discipline of Library and Information Science, a number of new concepts have emerged and are represented by new terms. In order to avoid ambiguity and confusion arising out of misinterpretation of terms, it is realised as necessary to standardise the terminology as far as possible. Thus the present effort is intended to aid in fixing more relevant meaning of the terms used in Library and Information Science.

In methodology, a comprehensive survey of published documents of all branches of LIS education was made to select the terms. These selected terms with brief explanation are arranged alphabetically in both the parts. To facilitate use with each term Hindi or English term follows as the case may be. The important contributions published in the area such as *Glossary of Library Science Technical Terms*, PN Gaur (1980), *Pushtakalaya Vigyan Kosh*, Prabhu Narayan Gaur (1961), *Glossary of Cataloguing Terms,* ISI (1959), *Pushtakalaya Vigyan Paribhasha Kosh* (1988), *Encyclopaedic Dictionary of Library and Information Science*, PP Parmar (1989), *Computers to-day*, Sanders (1983), *Dictionary of Audio Visual Terms,* BKSTS (1983), *MCC-mill Dictionary of Microcomputing*, Charles (1985), *Librarian's Glossary and Reference Book*, Harrod (1977), *Dictionary of Data Processing Terms,* Rodgers (1970) *Dictionary of Library and Information Science*, Sharma & Gupta (1986) were consulted. I am thankful to the contributors of the stated volumes.

The present work is unique in the sense that the terms selected also include the terms of new branches of discipline. The explanations are very brief and relevant only. The book is kept handy.

In case of borrowed explanation the name of the author or work is indicated in the end. In case of synonyms, 'see' and 'see also' entries are made. In spite of all, in continuing process of language advancement and subject expansion, there may be instances when users may have difference of opinion about the explanations recorded therein. Due to brevity it may also look like. Even then some efforts like brevity, expression and consistency will certainly leave a compact impression.

I am highly obliged to those whose contributions inspired

me to shape the present form of the work, also thankful to my professional friends, in particular Prof Naidu, consultant, INFLIBNET, whose constant encouragement enabled me to complete the work. I am thankful to my wife who has been always reminding me to work.

It gives me pleasure to place on record that the present shape of the work would not have been possible without the constant efforts of Concept Publishing Company.

I hope that the work will be useful for the scholars working for LIS education and services. Probably it will be a help to those who want to know LIS in national spirit.

O. P. GUPTA

A

Abbreviated Card: संक्षेपित पत्र *See* Abbreviated Catalogue Card.

Abbreviated Catalogue Card: संक्षेपित सूची-पत्र A catalogue card containing less information than the main card.

Abbreviated Catalogue Entry: संक्षेपित सूची प्रविष्टि Catalogue entry which contains selected information or an entry for selected information.

Abbreviated Name: संक्षेपित नाम The name in which initial letters or words are used. The method may be used for whole of the name or for a portion of it.

Abnormal: असामान्य Which is not commonly known.

Abnormal Size: असामान्य आकार A size of a document which is not common.

Abridged Edition: संक्षिप्त संस्करण A summarised edition of the original form or the work developed by taking essential features of the original work.

Abridgement: संक्षेपण Reduced form of a work, produced by removing details or by keeping main sense of the original work.

Absolute Address: संपूर्ण पता The complete or actual location in storage of data or the label assigned to a particular datablock.

Absolute Location: सम्पूर्ण स्थान *See* Fixed Location.

Absolute Size: सम्पूर्ण आकार *See* Perfect Size.

Absolute Value: सम्पूर्ण मूल्य More relevant to any subject.

Abstract: संक्षेप, सार The brief summary of the work. It is of two types: indicative and informative.

Abstract Bulletin: सार पत्रिका A bulletin containing abstract of currently published articles and works added to the library. It may appear after fixed intervals.

Abstract Journal: सार-पत्रिका See Abstracting Periodical.

Abstract Periodical: सार-पत्रिका *See* Abstracting Periodical.

Abstracting: सारकरण Method or art of preparing Abstract.

Abstracting Periodical: सारकरण पत्रिका A periodical on a stated subject and appearing in the current fascicles of periodicals, each entry being provided with an abstract of the article described by it. It may also include annotated entries of books currently published (Ranganathan).

Abstracting-Service: सारकरण-सेवा An organisation or individual who extends activity to provide abstracts.

Abstraction: पृथक्करण The process of separation for achieving grouping in classification.

Abstractor: सारकर्त्ता/संक्षेपकार A person who develops summary of the work or contribution.

Academic: शैक्षणिक Associated with education.

Academic Library: शैक्षणिक पुस्तकालय The library established by an educational institution such as university, college, school, etc., falls in this category. The kind of academic library may be ascertained on the nature of the institution to which it is attached.

Academy : अकादमी An organisation which works for the advancement of various branches of knowledge.

Academy Publication : अकादमी प्रकाशन The work/publication brought out by the Academy.

Access: प्रवेश/पहुँच Process for approaching to information or method by which a library document is searched. In computer it is a process of retrieving or locating information.

Access Point : पहुँच केन्द्र Identified unique heading or a term, name, phase, word or group of words under which a user of the library searches library collection to find out his or her information.

Access Time: पहुँच समय The time taken between transfer and selection of data/information from computer programmed data block.

Access Tool : पहुँच उपकरण A tool, generally a hard copy which consists access points to locate stored information.

Accession: अवाप्ति *See* Accession Number

Accession Arrangement : अवाप्ति संख्याक्रम An arrangement of books in a library in their order of receipt or in their collection order number.

Accession Book : अवाप्ति पुस्तक *See* Accession Register.

Accession Date : अवाप्ति तिथि The date on which a publication is listed in Library Accession Register.

Accession Department : अवाप्ति विभाग A department where acquisions of library are entered in Accession Register.

Accession Number: अवाप्ति संख्या The serial number given to the collections of a library as per the record register/Accession Register.

It is marked on every collection on the back of the title page and on secret page maintained by the library and also on stationery used on document to make it Institutional property.

Accession Number Section : अवाप्ति संख्या अनुभाग The section of an entry giving the accession number of its document. The place of which is decided on the basis of cataloguing code followed.

Accessioning : अवाप्तिकरण An act of doing accession which includes the verification of document and posting of information in record register and accession number on the document.

Accession Order : अवाप्ति क्रम The arrangement of documents on shelves in their acquision order or in order to the accession number assigned to these. *See also* Accession Arrangement.

Accession Record: अवाप्ति अभिलेख The progressive collection record of a library in which documents are entered as they are received. The information details are worked out by the monitoring authority of the library. It contains information about author, title, publication year, publisher, cost, source of collection etc. Some time it has a column to keep call number also. It may be either in book form or in card form. Popularly known as 'Accession Register'.

Accession Register: अवाप्ति पंजी This register is a basic and main record of any library. For details *See* Accession Record.

Accession Stamp: अवाप्ति मुहर/मुद्रा A stamp used to fix up accession number on a library document.

Accession List: अवाप्ति सूची A list of accession numbers generally prepared to perform internal jobs like verification.

Accounting: लेखाकरण A systematic record of income and expenditure.

Acronym: परिवर्णी शब्द A word framed from the initial letter or letters of a group of words such as ILA is framed from its name Indian Library Association. The formed term is always expressed in capital letters.

Acquisition: अधिग्रहण Acquisition is the continuous process for collection building of library records. It may be through purchase, gift, exchange etc.

Acquisition Department: अधिग्रहण विभाग The department of the library which has concern with identification, selection and collection of records/ books.

Acquisition Number: अधिग्रहण संख्या A serial number under which entry is made for the acquired document. *See also* Accession Number/Stock Number.

Acquisition Officer: अधिग्रहण अधिकारी An officer who has responsibility of collection building.

Acquisition Record: अधिग्रहण अभिलेख Such records are generally maintained in the form of Accession Register and acquisition files. These may have variety such as selection files, files for complete orders, files for outstanding orders and so on. The libraries may have separate accession register for purchased documents and documents received through various other sources such as gift, exchange etc.

Acquisition Work: अधिग्रहण कार्य The work relating to selection, approval, ordering and collection of the document.

Adaptation: **रूपान्तर** A version of a work, re-written for a particular purpose, provided it can not be deemed an independent work on the basis of the quality of its thought and expression. The adaptation may be either in the original language or in any other language.

Added Copies: **अतिरिक्त प्रतियाँ** Other copies of the titles which are already available in a library collection. It may be called duplicate or multiple copy.

Added Edition: **अतिरिक्त संस्करण** A different edition from the one already available.

Added Entry: **अतिरिक्त प्रविष्टि** An entry drived from the main entry to widen search approach through author, title, series etc. or duplicate entry with additional heading information. It is a supplementary entry which is generated from the main entry to help user in search.

Added Title Entry: **अतिरिक्त शीर्षक प्रविष्टि** An added title entry is made under the title only when the title is very prominent. In this type of entry title is used at tope line as search point.

Addenda : **परिशिष्ट** It is usually placed in the end to complete the text. It may also be called appendix.

Additional Librarian: **अतिरिक्त पुस्तकाध्यक्ष** A librarian who works directly to help the chief librarian.

Additional Copy: **अतिरिक्त प्रति** *See* Added Copies.

Additions: **संकलन** *See* Acquisitions.

Additions List: **अधिग्रहण सूची** A list of recently received library documents such as books, journals, reports etc. It may be in classified or alphabetical order.

Address: **पता** In computer it is a character or group of characters which identifies the data to communicate. It is a memory location.

Address Number: **पता संख्या** It is a location number assigned in computer programme to aid its memory.

Address Path: **पता रास्ता** The selection path for memory and input/output data.

Address Register: **पता पंजी** In computer it is a CPU register.

Add Time: **जोड़ समय** The time taken in adding data to the memory.

Add to Note: **सहयोगी टिप्पणी** Such notes are provided in classification schemes to direct to further divide a given class on the pattern of another class available in classification schedule. As DDC has used divide like in many places.

Adjustable Classification: समायोज्य वर्गीकरण Scheme of classification designed by James Duff Brown for smaller English libraries, with a notation of letters and numbers allowing for later insertions (Ranganathan).

Adjustable Shelving: समायोज्य व्यवस्थापन Shelves which can be raised or lowered by adjusting nuts and bolts to keep the books of various sizes.

Ad hoc Committee: तदर्थ समिति Committee constituted to suggest measures to deal with a sudden situation or to deal in detail with some specific assignment. Such committee works under fix terms of reference provided to it. Some times it is constituted from the main committee.

Administrative Office: प्रशासनिक कार्यालय The office which works to implement the policies to achieve the set goals of service.

Admission Card: प्रवेश पत्र It is a card or letter to use library or to get library membership. It is a introductory card/letter issued by competent authority after observing security. The card can be used to borrow fix number of library documents for a given period.

Admission Record: प्रवेश अभिलेख *See* Registration Record.

Admission Slip: प्रवेश पर्ची *See* Admission Card.

Adolescent Library: प्रौढ़ पुस्तकालय The library which works as bridge between the children and the adults.

Adult Education: प्रौढ़ शिक्षा Education imparted to the old age people.

Advance Copy: अग्रिम प्रति Copy which is received or moved before the announced date.

Advance Payment: अग्रिम भुगतान Payment which is given before receiving the item. The libraries are making such payment to collect periodicals and some times government publications.

Advertisement File: विज्ञापन फाइल The advertisements of various agencies on a particular subject are kept and the agencies are arranged alphabetically to facilitate.

Advisory Board: सलाह मण्डल Board of experts and prominent scholars to recommend or advice new methods to achieve efficiency in library services.

Advisory Services: सलाह सेवा *See* Reader's Service.

Advisory Committee: सलाह समिति The committee which is constituted to frame policies or to suggest guidelines to achieve efficiency in services. The librarian of the institution works as member secretary to it. Such committee is also appointed by Government to study the service needs and also to know status of library services during a particular period.

Aerial Photograph: हवाई चित्र The photograph which is taken from the space.

Affiliated College: सम्बद्ध विद्यालय (कालेज) The college which follow the guidelines framed by the university to run the courses. Though it functions with its own management.

Affiliating University: सम्बद्ध विश्वविद्यालय University which runs its course programmes through its various affiliated institutions.

Agency: प्रतिनिधि संख्या It may be a individual or a firm.

Agenda : कार्य सूची A plan outline of items to be discussed for framing guidelines on the given subject.

Agent: प्रतिनिधि A individual or a firm which is used to arrange library collections and other equipment.

Aggregate: समूह Collection of entities without any special arrangement of them (Ranganathan).

Agricultural Library: कृषि पुस्तकालय Agricultural library is maintained to disseminate information to agriculture sector and R & D units. In this category of library Indian Council of Agricultural Research Library and libraries of other such allied institutions can be kept.

Agricultural Research Information Centre (ARIC): एग्रीकल्चर रिसर्च इनफारमेशन सेन्टर अथवा **कृषि शोध सूचना केन्द्र** The centre is established to collect information of agricultural research of the country for creating data-base for onward transmission to data base known as AGRIS.

Agricultural Research Information System (AGRIS) : (एगरिस) कृषि शोध सूचना प्रणाली It is an acronym for agricultural research information system which is world-wide co-operative information system for current information in the field of agriculture, science and technology. It was set up in 1970-71 and using computer.

Aided Library: सहायता प्राप्त पुस्तकालय Aided library is a library which fulfils to the norms laid down to provide financial assistance from affiliating authority i.e. Government.

ALGOL: अलगोल An algebraic high level language.

Alien Region : असहयोगी प्रदेश Region in an arrangement consisting on either side of the umbral region, beyond the penumbral region concerned, consisting of classes of isolates or array, isolates not of interest to the reader at the moment (Ranganathan) or a subject totally irrelevant to the subject sought.

Alien-Penumbral-Umbral-penumbral-Alien (APUPA): अपूपा Arrangement complying with the pattern Alien, Penumbral, Umbral, Penumbral Alien, i.e. starting with the class or the isolate or the array isolate of primary interest to the reader at the moment or either side of it following successively the classes or the isolates, the array-isolates of progressively decreasing interest to him, until they fade out into classes or isolates or array-isolates not of interest to him. (Ranganathan) or it is arrangement pattern given by Dr. Ranganathan to sought relevant document in relation to less important documents. It recognises three types of documents such as non-relevant, partial relevant and totally relevant. The arrangement will put totally relevant documents in centre with partial relevant and non-relevant in both side from the totally relevant.

Alien Subject : असहयोगी विषय *See* Alien Region.

All Purpose Computer : बहु प्रयोजक कमप्यूटर *See* General Computer.

All Rights Reserved: सर्वाधिकार सुरक्षित It is a statement recorded on every document to reserve copyright or right of permitting-reproduction of the work. The right generally remains with author or publisher.

Allocate: निर्धारित करना Fixing of storage in a computer memory.

Allocation: आबण्टन Allocation of grants for meeting the anticipated demand or In classification providing the relevant place to a class among other classes.

Almanac: पंचाग An annual publication containing information about calendar/astronomy etc.

Alphabet: वर्णमाला Symbols with fixed value.

Alphabetic Coding: वर्णात्मक संहिता See Alphabetical Code.

Alphabetical: वर्णानुक्रमिक An arrangement achieved through alphabets.

Alphabetical Arrangement: वर्णानुक्रमिक विन्यास Arrangement of word entries in a catalogue by the alphabets.

Alphabetical Catalogue: वर्णानुक्रमिक सूची A catalogue in which all entries of author, title, subject, editor, translator are arranged in one alphabetical order.

Alphabetical-classed Catalogue: वर्णानुक्रमिक वर्ग सूची An alphabetical subject catalogue is in which subject entries are arranged in alphabetical order and under subject headings sub-divisions are also arranged alphabetically. In this arrangement all entries of the work are kept together.

Alphabetical Classed Filing System: वर्णानुक्रमिक वर्गीकृत फाइल प्रणाली A grouping of material into broad subject classes alphabetically arranged and subdivided by topics, arranged alphabetically within each class (Ranganathan).

Alphabetical Code: वर्णानुक्रमिक संहिता System of coding used in preparing information for input or storing in to a machine, so that information may be extracted in letters and words (Ranganathan).

Alphabetical Device: वर्णानुक्रमिक युक्ति The device using alphabets to achieve alphabetical sequence of names and names of items in a classification scheme.

Alphabetical Index: वर्णानुक्रमिका An index in which word/ names are arranged in one single alphabetical order.

Alphabetical Subject Catalogue: वर्णानुक्रमिक विषय सूची *See* Alphabetic Classed Catalogue.

Alphabetical Subject Index: वर्णानुक्रमिक विषय अनुक्रमाणिक *See* Alphabetical Classed Filing System. In this type subjects are put together in an alphabetical list.

Alphabetisation: वर्णानुक्रमण Arrangement of information in alphabetical order. It may have letters or words as the basis for arrangement.

Alternative Title: वैकल्पिक शीर्षक A sub-title introduced by 'or' or its equivalent, some times more than one language, or various types of type face are used to individualise.

Ambiguous Title: संदिग्ध शीर्षक A title which is not clear and creates confusion in understanding of work to which it belongs.

American Library Association: अमेरिकन लाइब्रेरी एसोसिऐशन (अमेरिकन पुस्तकालय संघ) It is the oldest and largest library association of the world founded in 1876. The office of the association is at Chicago. It is playing dynamic role in fostering library interests. It has thirteen divisions to carry responsibilities in more effective manner. In important activities it organises annual conferences and seminars on issues of professional concern.

Amplified Class: प्रवाधित वर्ग Class enriched by the addition of its pseudo entity (Ranganathan).

Ampere Classification: एमपेरे वर्गीकरण Scheme of class implied in the essay on philosophy of science (1834) of Ampere (Ranganathan).

Analog: एनालोग A physical system in which performance has the basis of mathematical problems.

Analog Computer: एनालोग कम्प्यूटर A computer in which operations are carried out in analog form, that is, using continuously variable physical quantities (DDPT) or a computer which deals with only electronic pulses and not with numbers to produce an analog signals.

Analysed Index: विश्लेषिक अनुक्रमणिका An alphabetical index under specific topics.

Analysed Title: विश्लेषित शीर्षक Title derived from kernal title by adding after each kirnel term. The symbol denoting the nature of its manifestation, or a title comprised of focal terms identified with fundamental category.

Analysis: विश्लेषण *See* Classification.

Analyst: विश्लेषक A person who analyses/defines subjects and develops solutions if desired.

Analytical Entry: विश्लेषिक प्रविष्टि Entry is supplementary to the main entry which is prepared for a part of the book/ periodical contributions/such other works for separate authorship. It includes the reference of the document which contains it.

Analytical Note: विश्लेषिक टिप्पण Part of the analytical entry which gives information about the document that contains the work entered.

Analytical Subject Entry: विश्लेषिक विषय प्रविष्टि *See* Subject Analytical.

Analytico Synthetic Classification: विश्लेषिक संश्लेषित वर्गीकरण Scheme of classification involving analysis of subject into its facets in the idea plane, transformation in the verbal plane, translation from the focal terms in the verbal plane to the focal numbers in the notational plane, and synthesis of the focal numbers into class numbers in the notational plane (Ranganathan).

Anglo-American Catalogue Code: एंग्लो अमेरिकन सूचीकरण संहिता A code containing cataloguing rules devised by the British Library Association and American Library Association and published in 1908.

Anglo-American Cataloguing Rule (AACR): एंग्लो-अमेरिकन सूचीकरण नियम These are the rules framed by British and American Library Associations to achieve uniformity and efficiency in cataloguing. First published in 1967 known as AACR-II and enlarged publication 1978 is recognised as AACR-II.

Annals: वृतान्त A periodical record of events which generally appears in chronological order.

Annotate: संक्षिप्त An art of preparing summary of the work.

Annotation: संक्षिप्तकरण A brief statement added at the end of an entry of a document, explaining/evaluating its contents.

Annual: वार्षिक A serial publication which is published yearly such as year books, annual reports and supplement annually brought out for multivolume books.

Annual Report: वार्षिक प्रतिवेदन A publication which gives report about the activities of the organisation for one year period. The information recorded in it is regarded as first hand authentic information.

Anonymous Book: अनामक पुस्तक The book which does not give an author statement.

Anonymous Work: अनामक रचना *See* Anonymous Book.

Anteriorising Common Isolate: पूर्वकारक सामान्य एकल Common isolate whose attachment to a class makes the resulting class have precedence, in arrangement, over the host class. These are directly applicable to host class number without a connecting symbol. These results the number vide which approach documents are placed before the subject concerned.

Anteriorising Common Isolate Idea: पूर्वकारक सामान्य एकल विचार *See* Anteriorising Common Isolate

Anteriorising Digit: पूर्वकारक अंक Digit, addition of which at the end of any class number makes the resulting class number precede the host class number.

Anterior Sub-division: पूर्व उप-विभाजन Sub-division of a subject to be placed interior or preliminary to a general treatment of subjects (Ranganathan).

Antonym: विलोम The opposite of synonym.

Aperture Card: छेद पत्र *See* Punched Card

Appendix: परिशिष्ट Subject matter supplementing the text of the document to which it attached.

Application File: आवेदन फाइल *See* Borrower's File.

Application Form: आवेदन-पत्र A printed/cyclostyled well designed form used to obtain library membership.

Apprentice in Library: पुस्तकालय प्रशिक्षु An effort to get acquainted with the practical operations of library before joining as professional in any institution.

Approach Material: अभिगम सामग्री The material which is used to understand the subject.

Approach Point: अभिगम केन्द्र *See* Access Point.

Approved Library School: स्वीकृत पुस्तकालय शिक्षण The agency imparting library education recognised within the frame work of the degree diploma awarded in the area.

Architecture: वास्तुकला The art of preparing the design to meet the requirement of library building and furniture.

Archives: अभिलेखागार Repository of public records with controlled conditions for the long time preservation.

Archivist: अभिलेखपाल A person who is responsible for the care of arehives.

Area Table: क्षेत्र तालिका A table of class numbers which are used to represent an geographical area.

Arrangement: विन्यास An enumeration of subjects according to the requirement.

Arrangement by Accession Number: अवाप्ति संख्या विन्यास When the collections of a library are arranged according to their acquision number.

Arrangement by a Combination of Sequences: सारिणी संयोग विन्यास When the arrangement is not unitary and a self arrangement has a combination of characteristics for arrangement.

Array: पंक्ति A set of classes arranged in the proper sequence and derived from a universe on the basis of a single characteristic at any step in the progress towards a complete assortment of the entities of their universe (Ranganathan) or a set of coordinate classes of its immediate universe. or set of related variables.

Array-Isolate Idea: पंक्ति एकल विचार Thought unit enumerated in a single array taken by itself (ISI).

Array Telescoping Point: पंक्ति अन्तर्वेधन केन्द्र Isolate in a telescoped array of which at least one succeeding isolate in the array is a sub-isolate (Ranganathan).

Arrester: कोष्टकान्तक Curve symbol inserted at the end of a subject device number of any other number which should be treated as if it were a single digit and should always be taken among with that symbol (Ranganathan).

Art-galleries: कला दीर्घा The galleries or the area of the library used for display or exhibit photographs, pictures and other forms of art.

Article: रचना Contribution of one or group of persons ready for publication.

Artificial Characteristic: कृत्रिम अभिलक्षण A quality which is possessed by a group of things in common, but is not a necessity of their being (Ranganathan).

Artificial Classification: क्रत्रिम वर्गीकरण The classification which is based on norms and characteristics used for fulfilling the goals.

Artificial Composite Book: कृत्रिम संयुक्त पुस्तक A composite book without a generic title, generally created by the binder. The books put together have their identity.

Artificial Digit: कृत्रिम अंक A digit used as substitute/assistance to notation adopted by a classification scheme.

Artificial Intelligence: कृत्रिम योग्यता The machnical process which looks like functioning of living beings.

Artificial Language: कृत्रिम भाषा A symbolic language used in any library classification. The language based on an arbitrary use and rules for its use are provided with it.

Ascending Order: आरोह क्रम

Aspect: **पहलू** *See* Facet

Assemblage: **समुच्चय** Formation of a new subject by bringing one subject into relation with another not capable of forming/sharpening the first subject device (Ranganathan).

Assemble: **एकत्रीकरण** A collection of subprogrammes which finally forms a complete programme

Assembly Language: **समुच्चय भाषा** A language based on machine code using memories or a language lies between high level language and machine language.

Assistant: **सहायक** Clerk who performs duties on direction of his supervisor.

Assistant Librarian: **सहायक पुस्तकाध्यक्ष** A library professional who assists the chief librarian and generally performs the specific duties assigned by the librarian.

Associated Book: **सहचारी पुस्तक** A book written about another book and also known as criticism.

Association of Government Librarians and Information Specialists (AGLIS): **गर्वन्मेंट पुस्तकालयाध्य एवम् सूचना विशेषज्ञों का संघ** AGLIS, formerly Government of India Librarians Associations (GILA) is dedicated professional association to the promotion of library and information science in India. It was founded in 1933 and present name was given in 1977. It has members throughout the country. To disseminate professional informations, it has one monthly and quarterly publications.

Association Library: **संघ पुस्तकालय** A library which is maintained by the association to up date its members in the areas of its working.

Association of Special Librarians and Information Bureaux (ASLIB): **एसलिब** This Association was founded in 1926 to develop co-ordination and systematic use of sources of knowledge and information in all public affairs, industry, commerce, art and sciences.

Assortment: **संयोजन** Process of the division of the entities of a universe into groups plus that of arranging the groups in a definite sequence. (Ranganathan).

Assortment Characteristic: **संयोजन अभिलक्षण** Characteristic preferred as the basis for assortment of a universe (Ranganathan).

Asterisk: **स्टरिक** A star like symbol which is used to indicate footnote.

Atlas: **मानचित्रावली** *Atlas* is a collection of maps and photographs. It may be a independent volume of maps or followed with description.

Attendant: **अनुचर** *See* Library Attendant.

Attendence: **उपस्थिति** Presence to work for assignment.

Attribute: **गुण, धर्म, लक्षण** Any property/quality of an entity.

Art-paper: **कला पत्र** Paper with smooth surface.

Audio: **श्रव्य** Concerned with sound recording and reproduction.

Audio Cassette: **श्रव्य कैसेट्** A compact cassette used for audio recording.

Audio Disk: **श्रव्य डिस्क** A disk used for audio recording such as gramophone record.

Audio System: **श्रव्य प्रणाली** Equipment which is used to record and reproduce voice.

Audio Tape: **श्रव्य टेप** Magnetic sound recording tape.

Audio-visual : **श्रव्य दृश्य** The document which is used on electronic device for getting the original voice or picture or both to hear or see as the case may be.

Audio-visual Aids: **श्रव्य दृश्य सहायक** Non-book material such as records, slides, gramophone, cassettes, tap etc. produced by educational technology.

Audio-visual Apparatus: **श्रव्य दृश्य यन्त्र** *See* Audio-visual Aids.

Audio-visual Centre: **श्रव्य दृश्य केन्द्र** A place where Audio-visual aids are used.

Audio-visual Communication: **श्रव्य दृश्य सम्प्रेक्षण** Communication through audio-visual media.

Audio-visual Education: **श्रव्य दृश्य शिक्षा** An education imparted to make use of audio-visual aids.

Audio-visual Equipment: **श्रव्य दृश्य साधन** Technical devices used to make use of electronic recording.

Audit: **लेखा परीक्षण** The service to check the correctness of expenditures and incomes of the organisation.

Auditing : **लेखा परीक्षण** Method of authentic examination of income and expenditure records of a body.

Auditor: **लेखा परीक्षक** An authority of checking the expenditures under the rules framed for the purpose.

Auditorium: **सभाभवन** A portion of the building used by the audience.

Authentic: **प्रामाणिक** Which is certified or works as the rules.

Authenticated Copy: **प्रामाणिक-प्रतिलिपि** A copy which has a certificate of responsibility.

Authenticity: **प्रामाणिकता** *See* Authentic.

Author: **लेखक** The person, persons or corporate body responsible for the works.

Author Analytical : **लेखक विश्लेषिक** Specific added entry referring from the name of the author and the title of his contribution forming a part of a document, to the host document and giving the place of occurrence of the contribution in the host document (ISI).

Author and Title Catalogue: लेखक तथा शीर्षक सूची Catalogue consisting author and title entries arranged in alphabetical order.

Author Bibliography : लेखक ग्रन्थ- सूची List of contributions of a author. It may also include the works published about him or his works.

Author Catalogue: लेखक सूची In this form of catalogue the added author entries of documents are arranged in alphabetical order.

Author Card: लेखक पत्र A catalogue card bearing an author entry. Top line gives the name of the author of the document

Author Copy: लेखक प्रति Complimentary copy of the book made available to author by the publisher.

Author Entry: लेखक प्रविष्टि The name of the author is traced on leading line to group all the contributions of a particular author.

Author Heading: लेखक शीर्षक *See* Author Entry

Author Index : लेखक अनुक्रमाणिका An index giving the names of authors.

Author Mark : लेखक चिन्ह Symbol used to represent author to identify the contributions of various authors in the same class. *See also* Book Number

Author Number : लेखक संख्या It may be letters/number assigned to each document to put in alphabetical order to all contributions of the same class or number used as translation to the name of the author.

Author Proof: लेखक संशोधन A proof passed on to author to make corrections.

Author Section: लेखक अनुभाग The section of an entry in cataloguing giving the name of an author of the document catalogued, or any substitute for the same.

Author Statement: लेखक विवरण Record, in a document, of the name of author and collaborator of its works, if any (ISI).

Authorised Edition: अधिकृत संस्करण An edition brought out with the consent of the author.

Authority Card: अधिकार पत्र A card issued for identification.

Auto-abstract: स्वतः संक्षेपण Select assemblage of key words from a document, by a machine method.

Autobiographer: आत्मकथा लेखक Writer of own life story.

Autograph: हस्ताक्षर The signature's given by the person himself.

Autobiography: आत्मकथा Authors contribution about his life and assignments.

Autographed Edition: हस्ताक्षरित संस्करण An edition of the document signed by the author.

Auto-Index: स्वतः अनुक्रमण Preparation of index with the help of mechanical device.

Autonomous Body : स्वायत्तशासी संस्था An institution which has its own board of management to take policy decision.

Automated Bibliography : स्वचालित ग्रन्थ सूची A bibliography stored in computer. Also known as database.

Automated circulation system: स्वचालित आदान-प्रदान प्रणाली A computer used system for arranging the circulation of library information collections.

Automated Dictionary: स्वचालित कोश A dictionary maintained as computer database.

Automated Glossary : स्वचालित शब्दकोश When a glossary is kept in computer for automatic use.

Automated Office: स्वाचालित कार्यालय An office which makes use of electronic devices and telecommunication technology for its functioning.

Automatic Programming : स्वचालित कार्यक्रम Technique in which computer is used to perform exercise in preparation of a program.

Automatic Record: स्वचालित अभिलेख Record of any phenomenon-natural or social-unmediated and uninterpreted by human intellect, for example instrument or photographic record, electronic record, or tele record (ISI).

Auxiliary Storage: उप-भण्डारण A storage that supplements the primary internal storage of a computer.

B

Bachelor in Library Science (B. Lib. Sc.): पुस्तकालय विज्ञान स्नातक Graduate level degree in library and information science education. *See also* Bachelor in Library and Information Science.

Bachelor in Library and Information Science (B.L.I. Sc.) : पुस्तकालय तथा सूचना विज्ञान स्नातक *See* Bachelor in Library Science.

Back: पश्च Binding edge of the book, in some cases on which author's name and title of the document is given.

Back cover: पश्च आवरण Cover portion, which remains in the back of the document and in some cases used to print information about author's qualification, present status and his other contributions.

Back Diskette: पश्च डिस्कैट *See* Floppy Disk.

Back File: पश्च फाइल Back numbers or issues of a periodical or original file.

Background Processing : पश्च संसाधन Program which works to prepare for goals.

Back Issue: पिछला अंक *See* Back File.

Back Margin: पश्च किनारा Left hand side margin of the document which is used to stich or bind the document.

Back Number: पश्च संख्या/अंक *See* Back File.

Back Order: पश्च खरीद आदेश An unexecuted order which is pending for future complians.

Back Page : पश्च पृष्ठ The other side of the page.

Back Space: पश्च स्थान When typing device is used to insert a digit in the back line and shifted to back space.

Back Title: पश्च शीर्षक The title printed on spine or back of the book.

Back up: पूर्तिकर In mechanical device computer to take precaution of current supply a multiple print device is used to preserve data. It is a alternative program. *See also* Back Up System.

Back up Copy : पूर्तिकर प्रति A copy obtained and preserved as back up.

Back up Program: पूर्तिकर कार्यक्रम A program prepared to keep backup.

Back up Services: पूर्तिकर सेवा Document/Readings in hard form are made available for the references selected.

Back up store: पूर्तिकर भंडार A store to hold the information records created by the computer.

Back-up System: पूर्तिकर प्रणाली A system which is a support system and that works parallel to the primary system to face the sudden down of electricity.

Backward Arrow: पश्च मुखी तीर It is a symbol used in colon classification scheme.

Bacon Classification : बेकन वर्गीकरण Scheme of classes implied in advancement of learning (1605) of Francis Bacon (Ranganathan).

Bad Copy : खराब प्रति A copy which is not written/printed well.

Balanced Collections: सन्तुलित संचय The collections, developed on some principles and have almost all important and relevant documents available in the field.

Banned Book: प्रतिवाधित पुस्तक The book which is not allowed for use. It may be due to its controversial thought contents or poor physical condition.

Base: आधार The total number of notation digits used in a scheme of classification.

Base Number: आधार संख्या A number to which another numbers in a classification scheme are added as per the guidelines available. Thus it is a initial number which can be further extended.

Base of a Notation: अंकन का आधार *See* Base.

BASIC: बेसिक (Beginners All-purpose Symbolic Instruction Code) Widely used a computer programming language developed by an American Jhon G. Kemeny in 1964 and popular for its simplicity.

Basic Book: मूल पुस्तक A book in which fundamentals of the subject are discussed or appeared first time.

Basic Class: मुख्य वर्ग Generic name for a main or a canonical class in a scheme of classification for the universe of knowledge (Ranganathan)

Basic Classification: मूल अथवा **आधारभूत वर्गीकरण** Version of a scheme of classification for the needs of macro thought and of libraries for general readers (Ranganathan).

Basic Entry: मूल प्रविष्टि *See* Main Entry.

Basic Fact: मूल पक्ष *See* Basic Class.

Basic Stock: मूल संग्रह Standard collection which is regarded essential to the objectives of the library.

Basic Subject: मूल विषय Main Subject.

Basis of Division: विभाजन का आधार The characteristics which are taken as variables of classification.

Batch : समूह A group of transactions carried out as a single unit.

Batch Number : समूह संख्या Identification number to the information having uniform characteristics.

Batch Processing : समूह संसाधान Techniques when data are batched for processing.

Bengal Library Association: बंगाल पुस्तकालय संघ It was formed to create library service awareness among the students and teachers.

Best Book : श्रेष्ठ पुस्तक A selected book on a subject.

Bibliographer: ग्रन्थ सूचीकार A person who has skill of preparing bibliographies.

Bibliographic Centre: ग्रन्थात्मक केन्द्र Place where bibliographic information is generated for dissemination among its users.

Bibliographic Classification: ग्रन्थात्मक वर्गीकरण Scheme of classification designed by Menry Evelyn Bliss and published for the first time in 1935. (Ranganathan) *See also* Close Classification

Bibliographic Database: ग्रन्थात्मक सूचना संकलन Computer information storage or collection of information/data on machine readable form.

Bibliographic Description: ग्रन्थात्मक विवरण Information record consists name of author, co-author, editor, translator, title, edition, publisher, series and publication date, etc.

Bibliographic Information : ग्रन्थात्मक सूचना *See* Bibliographic Data.

Bibliographic Record: ग्रन्थात्मक अभिलेख A block of information giving bibliographic data.

Bibliographic Record Format: ग्रन्थात्मक अभिलेख आकार Layout of bibliographic data on a mechanical device or computer.

Bibliographical Control: **ग्रन्थात्मक नियन्त्रण** Management of secondary publications.

Bibliographical Data: **ग्रन्थात्मक सूचना** *See* Bibliographical Description.

Bibliographical Description : **ग्रन्थात्मक विवरण** *See* Bibliographic Description.

Bibliographical Periodical : **ग्रन्थात्मक पत्रिका** Periodical giving a catalogue of books and articles currently published (Ranganathan).

Bibliographical Services: **ग्रन्थात्मक सेवा** The act of producing bibliographies.

Bibliographical Tool: **ग्रन्थात्मक उपकरण** The list of books, etc., used by the bibliographer.

Bibliography : **ग्रन्थ सूची** It is a useful systematic list of documents to keep user abreast with the development of the discipline for which it is prepared. It constitutes the basic material of the reference section of every library. It includes both macro and micro documents.

Bi-annual: **अर्धवार्षिक** A publication which is published twice in a year.

Bi-ennial : **द्वि-वार्षिक** A publication appears after every two years.

Bias: **पूर्वाग्रह** Relation between two groups/entities.

Bias Number Device: **अभिनत् संख्या युक्ति** Number device which is prejudice to some specific digits.

Bias Phase: **पूर्वाग्रह पक्ष** It is one kind of phase relation.

Bias Relation: **पूर्वाग्रह सम्बन्ध** Relation among phases, when one phase leave impact on another phase.

Bibliomania: **ग्रन्थ/सूचना संग्रह उच्च अभिलाषा** Strong desire for collection building in the area of interest.

Bibliometrics : **ग्रन्थात्मक सांख्यिकी** Statistical analysis of the literature/information of any subject.

Bill: **बिल** A draft of a proposed law to be placed in a legislative body or demand estimate against the supply of the items.

Bill Book: **देयक पुस्तक** A register in which bill record is kept or a book of blank performas of bill copies.

Bi-monthly: **द्वै-मासिक** A serial publication broughtout in alternate months or published after every two months.

Binary : **द्वि-अंगी** Computer used number system when zero (0) and one (1) are only used to represent entire base.

Binary Code: **द्वि-अंगी संहिता** A code that makes use of only two numbers, i.e., 0 (zero) and 1 (one).

Binary Digit: **द्वि-अंगी अंक** *See* Binary.

Binary Number: **द्वि-अंगी संख्या** *See* Binary and *see also* Bit.

Binary Number System: **द्वि-अंगी**

संख्या प्रणाली *See* Binary.

Binary Search : द्वि-अंगी खोज A search method in which only binary digits 0 and 1 are used.

Binder: जिल्द साज A person who binds documents or a folder which contains pamphlets and other loose papers.

Binder's Title: जिल्दसाज शीर्षक A short title tooled on the spine of a book.

Bindery: जिल्दसाजी केन्द्र A place where books are bound.

Binding : जिल्द The protection cover of the volume.

Binding Edge: जिल्द किनारा The edge of the document used to attach with binding.

Binding Record: जिल्द अभिलेख Record maintained to take up binding work which may be in the form of cards or register.

Binding slip: जिल्द पर्ची Slips used for keeping records/information of individual volume to be got bound.

Birth Date: जन्म तिथि The year of birth of author which is generally traced in catalogue entry to identify the author.

Biscoe Time Number: बिस्को समय संख्या A book number expressing a date in abbreviated form, from a scheme devised by WS Biscoe for arranging books on shelves chronologically rather than alphabetically (Ranganathan).

Biographer : जीवनी लेखक A person who writes biography.

Biographical Dictionary: जीवनी कोश Systematic collection of selected biographical information of prominent persons of various fields of knowledge. In each entry summarised information about their native place, education and life achievements and special field of work is included.

Biography: जीवनी A written account of important events of a person's life.

Bit: बिट A single unit of word in machine language or the basic element for representing data in computer, or a single binary digit.

Bi-weekly: अर्ध साप्ताहिक *See* Fortnightly or Semimonthly.

Black List: बदनाम Identification of the users who have not honoured the library rules.

Blank Cover: खाली आवरण The cover of the volume which has nothing written/printed on it.

Blank Page: खाली पृष्ठ A page in a document on which nothing has been written/printed.

Block: खण्ड A set of words/similar digits/characters/records etc. which can be used as one unit record in computer system. It may have one or more records.

Block Arrangement: खण्ड विन्यास Where the shelf is marked to keep particular type of documents or documents on a specific subject.

Block-in-Heading: खण्ड शीर्षक A word group in a heading taken alongwith its individualising element.

Blue Book : अधिकृत पुस्तक An important book and this term is also popularly used for Government publications.

Board of Trustees: संरक्षक मण्डल A group of persons responsible to frame guidelines to run an institution. It may also be known as Board of Directors.

Body of the Book: ग्रन्थ की विषय-वस्तु The main text of the book which includes illustrations, appendices and footnotes, etc.

Bold Face: सुस्पष्ट This face is usually used to give emphasis to words/headings in the text.

Bombay Library Association: बम्बई पुस्तकालय संघ The Association was founded on 9th Dec., 1944 to promote library services and librarianship within the municipal limits of the Bombay city.

Bond Paper: बाण्ड कागज A good quality paper used for preserving contributions for many years.

Book: पुस्तक A physically independent other than a periodical publication, completed or intended to be completed in a finite number of volumes or book means any volume, part of it, in library it may be printed form, manuscript, photocopied, microfilmed, audio-vedio cassettes, photograph, map, newspaper, periodical and tape etc. Thus it is a macro document which deals subject in great extension and less intention.

Book Bank: पुस्तक बैंक *See* Text Book Library.

Book Binder: जिल्द साज *See* Binder.

Book Budget: पुस्तक अनुदान The amount made available to increase library collections. *See also* Book Fund.

Book Card: पुस्तक पत्र A card keeping selected information about the book and kept either in book/book pocket to use it at charging time. It may be called charging card/charging slip. At time of loaning the document in a few cases the date of issue or due date is indicated on it.

Book Capacity: पुस्तक क्षमता *See* Shelf Capacity.

Book Catalogue: पुस्तक सूची A catalogue produced in book form and also known as printed catalogue.

Book Case: पुस्तक मंजूषा A case used to hold books for proper display.

Book Classification: पुस्तक वर्गीकरण *See* Classification

Book Clubs: पुस्तक क्लब Group of persons who are producing/distributing/using books.

Book Cover: पुस्तक आवरण Paper Cover used to protect the volume. *See also* Jacket.

Book Collection: पुस्तक संग्रह Collections of a library, it may have all types of print non-print documents.

Book Charging : पुस्तक निर्गम Method of loaning of library books.

Book Charging Slip: पुस्तक निर्गम पर्ची A slip which contains the details of the document loaned.

Book Deposit Centre: पुस्तक संग्रह केन्द्र A place where books are kept.

Book Display: पुस्तक प्रदर्शनी Exhibition of new arrivals to attract users.

Book Exchange : पुस्तक विनिमय *See* Inter Library Loan.

Book Exhibition: पुस्तक प्रदर्शनी Display of books to give more publicity among users. It can also be called Book Fair.

Book Fund: पुस्तक कोश An amount generated to purchase books in a library.

Book Issue: पुस्तक निर्गम *See* Book charging.

Book Jacket: पुस्तक आवरण The outer paper cover of the book which usually contains information about book and its author.

Book Label : पुस्तक लेबल A label used on the spine of the book.

Booklet: पुस्तिका A small book in paper cover.

Book Lifter: पुस्तक वाहक A person/machine that transports library documents from one place to another.

Book List: पुस्तक सूची A list of books complied for some specific use.

Book Maker: पुस्तक रचियता *See* Author.

Book Market: पुस्तक बाजार A market where book shops and publishing houses are in operation.

Book Mobile : पुस्तक वाहिका A large motor vehicle equipped with shelves and goes to the users to provide books.

Book Number: पुस्तक संख्या Ordinal number which fixes the position of a document in a library relative to the other documents having the same ultimate class (Ranganathan), or a set of numbers, digits, symbols or combination of all used to distinguish an individual document from every other documents of the same class to put it on the shelves in desired manner.

Book Order List: पुस्तक क्रयादेश सूची A list of selected titles of the books to be purchased by a library.

Book Piracy: रचना चोरी When a author of the work copies the thought contents of others with-out showing their reference.

Book Plate: पुस्तक-पर्ची A paper plate pasted on a book to indicate the name of the library to which the document belongs.

Book Pocket: पुस्तक जेब It is a paper pocket pasted inside the cover of the document to hold the book card.

Book Post: पुस्तक पोस्ट The term is used by the post office to claim ordinary parcel rates which are less for printed matter under Government policy.

Book Processing: पुस्तक संसाधन The classification, cataloguing of the document and also other services required to make the volume available for use.

Book Processing Centre: पुस्तक संसाधन केन्द्र A place where books are processed for use or for circulation.

Book Purchase: पुस्तक खरीद A method of acquiring books on cost payment.

Book Rack: पुस्तक रैक A shelf which is holding books.

Book Record: पुस्तक अभिलेख Record of the holdings of a library.

Book Repair: पुस्तक सुधार It includes various techniques which gives protection to the book.

Book Replacement: पुस्तक प्रतिस्थापन्न The substitute to a document. It is generally a photocopy of the whole document.

Book Report: समीक्षा A brief account written about a book.

Book Rest: पुस्तकाश्रय Device which is attached with the table/stand to hold the book.

Book Room: पुस्तक कक्ष A room keeping book collections.

Book Review: पुस्तक समीक्षा An evaluation of the work.

Books are for use: पुस्तक प्रयोग के लिए हैं It is first law of library science formulated by Dr. S.R. Ranganathan. This law advocates for use instate of preservation of library documents. The law demands that all situations like location, hours, staff, building etc. should satisfy the requirement of the law.

Books on Approval : अनुमोदन पुस्तक The books submitted by the book sellers/publishers for consideration/approval to market these for libraries.

Book Selection: पुस्तक चयन The process of identification of useful books.

Book Selection Card: पुस्तक चयन पत्र A card comprising data about a document which is to be taken in consideration of selection.

Book Sellers Catalogue: विक्रेता सूची A catalogue developed by the bookseller for his holdings or for the holding which he can arrange on demand.

Book Seller: पुस्तक विक्रेता The person who sells books.

Book Slip: पुस्तक पर्ची A slip containing bibliographic data of the document.

Book Stall: पुस्तक क्रय केन्द्र The place where the books are sold also known as bookshop.

Book Stamp: पुस्तक मुहर/मुद्रा Stamp used to fix up ownership. It may be of rubber or metal.

Book Stand: पुस्तक प्रदर्शक Stand for displaying books.

Book Stock: पुस्तक भण्डार A room which is equipped to shelve the collections. *See also* Book Room.

Book Supporter: पुस्तक संयोजक A L or T shaped piece of metal to keep books properly on shelves.

Book Talk: पुस्तक वार्ता A talk about books/to create awareness about the new books added to collections.

Book Trade: पुस्तक व्यवसाय Method of selling books to distributors and individual buyers.

Book Trade Journal: पुस्तक व्यवसाय पत्रिका A periodical, brought out by a publisher or a group of publishers to give publicity to their current publications.

Book Tray: पुस्तक ट्रे A tray used for carrying books.

Book Trolly: पुस्तक वाहक A set of shelves on wheel to carry collections within the library.

Book Turn Over: पुस्तक परिवर्तन Ratio of the books used among the volumes available in any centre.

Book Week: पुस्तक सप्ताह A week in which exhibitions and talks about books are arranged to create interest among users.

Book Worm: पुस्तक के कीड़े Kind of insects found in books.

Book Van: पुस्तक वाहन A van used to carry books. *See also* book mobile.

Booting: बूटिंग A process of getting computer system in working condition.

Borrower: उधार लेनेवाला/उधारग्राही A user who is allowed library books outside the premises. *See also* User or Reader.

Borrower's Card: उधार प्राप्ति पत्र/उधार ग्राही पत्र The membership card or cards permitting the holdor carrying books from the library. May also be known as library card.

Borrower's File: उधार प्रयोक्ता फाइल Membership forms are arranged in alphabetical order and it can also be recognised as Registration File.

Borrower's Number: उधारग्राही संख्या The registration number assigned to the individual member of the library.

Borrower's Record: उधार ग्राही अभिलेखन *See* Borrower Register.

Borrower's Register: उधारग्राही पंजी A register containing particulars and address of the borrowers.

Borrower's Ticket: उधार प्राप्ति पत्र *See* Borrower's Card.

Bottom Edge: अन्तिम किनारा Lower edge of the document.

Bottom Note: अन्तिम टिप्पणी *See* Foot-note.

Bound Volume: जिल्द युक्त खण्ड Volume which has hard binding or loose issues like periodical issues when bound together to get volume.

Bound With: जिल्द के साथ Note used by the cataloguers referring to books published separately but subsequently bound together.

Bracket: कोष्टक Standard symbol used by cataloguer to distinguish recorded information.

Braille Library: अन्धों का पुस्तकालय A library which has collections used by blind.

Branch Library: शाखा पुस्तकालय *See* Extension Library.

British Library: ब्रिटिश पुस्तकालय British library is the national library of the United Kingdom. It is seving as centre to scholarship, research and industry of the country.

British National Bibliography: ब्रिटिश राष्ट्रीय ग्रन्थ सूची It is a list of books published in Great Britain. The entries are available on international size cards. The list is compiled on the basis of publication received under copyright act.

Broad Classification: व्यापक वर्गीकरण Arrangement of subjects in a classification system in broad general divisions with minimum of sub-divisions (ISI)

Broken File: भंग फाइल Incomplete file.

Broken Order: भंगक्रम To achieve more helpful sequence when the order of chosen classification scheme is broken is known as broken order.

Brochure: विवरणिका A short printed work of few leaves stiched together.

Brown's Book Charging : ब्राउन पुस्तक निर्गमन A method given by brown for charging library documents. It is also known as two card system.

Brunet Classification: ब्रनेट वर्गीकरण Scheme of classification designed by Jacques Charles Brunet and published for the first time in 1809 in his manual du libraire et de I amateur de lovers (Ranganathan).

Budget: बजट An estimate of income and expenditure for anticipated future needs.

Budget Allocation Register: बजट आवण्टन पंजी The register maintained to keep records of budget allocations.

Building Department: भवन विभाग A library department responsible for the maintenance of building.

Bulk of A Book: पुस्तक आकार Thickness of the book.

Bulletin: पत्रिका A publication appears at regular intervals as a serial publication.

By-laws: उप-नियम A set of guidelines

Byline: अधिकार रेखा A line at the head of a newspaper or magazine article showing its authorship.

Byname: उपनाम A name other

then the actual name.

Byte: बाइट A byte is one character of data which is operated as a unit. *See also* Bit. Generally it consist 8 bits to represent one unit.

C

CDS/ISIS: सी डी एस/आई एस आई एस It is a computer used software conceived and developed by UNESCO for managing documentary databases. It is especially designed programe for storage and retrieval of information culled from textual records. In India distribution is available from NISSAT.

Cobol: कोबोल An acronym for common business oriented language. Commonly papular computer programming language.

CD-ROM: सी. डी. रोम Compact disk read only memory is an optical storage medium which only allows for reading of information.

Cabinet: पेटिका *See* Card Cabinet

Calendar: दिन दर्शिका Chronological schedule of events or an almanac giving list of days and months.

Call Number: आह्वान संख्या Call number is the ordinal number which fixes the relative position of a document in a library. It comprises of class number, book number and collection number.

Call Number Entry: आह्वान संख्या प्रविष्टि This entry starts with call number as leading section. In classified catalogue code it is regarded main entry.

Call Number Section: आह्वान संख्या अनुभाग The section of an entry, giving the call number of its document (ISI).

Calculator: गणक A device especially designed for performing arithmetic operations.

Calligraphy: सुलेखन The art of beautiful writing.

Cancel: निष्काशन A correction slip used to replace errors detected at any stage.

Canon: प्रनियम Guiding principles framed by Dr. Ranganathan for the help of classificationist.

Conon of Ascertainability: सुनिश्चितता का प्रनियम A characteristic used as the basis for the classification of a universe should be definitely ascertainable (Ranganathan).

Canon of Book Number: पुस्तक संख्या का प्रनियम A scheme of document classification should be provided with a scheme of book numbers to individualise the documents having the same class of knowledge as their ultimate class (Ranganathan).

Canon of Classics: स्ववर्गी ग्रन्थ प्रनियम A scheme of classification should have a device to bring together all the editions, translations and adaptations of a classic, and next to them all the editions, etc., of the different commentaries of it, those of a particular commentary coming together, and next to each commentary all the editions, etc. of the commentaries on itself (Ranganathan).

Canon of Collection Number: **संग्रह संख्या का प्रनियम** A scheme of document classification should have provision for a schedule of collection numbers to individualise the various collections of special documents to be formed on the basis of the peculiarities of their gross bodies or their rarely, or service exigency, or for other reasons (Ranganathan).

Canon of Concomitance: **समानधर्मिता का प्रनियम** No two characteristics used in succession as the basis for the classification of a universe should be concomitant, that is they should not give rise to the same array of classes (Ranganathan).

Canon of Consistency: **समरूपता का प्रनियम** Characteristics used as the basis for the classification of a universe should be used successively in the same sequence, so long there is no change in the purpose of classification (Rananathan).

Canon of Consistent Sequence: **समरूपी तारम्यता प्रनियम** If similar classes occur in different arrays, the sequence should be parallel in all the arrays, unless there is a positive difference in purpose and helpfulness (Ranganathan).

Canon of Contact: **प्रासंगिकता का प्रनियम** The denotation of a term in a scheme of classification should be determined in the light of different classes of lower order (upper links) belonging to the same primary chain as the class denoted by the term in question (Ranganathan).

Canon of Co-ordinate Classes: **समकक्ष वर्गों का प्रनियम** Among the classes no class with less affinity should come between two classes or arrays with greater affinity (Ranganathan).

Canon of Currency: **साम्प्रतिकता का प्रनियम** The term used to denote a class in a scheme of classification should be one currently accepted by those specializing in the universe to which the scheme is applicable (Ranganathan).

Canon of Decreasing Extension: **ह्रासमान विस्तार का प्रनियम** While moving down a chain of classes, form its first link its last, the intention of the class should increase and their extension should decrease at each step (Ranganathan).

Canon of Differentiation: **विभेदीकरण का प्रनियम** A characteristic used as the basis for the classification of a universe should differentiate some of its entities, that is it should give rise at least to two classes (Ranganathan).

Canon of Distinctiveness: सुस्पष्टता का प्रनियम In a scheme of library classification, the class number, the book number, and the collection number, should be written quite distinct or apart from another (Ranganathan).

Canon of Enumeration: परिगणना का प्रनियम The denotation of term in a scheme of classification should be determined and be left to be determined in the light of or through the sub-classes (lower links) enumerated in the various chains having the class denoted by the term in question as their common link (Ranganathan).

Canon of Exclusiveness: अन्यता का प्रनियम Classes in an array of classes should be neutrally exclusive (Ranganathan).

Canon of Exhaustiveness: पूर्णता का प्रनियम Classes in an array of classes should be totally exhaustive of their immediate universe (Ranganathan).

Canon of Expressiveness: अभिव्यंजना का प्रनियम There should be in a class number a digit to represent each of the characteristics used in constructing the class number (Ranganathan).

Canon of Favoured Sequence: वांछित क्रम का प्रनियम In arrangement precedence should be given to a class, whatever be its natural position in the normal sequence, so as to be of greater help to those for whom it is intended (Ranganathan).

Canon of Helpful Sequence: सहयोगी क्रम का प्रनियम Classes in array should be helpful to those to whom it is intended (Ranganathan).

Canon of Hospitality in Array: पंक्ति में समायोजन का प्रनियम The construction of a class number or an isolate number should admit of an infinite a number of new co-ordinate classes or isolate being added to array to which it belongs at appropriate filiatory places, without disturbing the existing class numbers or isolate numbers in any way (Ranganathan).

Canon of Hospitality in Chain: शृंखला में समायोजक का प्रनियम The construction of a class number or an isolate number should admit of an infinite number of new class numbers or isolate numbers being added at the end of the chain to which it belongs, without disturbing the existing class numbers or isolate numbers in any way (Ranganathan).

Canon of Mixed Notation: मिश्रित अंकन का प्रनियम The notation of a scheme of classification should be a mixed one (Ranganathan).

Canon of Modulation: अनुविम्बन का प्रनियम A chain of classes should be divided from the universe with the use of correct resolving power at each stage of division (Ranganathan).

Canon of Non-hierarchical Notation: अपदानुक्रम अंकन का प्रनियम In the class number there should not be a digit to represent each of the characteristics used in constructing the class number (Ranganathan).

Canon of Permanence: स्थायित्व का प्रनियम A characteristics used as the basis for the classification of a universe should continue to be unchanged so long as there is no change in the purpose of classification (Ranganathan).

Canon of Pure Notation: शुद्ध अंकन का प्रनियम The notation of a scheme of classification should be a pure one (Ranganathan).

Canon of Reticence: संयमन का प्रनियम The term used to denote a class in a scheme of classification should not be critical, that is express any opinion of the classificationist (Ranganathan).

Canon of Relativity: सापेक्षता का प्रनियम The number of digits in a class number should be proportional to the order of the class it represents (Ranganathan).

Canon of Relevance: औचित्य का प्रनियम A characteristic used as the basis for the classification of a universe should be relevant to the purpose of the classification (Ranganathan).

Canon of Relevant Sequence: औचित्यक्रम का प्रनियम Characteristic used as the basis for the classification for a universe should be used successively in a sequence relevant to a purpose of the classification (Ranganathan).

Canon of Scheduled Mnemonics: सारणी स्मृति सहाय्य का प्रनियम A scheme of classification should include a set of schedules of common isolates likely to occur in an array of some order or other of all or several classes, or that it should refer any recurrent set of isolates to the one schedule of them given in connection with an appropriate basic class (Ranganathan).

Canon of Seminal Mnemonics: समजीवी स्मृति सहाय्य प्रनियम A scheme of classification should use one and the same digit to represent seminally equivalent concepts in whatever array of whatever facet of whatever class they may appear, though the concept may be denoted by different terms in different contexts of arrays (Ranganathan).

Canon of Sub-ordinate Classes: अधीनस्थ वर्गों का प्रनियम All the sub-ordinate classes of a class, in whatever chain they may occur, should immediately follow it without being separated from it or among themselves by any other class (Ranganathan).

Canon of Systematic Mnemonics: सुव्यवस्थित समृति सहाय्य प्रनियम A scheme of classification should use one and the same sequence of digits to represent the isolate in an array, arranged according to each one of the principles, such as later-in-time, special contiguity (Ranganathan).

Canon of Uniformity: समरूपता का प्रनियम The number of digits in a class number should be constant whatever be the order of the class it represents (Ranganathan).

Canon of Verbal Mnemonics: शाब्दिक स्मृति सहाय्य प्रनियम The alphabetical device may be used to represent any isolate or array isolate, when arrangement on the basis of any characteristic other then the name, is not more helpful (Ranganathan).

Canonical Class: आप्त वर्ग Traditional sub-class of a main class, enumerated as such in a scheme of classification for the universe of knowledge, and not derived on the basis of definite characteristics (Ranga-nathan).

Canonical Order: आप्त क्रम The order in which sub-classes of a main class are arranged.

Canonical Sequence: आप्त सारणी Traditional arrangement of subjects which is not derived on the basis of any definite characteristic.

Capacity: क्षमता The number of characters accommodated in a storing device.

Capacity of a Notation: अंकन की क्षमता The capacity of a notation is the number of classes that can be individualised by it.

Capitals: बड़े आकार के अक्षर The large size letters.

Caption: अनुशीर्षक A written identification. *See also* Heading.

Caption Title: अनुशीर्षक The title printed at the top of every page which is also known as text title.

Carbon Paper: कार्बन कागज A thin chemical coated paper used for obtaining multiple copies.

Card: पत्र *See* Catalogue Card.

Card Cabinet: पत्र पेटिका A set of drawers in which cards are filed in vertical order.

Card Catalogue: पत्र सूची A catalogue prepared on standard uniform 5"X 3" size cards. Each entry has complete information according to approach and these are kept in dictionary order or in classified order as the case may be. It is a unit of card filing drawers made of either wood or steel.

Card Catalogue Cabinet: पत्र सूची पेटिका *See* Card Cabinet.

Card Drawer: पत्र दराज Steel or wooden drawers for holding catalogue cards to keep these in a Card Cabinet.

Card Form Catalogue: पत्र आकार सूची *See* Card Catalogue.

Card Index: पत्र अनुक्रमणिका An index prepared on cards.

Card Issue System: पत्र निर्गम प्रणाली To arrange circulation of library document, cards are introduced for identification of the borrower and also for document loan, number of cards are issued on the basis of the policy followed.

Card Tray: पत्र ट्रे A drawer which holds cards to keep these in a card cabinet.

Cardex: कारडैक्स It is a record keeping library equipment which is mainly used to keep the records of periodical acquisitions. A separate card is introduced for each title.

Cardinal Number: मूल संख्या

Cardinal Value: आधार भूत मूल्य

Care of Books: पुस्तकों की देख-रेख The books should be saved from dust, femigation and from abnormal weather conditions.

Cartographer: मानचित्रकार One who prepares maps/charts on the basis of data available.

Cartography: मानचित्र विज्ञान An art of making maps/charts.

Cash Book: रोकड़ बही, कैश बुक Record of daily transaction of income and expenditure of a library.

Cassette: केसेट्स Package of film. It may be blank or recorded.

Cassette Recorder: कैसेट अभिलेखक A device designed to use cassette.

Catalogue: सूची Catalogue is a list of holdings of a library which is developed with definit purpose. It is a key to collections arranged on a set plan as the documents on shelves. One can know by it which publication at what rack is available in a library. It may be for one library or for a group of libraries.

Catalogue Cabinet: सूची पेटिका It is made of wood or steel in standard size to hold catalogue cards.

Catalogue Card: सूची पत्र It is a standard size 12.5 cm x 7.5 cm white ruled or blank paper card used for preparing entries of library records for vertical filing.

Catalogue Code: सूची संहिता A set of rules for guidance of cataloguers to achieve uniformity popularly used codes are AACR & CCC.

Catalogue Entry: सूची प्रविष्टि An entry which is prepared for a document to include it in a catalogue.

Cataloguer: सूचीकार A person who prepares catalogue entries and knows cataloguing rules.

Cataloguing: सूचीकरण An art of making entries for a catalogue.

Cataloguing Department: सूचीकरण विभाग The department, process documents for cataloguing.

Cataloguing in Publication: प्रकाशननान्तर्गत सूचीकरण When catalogue entry is either published in the book or printed cards are made available with its publication.

Cataloging Rules: सूचीकरण नियम *See* Catalogue Code.

Cataloguing in Source: प्रकाशन के साथ सूचीकरण The cataloguing is performed by central agency from proof copy which are made available by the publisher. These entries are published on the document itself or made available with the published book.

Cataloguing Technique: सूचीकरण तकनीक The method adopted under the rules to develop catalogue entries.

Catalytic Material: उत्प्रेरक समान Natural or near natural material or an intermediate commodity, whose mere presence is essential in the process of arriving at the ultimate commodity if it is the next stage or into the intermediate commodity of the next stage in its progress towards the stage of ultimate commodity (ISI).

Catch Word Title: ध्यानाकर्षी शब्द शीर्षक A title comprised of striking words.

Catchy Title: ध्यानाकर्षी शीर्षक *See* Fanciful Title.

Catechism: प्रश्नोत्तरमय Work in the form of question answers.

Category: श्रेणी A fundamental concept to group knowledge in desired manner. *See also* Facet.

Caution Money: जमानती धन The money collected to provide security to library documents and the same is returned on discontinuation of membership.

Cell: अंश, भाग Storage for single element of information, usually one character or machine word (ISI).

Central Catalogue: केन्द्रीय सूची A catalogue of the library system which has the entries of the documents available even in extension libraries. It can be called main catalogue or a catalogue for the collections of library system.

Centralised Cataloguing: केन्द्रीकृत सूचीकरण Cataloguing of all the collections of a library system or of group of libraries by a central agency to achieve uniformity.

Centralised Processing: केन्द्रीकृत संसाधन A library staff unit works for purchase/acquisition/cataloguing/classification at one place to achieve economy and standardisation in services.

Centralised Registration: केन्द्रीय पंजीयन Registration of library members at one place to use a library system.

Central Library: केन्द्रीय पुस्तकालय The main monitoring library of the system or a library which has number of branches.

Central Processing Unit (CPU): केन्द्रीय संसाधन इकाई It is a primary data storage of a computer which is regarded as computer brain. It is a control unit which directs the sequence of operation. It receives data and transfers data. Thus it co-ordinates and controls data loading in first instance. It is a principle operating part of computer.

Central Registration: केन्द्रीय पंजीयन *See* Centralised Registration.

Central Shelf List: केन्द्रीय शैल्फ सूची A shelf list developed for the holdings of the library system which may be known as main shelf list or union shelf list.

Certification: प्रमाणीकरण Action of certifying.

Cess: उपकर *See* Tax.

Chain: शृंखला It is a sequence of subordinate classes of decreasing extension and increasing intention achieved by successive divisions of any universe. Chain can be derived from its immediate class.

Chain Indexing: शृंखला अनुक्रमणीकरण A mechanical process of achieving index through analysis of class number into its digits representing subjects. It was originated by Dr. Ranganathan.

Chain Procedure: शृंखला प्रक्रिया Procedure for determining the class index entries, the specific subject entries and see also subject entries of a document from its class number and the class number of the cross reference entries provided for it (Ranganathan) or it is a systematic method of driving class index entries from a given class number.

Change of Title Note: परिवर्तित शीर्षक टिप्पण A note mentioning the alternative title, if any, under which the work may have appeared earlier (ISI).

Change Record: परिवर्तन अभिलेख It is a master record in which amendments are incorporated as and when released.

Changed Name: परिवर्तित नाम When a author contributes under various adopted names then for all such names a note is made in cataloguing.

Changed Title: परिवर्तित शीर्षक A different title then the title appeared in the previous edition.

Channel: वाहिका अथवा पथ A device, either manual, mechanical or electrical, for transducing informative signals from one place to another (ISI). or A track on a magnetic tape for carrying signals.

Channel Capacity: वाहिका क्षमता The maximum number of binary digits or elementary digits to other bases which can be handled in a particular channel for unit time (ISI).

Chapter: अध्याय A part of contribution.

Chapter Heading: अध्याय शीर्षक Heading used in the beginning of the chapter to represent contents recorded.

Character: प्रतीक, करैक्टर Any symbol, digit/letter which is used to represent data in computer.

Characteristic: अभिलक्षण An attribute/distinctive property/feature by which things are put together or identified in a classification.

Charge: निर्गम A record of the circulated book.

Charging: निर्गम Method of loaning library documents.

Charging Department: निर्गम विभाग *See* Circulation Department.

Charging Desk: निर्गम डैस्क Counter from which circulation services are operated.

Charging File: निर्गम फाइल Record of documents loaned.

Charging Guide: निर्गम दर्शक *See* Date Guide.

Charging Method: निर्गम विधि Method of loaning library documents also known as issue system.

Charging Slip: निर्गम पर्ची A slip containing details of the document and preserved as receipt when book is loaned.

Charging System: निर्गम प्रणाली *See* Charging Method.

Charging Tray: निर्गम ट्रे The tray used to hold issue record. Also known as Issue Card Tray.

Chart: चार्ट A specially designed layout on paper to display information.

Chattopadhyay (D. P.) Committee: चट्टोपाध्यय डी पी समिति A committee appointed by the Government of India to study and suggest the scales of pay for library professionals in continuation of 4th Pay Commission exercise.

Cheap Edition: सस्ता संस्करण An edition of a document brought out on cheaper price which is generally in paper back.

Checking: निरीक्षण Process of knowing the correctness of the things.

Check List: निरीक्षण सूची A list of documents with details used for verification.

Chief: मुख्य A person who is responsible for supervising the entire services.

Children's Library: बाल पुस्तकालय A library in which major part of collections are for the use of children.

Children's Book Trust: बाल पुस्तकन्यास It is a non-profit making effort in which books in English and Hindi language are sold on subsidised price.

Chip : चिप An electronic entity comprised of one or more semiconductors on a wafer of silicon or a short blim.

Chronological Device(Idea Plane): कालानुक्रमिक युक्ति (विचार तल) Device for forming an isolate or sharpening a host focus in the form of an isolate or an array isolate with the help of chronological characteristic (Ranganathan).

Chronological Device (Notational Plane): कालानुक्रमिक युक्ति (अंकन तल) Device of using a chronological number as an isolate number or adding to a host isolate number a chronological number to implement the chronological device of the idea plane (Ranganathan).

Chronological Order: कालानुक्रम An arrangement achieved by choosing time and date as characteristic.

Circular Brackets: घुमावदार ब्रेकिट्स Curves or round brackets in which first is called starter and last is called arrester. These are used with notation to identity subject device use.

Circular Letter: परिपत्र An official letter which is used to convey a policy or revision of previous decision among the effected people.

Circulation: आदान-प्रदान Loaning of library documents.

Circulation Control: आदान-प्रदान नियंत्रण All activities relating to issue and return of library documents are looked after.

Circulation Department: आदान-प्रदान विभाग The department of a library in which documents are received back after use and loaned on demand for use.

Circulation Desk: आदान-प्रदान डैस्क *See* Circulation Department.

Circulation Record: आदान-प्रदान अभिलेख Record of the loaned documents of a library.

Circulation Statistics: आदान-प्रदान सांख्यिकी Statistical profile for the book circulated by a library.

Circulation Work: आदान-प्रदान कार्य Service by which books reach the users.

Circuit: परिपथ An electrical network in which there exist one or more paths through which current can flow (DDPT).

Citation: उध्दरण An information in an entry about a document in which information originally appeared or a note of reference to a work from which passage has been quoted.

Citation Index: उध्दरण अनुक्रमणिका Index to the documents cited in works.

Citation Order: उध्दरण क्रम The order of class number in which characteristics of any class are recognised. *See also* Facet Formula.

Class: वर्ग An original field of study which has common characteristics.

Class Index Entry: वर्ग अनुक्रमाणिका प्रविष्टि Index entry in a classified catalogue giving the class number for a class (ISI).

Class Number: वर्ग संख्या It is the translation of the subject embodied in a document from natural language to classificatory language or it is a symbol fixing the position of a subject document relating to other documents of the same and also with other subject (Ranganathan).

Class Number: वर्ग संख्या A number used to denote a class in a classification scheme.

Classic: स्ववर्गीग्रन्थ Work usually appearing in several versions or having several adaptations and translations, inspiring other works on itself, and repeatedly coming in print even long after its origin (Ranganathan).

Classic Device: विशिष्ट व्यंजक युक्ति A device used to group classic documents.

Classical Author: स्ववर्गी लेखक An author who's works are evaluated and has acceptance through ages and got acceptance as independent class.

Classification: वर्गीकरण Classification is a systematic arrangement on common characteristics, or it is arranging of things according to likeness and unlikeness. *See also* Library Classification.

Classification Code: वर्गीकरण संहिता A book of classification rules used to operate a classification scheme.

Classification Number : वर्गीकरण संख्या *See* Class Number.

Classification Scheme: वर्गीकरण पद्धति A scheme of keeping library documents in helpful subject arrangement to extend efficient library service.

Classificationist: वर्गीकरण विद् One who makes classification scheme.

Classificatory Language: वर्गीकरणत्मक भाषा Artificial language of the ordinal numbers used in a Scheme of classification. (Ranganathan)

Classified Arrangement: वर्गीकृत क्रम Arrangement in which documents are kept in their respective class identified by the classification scheme implemented. It is decided on the basis of characteristics which helps in arranging all the relevant subject documents at one place to facilitate.

Classified Catalogue: वगीकृत सूची It comprises two parts-classified and alphabetical. In classified part subject or number entries are arranged in subject order and in alphabetical part remaining word entries are arranged in alphabetical order. It forms a subject catalogue on the basis of subject classification adopted by the scheme implemented.

Classified Catalogue Code: वर्गीकृत सूची संहिता A catalogue code which contains rules for preparing classified subject entries. The code was formulated by Indian library scientist, Dr. S. R. Ranganathan.

Classified Library: वर्गीकृत

पुस्तकालय A library in which collections are arranged in their desired groups.

Classified Subject Catalogue: **वर्गीकृत विषय सूची** *See* Classified Catalogue.

Classify: **वर्गीकरण** The process of grouping collections in their subject order or in any order which will suit to the useser.

Classifying: **वर्गीकरण** An act of grouping entities on the basis of characteristics.

Clay Tablet: **क्ले टैबलेट** An ancient form of information record.

Clerical Assistant: **लिपिक सहायक** A person who undertakes secretarial duties under supervision.

Clientele: **पाठक** *See* User, *See also* Borrower; Reader.

Clipping : **कतरन** A printed paper piece clipped from a news paper or magazine which contains some specific information on a given subject.

Clipping Service: **कतरन सेवा** Service generated on the basis of the clippings. Generally the clippings in subject order are provided to the specialist users to know the current trend of their subject.

Close Classification: **निकटतम वर्गीकरण** A classification which takes care of minute subdivisions of topics.

Closed Access: **बाधित प्रवेश** Where the user has no free access to the documents.

Closed Array: **अवरुद्ध पंक्ति** An array of classes not accepting new classes and which cannot be extended further more.

Closed Entry: **पूर्ण प्रविष्टि** An entry which consists total information about a document and no addition is required.

Closed Notation: **अवरुद्ध अंकन** A notation which does not accept new digits to represent new classes.

Closed Shelves: **बाधित अलमारी** *See* Closed Access.

Closed Sequence : **बाधितक्रम** *See* Closed Array.

Cloth Binding: **कपड़ा जिल्द** A binding in which cloth is used with hardboard to protect document.

Co-author: **सह-लेखक** *See* Joint Author.

COBOL: **कोबोल** (Common Business Oriented Computer Language) used for business data processing purpose.

Code: **संहिता** A set of rules or symbols specifying their use in particular situation.

Code Dictionary: **संहिता कोश** Dictionary giving code symbols of the technical terms usually occurring in learned papers and their abstracts (ISI).

Code of Conduct: **आचार संहिता** A set of library rules.

Coding: **चिन्हांकन** Rendering the index entires into nongraphic symbols suited to the machine(ISI).

Coextensiveness: **सहवितरणशीलता**

The expression in a class number of the measure of incidence of each of the relevant characteristics of the subject embodied in the document concerned.

Collaborator: **सहयोगी लेखक** A person or a corporate body associated with a work or its author in the capacity of director, assistant, commentator, illustrator, engraver, translator, revisor, editor, writer of introduction, epitomiser, adapter, librettist writer of the words in a musical composition, or in any other similar secondary capacity not amounting to authorship (ISI).

Collateral Arrays: **समानान्तर पंक्तियाँ** Arrays of the same order derived from the same universe (Ranganathan).

Collateral Classes: **समानान्तर वर्ग** Classes of the same order but not belongs to one and the same array, derived from the common universe (Ranganathan).

Collation: **पृष्ठादि विवरण** The description of document to present physical form such as volume, page, illustration size, etc.

Collected Work: **संम्पूर्ण रचना** Complete collections of a author which generally appear in member of volumes.

Collection: **संकलन** Number of documents acquired by a library.

Collection Development : **संचय विकास** *See* Acquisition.

Collection Number: **संचय संख्या** A number used to represent library holdings. *See also* Accession Number.

Collective Biography: **सामूहिक जीवनी** A work consists of biographies of the persons of various disciplines.

Collective Cataloguing: **सामूहिक सूचीकरण** *See* Co-operative Cataloguing.

Collective Entries: **सामूहिक प्रविष्टियाँ** All type of entries for all authors and works put together.

Collective Title: **सामूहिक शीर्षक** A title which is assigned to the contributions of various authors appearing together or common to all volumes of a work. *See also* Generic Title.

College Library: **कालेज पुस्तकालय** It is a library to support academic activities and courses conducted by the college to which it is attached. Thus it is to satisfy a variety of demands of large number of teachers and students.

Colon: **द्वि-बिन्दु** It is a symbol used by universal decimal classification and very intensivally by colon classification scheme.

Colon Book Number: **द्वि बिन्दु पुस्तक संख्या** The number may consist of one or more from the successive facet like language, form, year, acquisition, volume, supplement, copy, evaluation and evaluation acquisition number (Ranganathan).

Colon Classification: द्वि बिन्दु वर्गीकरण It is a freely faceted and analytico synthetic scheme of classification first published in 1933. It has a very sound theory to understand it. The scheme has good number of principles and postulates to analyse and synthesis the subject into five fundamental categories (Ranganathan).

Column: स्तम्भ अथवा **कालम** Any vertical arrangement of characters/sets of characters/image or the like (DDPT).

Comma: अर्ध विराम चिन्ह Punctuation mark used to separate the clauses.

Command: आदेश In computer electronic signal/signals to continue operations.

Commentator: भाष्यकार A person who does commentary.

Commentary: समालोचना Explanatory note on a work.

Committee: समिति *See* Library Advisory Committee.

Commodity-Raw Material Transformation-Prinicple: वस्तु अपिरिष्कृत सामग्री परिवर्तन सिद्धांत If facet A is commodity: got out of the raw material farming facet B by the process of transformation forming facet C of the same subject then the three facets should be arranged within the class and the class number of the subject in the sequence A,B,C (Ranganathan).

Common Auxiliaries : सामान्य सहयोगी सारणी Auxiliaries tables are provided with the classification schemes.

Common Communication Format (CCF): सामान्य सम्प्रेषण आकार It is a standard format to exchange bibliographic records.

Common Facet: सामान्य पक्ष A facet which can occur in any of the class in a classification.

Common Isolate: सामान्य एकल *See* Common Isolate Idea.

Common Isolate Idea: सामान्य एकल विचार Isolate idea that can be attached to several host classes, but is denoted by the same isolate term, and represented by the same isolate number, whatever be the host class (ISI).

Communication: संदेश Transfer of information between two or more points.

Communication Channel: संदेश पथ A channel which is used for transmitting information for main point to other.

Community Library: सामाजिक पुस्तकालय A library which is for the use of the community as a whole. *See* public library.

Compact Disk: सघन डिस्क A storage device used in computer.

Comparison Relation : तुलनात्मक संबंध Phase relation in which phase 1 is compared with phase 2 (Ranganathan).

Compatibility: तुलनात्मकता Quality which can be compared with other item of same kind.

Compendium: सार संग्रह A work comprised only important points of a larger work.

Competent Authority: सक्षम अधिकारी Any person/persons authorised to carry out the work to satisfy the guidelines available on the subject.

Compilation: संयोजन A work developed by collecting relevant material from available works.

Compiler: कम्पाइलर Software form that translates a complete program into machine language or checks errors of the program.

Compiler: संयोजक A person who collects matter from various sources and puts it in order to use.

Complete Bibliography: पूर्ण ग्रन्थ-सूची Up to date list of documents on a particular subject.

Complete Chain: पूर्ण शृंखला Loose primary chain that is a chain with the original universe has its first link and a unitary class as its last link (Ranganathan).

Complete Division: पूर्ण विभाग Process of continuing the division of the entities of a universe on the basis of a sequence of characteristics, until no multiple group is felt (Ranganathan).

Complete Series: पूर्ण ग्रन्थ-माला A complete set of publications appeared under a Series.

Completely Amplified Class: पूर्ण विस्तृत वर्ग Any class amplified by the pseudo entities corresponding to all the multiple classes arising in the course of its complete assortment (Ranganathan).

Completely Amplified Universe: पूर्ण विस्तृत ज्ञान जगत Original universe amplified by the pseudo entity corresponding to its self and by the pseudo entities corresponding to all the multiple classes arising in the course of its complete assortment (Ranganathan).

Complex Array Isolate: मिश्रित पंक्ति एकल Array isolate framed by the combination of two or more array isolates in one and the same array to express the relation between them but excluding the case of their superimposition. (Ranganathan)

Complimentary Copy : उपहार प्रति A copy received without payment which may be for publicity or to get the work evaluated.

Complex Class: मिश्रित वर्ग Class framed by the combination of two or more basic or compound classes and made to express the relation between them, but excluding the case when one of the classes forms an isolate of the other, formed by subject device (Ranganathan).

Complex Subject: मिश्रित विषय A subject with one basic class and one or more isolate ideas. Thus the subject which has more than one characteristics.

Composite Author: संयुक्त लेखक An author responsible for the contributions included as a part of composite book.

Composite Book: संयुक्त पुस्तक A book with two or more contributions, not forming a continous exposition, and often, through not necessarily, by different authors. These are of two type — ordinary composite book and artificial composite book.

Composite Classification: संयुक्त वर्गीकरण A classification scheme which is used by mixing more than one scheme.

Compound Base: यौगिक आधार A base consisting of two or more simple base.

Compound Class: यौगिक वर्ग Class with a basic facet and one or more isolate facets (Ranganathan).

Compound Name: यौगिक नाम A proper name formed from two or more single-worded proper names after connected by a hyphen, a conjunction or a preposition (ISI).

Compound Subject: यौगिक विषय A subject closely associated with another subject or which is the result of combination of more then one subjects.

Comprehensive Abstracting Service: व्यापक सार-सेवा An abstracting service in which all important contributions of a given subject are covered.

Comprehensive Bibliography: व्यापक ग्रन्थ सूची A bibliography prepared for every thing brought out in a subject.

Comprehensive Collection: व्यापक संचय The collections which are sufficient to meet the requirements of the users.

Comprehensive Work: व्यापक रचना A work which includes all important aspects of the subject.

Computer: कम्प्यूटर A machine capable of accepting data and processing it by the application of mathematical and/or logical operations (DDPT).

It is a powerful form of electronic gadget/machine which translates one kind of language suitable to a machine into another kind of language also suitable to a machine (ISI) or it is an electronic device that can receive and store data to operate it in desired manner through a set of instructions. Thus computer is a widely used data processing machine or is a series of machines which performs assigned task with tremendous speed and accuracy. The capacity can be used for storing, processing and retrieving information. Mainly these can be of three types digital, analog and hybrid computers.

Computer Applications: कम्प्यूटर प्रयोग Use of computers for various sources and operations.

Computer Centre: कम्प्यूटर केन्द्र A computer equipped location.

Computer Communication System: कम्प्यूटर सम्प्रेषण प्रणाली *See* Microcomputer System.

Computer Language: कम्प्यूटर भाषा A language used to establish communication through computer.

Computer Network: कम्प्यूटर तन्त्र A set of computers connected through communication lines forms a computor network.

Computer Operator: कम्प्यूटर प्रयोगकर्ता One who makes use of computer.

Computer Output: कम्प्यूटर परिणाम The results achieved with the application of machenical process.

Computer Programe: कम्प्यूटर योजना A set of instructions organised to deal with the work performance of the computer.

Computer Science: कम्प्यूटर विज्ञान The subject dealing with the design and use of computers.

Computer System: कम्प्यूटर प्रणाली Total unit of the computer which includes a number of machine parts such as CPU, Monitor and keyboard, etc. *See also* Computer.

Computer word: कम्प्यूटर शब्द A series of bits or characters that is treated as an unit and which in particular, occupies a single storage location (DDPT).

Computerised Databases: कम्प्यूटरकृत सूचना संग्रह The information collection in machine readable form or information storage in computer.

Computing Unit: गणक युक्ति इकाई The part of a computer that performs arithmetic operations and logic operations and makes decisions: the central processor (DDPT).

Concordance: शब्दानुक्रमाणिका An alphabetical index for the words in a document.

Concrete Entity: निश्चित सत्ता Entity existing physically in space-time, mesh, outside the mind of the knower, as it is commonly understood. It is either recognizable with the aid of the primary senses or inferable from data obtained with the aid of primary senses(ISI).

Condemned Book: नष्ट पुस्तक *See* Weeded Book.

Conference: सम्मेलन A meeting to discuss certain identified issues.

Conference Room: सम्मेलन कक्ष A room used to arrange conference.

Confidential File: गोपनीय फाइल A file which contains very important paper and only used under definit restrictions.

Connect Time: **संयोजी समय** In computer use the time in which a user is logged on.

Connecting Digit: **संयोजक अंक** A digit used as a connector in a class number, that is as a conjection in a classificatory language (Ranganathan).

Connecting Symbol: **संयोजी चिन्ह** Any symbol used in a class number to add a facet to back class or with other facets.

Connotation: **जातिबोध** All the characteristics comprised in a class term.

Conservation of Document: **अभिलेख सुरक्षा** Preservation of documents from loss.

Consolidated Entry: **संयुक्त प्रविष्टि** Two or more entries consolidated into a single entry.

Consolidation: **संयोजन** A process of achieving comprenensive account by murgering one or more records.

Contents: **विषय विन्यास** A list of chapter headings under which text is developed

Contents Page: **विषय विन्यास पृष्ठ** A page containing contents.

Continuation Card: **पूरक पत्र** Second and subsequent card which carry on its top the reference that is classification number and entry word as in main card to follow remaining part of the main entry which was not covered in first card due to pository of space.

Continuation File: **पूरक फाइल** This is also called part II and III as the case may be.

Continuing Education: **सतत् शिक्षा** Non-formal education for the benefit of working professionals/working class to improve their skill or to update them in the area of their work.

Continuous Array: **सतत् पंक्ति** An array of classes not admitting of interpolation but open to add more new classes.

Contribution: **अंशदान** A work forming a part of a composite book/periodical/serial/ thought embodied in a host document in the form of an article in a periodical or of a section or a paragraph in a book (Ranganathan), or a portion of the amount or service.

Control: **नियमन** The parts/devices of computer which carry out instruction.

Control Program: **नियमन योजना** A specially designed program of instructions to guide central processing unit.

Control Unit: **नियमन इकाई** Section of the central processing unit that selects, interprets and controls the execution of program.

Conventional Name: **प्रचलित नाम** Name which is other than real name

Conversion Rate: **परिवर्तनीय दर** The rate of Indian currency for marking payment for foreign publications.

Co-operative Acquisition: **सहकारी संकलन** Joint approach for achieving effective collections with limited funds.

Co-operative Cataloguing: सहकारी सूचीकरण Collective effort by a group of libraries to achieve economy and uniformity. Manpower and expenditure is also shared by participating libraries. It avoids duplicate working.

Co-operative Storage: सहकारी संग्रह It is an effort to improve the quantum of information without hindrance of space and distance.

Co-opted Member: सहयोगी सदस्य A member in a committee to help in the field of his specialisation.

Co-ordinate Classes: समकक्षवर्ग Classes belonging to one and the same array (Rangnathan).

Copy: प्रति A single document or a duplicate copy of a document or unchanged transfer of data from original source to another place for use.

Copy Filing: प्रति क्रमांकन When the copies are arranged in a file.

Copy Number: प्रति संख्या Number within the book number of a copy of a document of which there are two or more copies, individualizing the said copy (Ranganathan).

Copyright: स्वत्वाधिकार Right of an author/publisher/any other body under rule on a contribution.

Copyright Date: स्वत्वाधिकार तिथि The date on which copyright of a book is extended, generally printed on the back of title page.

Copyright Library: कापीराइट पुस्तकालय A library which is entitled to receive a free copy of every published document under Copy Right Act.

Corporate Author: सामूहिक लेखक Corporate authorship is an effort where group of persons are identified by a particular common name and associated for common cause. The authorship lies with institution or other such body.

Corporate Body: सामूहिक निकाय A group of individuals associated together as an organised unit with common objectives.

Corporate Entry: सामूहिक प्रविष्टि An entry which is rendered under a corporate body.

Corrected Edition: संशोधित ससंकरण A new edition after incorporating corrections.

Cost Benefit: मूल्य लागत लाभ Relationship between cost involved and service generated by the programme.

Cover: आवरण Paper or any other material like cloth, leather etc. to protect document.

Cover Title: आवरण शीर्षक On the back or spine of the document short title is printed to identify the document or title available on cover page.

Cow-calf Principle: गाय बछड़ा सिद्धांत If facet A and another facet B belonging to the same subject are not to be separated though they are distinct from each other and separable, they should be kept together within one and the same round as a milking cow and its unweaned calf are not separately sold out though are distinct entities and are thus separable, but are kept together with one and the same owner (Ranganathan).

Cross Classification: पारगामी वर्गीकरण Use of more or two characteristics to form one and the same array leading to the violation of the canon of consistency and the canon of exclusiveness (Ranganathan).

Cross Reference Entry: संदर्भ प्रविष्टि Specific added number entry in classified catalogue, referring from the class number of a subject forming only a part of the document, to the host document and giving the place of occurrence of the subject in the host document (Ranganathan) or entries connecting to related entries

Cross Reference Index Entry: संदर्भ अनुक्रमाणिका प्रविष्टि General added entry referring from one word or set of words to another word or set of words. It may draw information outside the document catalogued. The second word or set of words may be a synonym of the former; or it may be an alternative name to denote the same entity as one denoted by the former. It occurs in dictionary catalogue in classified catalogue (ISI).

Cumulation: संचयन Progressive indexing of entries in a predetermined order and which are circulated for use after a fixed period.

Cumulative Index: संचित अनुक्रमणिका An index resulted by combining separately published indexes.

Cumulative List: संचित सूची A list developed by murging the lists prepared separately.

Current Awareness Service (CAS): साम्प्रतिक सूचना सेवा Service to keep sepecialist users abreast about additions in areas of their interest.

Current Bibliography: साम्प्रतिक ग्रन्थ सूची A bibliography compiled for the recent published books.

Current Content: साम्प्रतिक विषय सारिणी It is a kind of reference service in which current contents of the works are provided to the specialist users.

Current Directory: साम्प्रतिक निदेशिका Directory which contains the information of current nature.

Current Information: साम्प्रतिक सूचना An information of immediate value.

Current List: साम्प्रतिक सूची A list provides information about acquisitions of a library.

Current Number: साम्प्रतिक संख्या The last published number/ issue of a publication.

Current Reviews: साम्प्रतिक समीक्षा The latest reviews which are used to evaluate the contribution.

Cutter Number: कटर संख्या It is also known as author number/book number from cutter table. It is used to individualizes document within the same class.

Cursor: करसर Electronic device displayed on the monitor of the computer to highlight the location of the next character.

Custodian: रक्षक A person who is incharge of something.

Cybernetics: साइबरनेटिक्स Study of communication system made of a mechano-electrical system, such as a computing machine (Ranganathan).

D

Daily: दैनिक A publication brought out every day to disseminate current news.

Damaged Book: क्षतिग्रस्त पुस्तक A book which has become uncervicable due to continous use and that needs repair or replacement.

Dash: रेखा अंश A line used to connect two words.

Data: सूचना इकाई A term used for un processed or unorganised information in computer. It is a raw form of information. In its general sense it is a form of statistical profile. *See also* Information.

Data Acquisition Control System: सूचना अधिग्रहण प्रशासनिक प्रणाली It is a system which is designed to obtain data from number of remote stations and transmit data to them under programe control.

Data Bank: सूचना संग्रह Unprocessed large store of organised information or a collection of information on a given subject. *See also* Database.

Database: सूचना संग्रह Collection of structural and organised related information which is accessible to the user on demand in automatic search by the use of the computer. *See also* Data Bank.

Database Management system (DBMS): सूचना-संग्रह प्रशासन प्रणाली A collection of software that helps in managing database; or comprehensive software system that builds, maintains and provides access to a database.

Data Centre: सूचना केन्द्र An organisation where information/data acquired and processed for dissemination

Data Compilation: सूचना संयोजन Organisation and collection of information/data according to requirement.

Data Code: सूचना संहिता A set of characters structured in such a way as to represent the data items of a data element. (DDPT)

Data Collection: सूचना संग्रह Transfer of information from various points to a central point.

Data Communication: सूचना सम्प्रेषण The transmission of data between points, generally by means of telecommunication system (DDPT)

Method of transferring data to processing site.

Data Communication Control Unit: सूचना सम्प्रेषण प्रशासनिक इकाई The unit that scans the central terminal unit buffers for massages and transfers them to the central processor (M.D.).

Data Communication Network: सूचना सम्प्रेषण तंत्र An interconnected group of computer systems. *See also* Computer Network.

Data Communication System: सूचना सम्प्रेषण प्रणाली A system of data processing in which terminal devices and special interfacing equipment is used.

Data Conversion: सूचना परिवर्तन The change of data from one format to another

Data Design: सूचना संयोजन Layout/format of information.

Data Element: सूचना तत्व Category of the information based on its characteristics. Unit of information is also regarded as data element in cataloguing

Data Entry Operator: सूचना निवेशकार One who inputs data in computer.

Data Error: सूचना गलती A mistake in data.

Data Field: सूचना क्षेत्र An area allocated to a data record in main memory of the computer.

Data File: सूचना सारणी/फाइल Arranged order of various sets of data.

Data Flowchart: सूचना अंकन रुपरेखा A flowchart showing the path of the data through a system.

Data Format: सूचना आकार The way in which data kept in a file.

Data Input: सूचना निवेश The process of recording data in computer device.

Data Processing: सूचना संसाधन Generic term used for all the operations carried out to use/handle data.

Data Register: सूचना पंजी Computer CPU where provision is available for the temporary storage.

Datamation: आंकड़ाकरण Automatic Data Processing, or the manipulation of information by machines, resulting in a column reduction and simplification, to meet a more understandable, rational or meaningful. Commonly applied to a logical sequence for rapid access (Ranganathan), or it is a data storing and retrieving system.

Date: तिथि, दिनाँक A statement of time/period on a letter, book, document, etc.

Date of Accession: अवाप्ति दिनाँक A date on which document enters to the library records.

Date Card: तिथि पत्र *See* Book Card

Date Guide: तिथि दर्शक A guide card used to indicate the date of loan of documents.

Date of Issue: देय तिथि A date on which a book is given on loan to the borrower.

Date of Publication: प्रकाशन तिथि Year in which a document is published.

Date Slip: तिथि पर्ची A paper slip generally pasted inside the cover of the document to indicate circulation mark.

Date Stamp: तिथि मुहर A stamp used by the library circulation counter to fix up either date of issue or date of return on the loaned document.

DBS III: डी. बी. एस. थ्री Database management system for micro-computers and popular in use on IBM PCs.

Death Date: मृत्यु तिथि The year of death is traced in catalogue entry to highlight the period of the contribution.

Decentralisation: विकेन्द्रीकरण The operations are carried out at various points to complete service.

Decimal: दशमलव Property of the digit, in which there are ten possibilities.

Decimal Classification: दशमलव वर्गीकरण It is a widely used library classification scheme devised by Melevil Dewey and first published in 1876. In four volume 20th revised edition has been brought out to make scheme more effective and workable. It has used Indo Arebic numeral notation in decimal fraction, the universe of knowledge is classified in ten class orders.

Decimal Fraction Device: दशमलव अंश युक्ति Device of taking the place value of each digit in a number as in a pure decimal fraction, though the decimal point to its equivalent mark is not actually put in front of the number (Ranganathan).

Decimal Notation: दशमलव अंकन Decimal notation is widely used in deway decimal classification seheme and digits are grouped in three.

Dedication: समर्पण Author statement in his work for paying respect to someone.

Defaulter: विलम्बी A person who fails in returning library documents on due date.

Defective Copy: दोषयुक्त प्रति A copy which have some defect in printing/binding.

Defence Science Information and Documentation Centre (DESIDOC) : रक्षा विज्ञान सूचना एवम् प्रलेखन केन्द्र The centre is functional under the defence research and development organisation to serve the requirement of DRDO scientists. It is collecting information from published and unpublished sources to disseminate it to defence establishments. It has official organs like news letter and bulletin to provide current information in the field of defence science and technology.

Definition: परिभाषा Description of the word.

Delegation of Powers: अधिकार हस्तान्तरण When powers are transfered on a particular level.

Delete: समाप्त A command used in computer to remove a program character from the memory of the computer.

Delivery Van: वितरक वाहन A vehicle used for transporting documents of a library.

Deluxe Binding: विशेष बड़ी जिल्द An artistic larger size binding.

Demonstration : प्रदर्शन Presentation of services to focus the value.

Denudation: निएवरण Progressive decrease of the extension and the increase of the intention or the depth of a subject or an isolate and there by producing a chain of new subjects or isolates (Ranganathan).

Department: विभाग It is a section of the institution like library.

Departmental Catalogue: विभागीय सूची A catalogue consisting of entries for books of a department for which it is developed.

Departmental Collection: विभागीय संचय A collection which is developed to satisfy the requirements of the department or collection of documents generated by the department.

Departmental Library: विभागीय पुस्तकालय This category library is maintained almost by all the ministries and subordinate departments or the library maintained as extension in the departments of university/college.

Departmental Publication: विभागीय प्रकाशन The publications generated by the department. These are generally research reports/project reports.

Dependent Work: आश्रित कार्य Work got by some modification of another work or by the augmentation of it (Ranganathan).

Depository: संग्रह स्थल A place where things are stored for safty.

Depository Library: संग्रह पुस्तकालय A library in which less used documents are shifted or a library which receives document free of cost under the provision of law.

Depth Classification: गहन वर्गीकरण Version of a scheme of classification sufficiently worked out for the needs of micro-thought and of documentation work and service (Ranganathan), or classification to identify its smallest/ micro aspect.

Deputy Librarian : उप पुस्तकाध्यक्ष One who works direct in subordination of librarian and responsible to act as librarian in his absence.

Description: विवरण The detailed record.

Descriptive Cataloguing: विवरणात्मक सूचीकरण Part of the catalogue which has more concern with physical description.

Descriptive Bibliography: विवरणात्मक ग्रन्थ सूची It is a type of bibliography in which information is covered in more detail.

Descriptive Element: विवरणात्मक तत्त्व Terms added after the name of a person or a corporate body, inclusive of individualizing term, to denote the role played (ISI).

Descriptor: विवरणकार A word or symbol used to represent the document.

Device: युक्ति It is a technique.

Devised Array-Isolate: उत्पन्न पंक्ति एकल Array-isolate of an array got by chronological or alphabetical or subject device.

Devised Common Isolate: उत्पन्न साधारण एकल Common Isolate got by subject device.

Dewey Decimal Classification: ड्वे दशमलव वर्गीकरण American devised library classification published in 1876. It divides knowledge into ten groups. To represent classes Indo-Arabic numerals in decimal are used in three figures. 20th edition of the scheme in four volume is available for use.

Diagram: रेखाचित्र An outline figure/scheme/record traced by an automatic indicator.

Diary: डायरी Record of events.

Dictionary: शब्द कोश The book containing the words of a language, arranged in alphabetical order with their explanation.

Dictionary Catalogue: शब्द कोश सूची Catalogue in which all word entries are arranged in alphabetical order. This comprises one part of catalogue.

Digest: डाइजेस्ट A publication consisting information on a topic with related topics in very condensed form.

Digit: अंक Each one of the distinct symbol, taken by itself, found in a class number or used in constructing/it (Ranganathan)/smallest unit in a notational system.

Digital Computer: डिजिटल कम्प्यूटर A computer that process information in numerical or coded form, rather then in the form of directly measurable quantities. (DDPT)

Digital Signal: डिजिटल संकेत A signal that represents digital data generally one in which various states are represented by discrete level of some physical para meter. (DDPT)

Dimension of a Class: वर्ग के आयाम Number of facets including the basic facet in a compound class; and the total of the number of facets in all the constituents of a complex class.

Diploma Course in Library Science: पुस्कालय विज्ञान शिक्षा में डिप्लोमा Library science education to begin with the professional services.

Direct Access: सीधी पहुँच Access to the data without any reservation.

Direct Processing: सीधा संसाधन Technique of locating, retrieving and updating of records in computer without reading proceedings.

Disk: डिस्क A revolving platter upon which information/data is recorded (DDPT).

Direct Entry: सीधा प्रवेश An entry without any barrier. *See also* Open Access.

Direct Printing: सीधी छपाई Process in which machine readable data transferred direct on paper without loading it to another machine.

Direct Sub-division: सीधा उप विभाग Sub-division brought-out of a division directly.

Director: निर्देशक The chief executive/head of the institution.

Directory: निदेशिका A alphabetical list of names, places countries, institutions, etc., with brief information.

Directory of Libraries: पुस्तकालय निदेशिका An alphabetical list of the libraries with brief information about each of library included in it, such directories are brought out by ILA and Raja Ram Mohun Roy foundation.

Discharging Desk/Discharging Counter: निर्गम डैस्क/मेज *See* Circulation Department.

Discipline: विषय An organised field of learning.

Discipline: अनुशासन *See* Library Discipline

Discharge: निर्गम An act of cancellation of loan record of library document's when it is received back by the library.

Discharging: निर्गम *See* Discharge.

Discharging Tray: निर्गम ट्रे A tray used to keep records of the documents operated by circulation desk.

Discount: छूट The rebate on printed price.

Discontinued Publication: विच्छिन्न प्रकाशन A publication which is stopped.

Discontinued Array: बाधित/विच्छिन्न पंक्ति An array of classes, not admitting of interpolation.

Disjunctive Treatment: विभाजक व्यवहार Treatment of a subject in a work in such a way that the treatment of its subdivisions are separable and admit of each being made a work by itself independently of the other subdivisions and of the whole work.

Disk Drive: डिस्क ड्राइव Device which keeps disks for use in computer. It is a secondary storage that provides additional memory capacity to a microcomputer system.

Diskette: डिस्केट *See* Floppy Disk

Display: प्रदर्शन Presentation of document/information for exhibition, or calling of data on monitor in computer, or an output device to view the data.

Display Board: प्रदर्शन पट्ट A board used to publicise new aquisitons or exhibition of important topics on special occasions.

Display Case: प्रदर्शल मंजूषा *See* Book Display Case. *See also* Exhibition Case.

Display Stand: प्रदर्शक आधार A stand used to exhibit library documents.

Dissection: विच्छेदन Breakdown of a subject or an isolate into several subjects or isolates of smaller extension on the basis of a characteristic and there-by creating an array of new subjects or isolates (Ranganathan).

Dissemination of Information: सूचना सम्प्रेषण It is the service arranged with communication system to keep information within the reach of the user.

Dissertation : शोध प्रबन्ध An original work brought out by the researcher. *See also* Thesis.

Distinctive Name of Corporate Body: सुस्पष्ट नाम समष्टि निकाय Name of corporate beginning with the name of a person or of a geographical entity.

District Central Library: जिला केन्द्रीय पुस्तकालय Main district public library established under an act framed by the state government.

District Library: जिला पुस्तकालय It is a public library which functions at district headquarters.

Divide like: विभाजन जैसे An instruction used in classification to develop parallel sequence by using the available pattern.

Division: विभाग Process of sorting the entities of a universe into sub-aggregates on the basis of a preferred characteristic, putting like entities into the same sub-aggregate and the unlike entities into different sub-aggregates (Ranganathan).

Division Characteristic: विभाजक गुण Characteristic preferred as the basis for the division of the entities of a universe (Ranganathan).

Doctoral Thesis: शोध प्रबन्ध See Thesis.

Document: अभिलेख The document is the record of knowledge/information which may be in print/non-print form. In computer a non book medium that contains stored information for further use.

Documentalist: प्रलेखक An officer who is concerned with the documentation to facilitate information dissemination to specialist reader.

Documentation: प्रलेखन Collection, organisation of recorded information exhaustively, expeditiously and pin-pointed for use of the researchers.

Documentation Centre: प्रलेखन केन्द्र It is an organisation engaged in collection, evaluation, organisation and repackaging of information for quick retrieval on demand. It generates publications such as abstracts, indexes, annotations lists etc.

Documentation List: प्रलेखन सूची List of documents prepared for a specific purpose. The purpose is usually to bring to the reader close to a exhaustive/select list of document relevant to his enquiry/study. This term is used to emphasise the inclusion of micro documents in listing.

Documentation Research and Training Centre (DRTC): (डी आर टी सी) The centre is situated at Bangalore and engaged in the advanced research and training in the field of Library and Information Science.

Documentation Service: प्रलेखन सेवा Service vide which abstracting, indexing etc. are provided to the user.

Documentation Science: प्रलेखन विज्ञान It is a science of controlling the enormous growth of information and of generating secondary sources.

Documentation Work: प्रलेखन कार्य Method of preparing lists, abstracts etc.

Document Delivery Service: प्रलेख प्रदाय सेवा A service which arranges documents/information at the user's place.

Document Procurement Service: प्रलेख प्राप्ति सेवा Service in which photocopies of the documents are obtained to make available to the user.

Document Profile: प्रलेख विवराणिका Machine readable bibliographic record.

Document Supply: प्रलेख पूर्ति *See* Document Delivery Service.

Donation Record: दान-अभिलेख Record for gifts received. It may contain record for cash/items or for both.

Dormitory Library: डारमेटरी पुस्तकालय When a library collections are operated in dormitory.

Down Loading: उतारना Transfer of data from one computer unit to another computer unit.

Downtime: उतार समय Time taken by the computer in transfer of data.

Draft: प्रारूप First step writing which requires modification and corrections.

Drive: संचालन Refers to a disk drive which is used to load a storing device.

Due Date: देय तिथि Date on which a document is due for return to the library from which it was borrowed.

Dummy: नमूना A substitute to the original. It is generally prepared to publish a work.

Duplicate: प्रतिलिपि Exact copy of the original.

Duplicate Entry: पुनः प्रविष्टि An additional entry.

Duplication: प्रतिलिपिकरण A process of obtaining of number of copies from the original.

Duplicator: प्रतिलिपिकारक A machine used to obtain multiple copies of the original.

Dusting: धूल निवारण An act of removing dust from collections.

E

Edit: संशोधन Adjustment of information/data into required format.

Edited: संम्पादित The work prepared for publication by the person other than author.

Editing: सम्पादन It is an activity of incorporating correction at the stage of creation of a work or selection of relevant material in its sequences.

Edition: संस्करण Copies of the document published first time.

Edition Statement: संस्करण विवरण An information pertaining to the edition of the document generally made in a catlogue card.

Editor: सम्पादक A person who prepares contributions for publication, and the contributions are not his own. He makes only changes and corrections wherever necessary.

Editorial: सम्पादकीय A statement in which current matters are presented by the editor, or the point of view of the work.

Editor Reference: सम्पादक संदर्भ Information about editor traced in catalogue card.

Education: शिक्षा It is to promote full awareness of social and human values, so that one can develop a strong character and livo better life and can function as responsible member of the society.

Education for Librarianship: पुस्तकालय विज्ञानी शिक्षा *See* Library Science Education.

Effective Link: प्रभावी कड़ी *See* Sought Link.

Electronic Document Delivery System: इलैक्ट्रोनिक प्रलेख प्रदाय प्रणाली When through the computer information/data is approached on line and is retained on electronic device, if required.

Electronic Library: इलैक्ट्रोनिक पुस्तकालय Electronic library is one which uses latest modern technologies to store and retrieve information with a speed.

Electronic Mail (E Mail): इलैक्ट्रोनिक मेल Method of transmitting message electronically. It is a computer and telecommunication facility used advanced program then the telex services.

Electronic Media: इलेक्ट्रोनिक माध्यम Apparatus-like computer and communication devices.

Electronic Ordering: इलेक्ट्रोनिक खरीद आदेश It is a on line ordering technique.

Elimination Factor: निष्कासन कारक Ratio of the number of rejected documents to total number of documents searched (Ranganathan).

Embossed Book: उत्कीर्ण पुस्तक A book prepared for the use of blind by embossing characters.

Empty Digit: रिक्त अंक A digit which has no semantic value, but it retains the ordinal value and generally used to expend notational capacity.

Empty and Emptying Digit: रिक्त एवम् रिक्तकारक अंक A digit with ordinal value, without representing any specific focal idea, and depriving the preceding digit of focal idea. (ISI)

Emptying Digit: रिक्तकारक अंक A digit with ordinal value and also depriving the preceding digit of its focal idea (ISI).

Emptying Substantive Digit: रिक्त कारक गर्भित अंक A digit with ordinal value representing a focal idea, and depriving the preceding digit of its focal idea.

Embodied Thought: अन्तर्निहित विचार Record of the work on paper or other material, fit for physical handling, transport across space, and preservation through time (ISI).

Encyclopaedia: विश्व कोश A publication consisting information on universe of knowledge or on all possible aspects of the branch of knowledge for which it is developed. It is usually arranged alphabetically. The publication may appear in number of volumes.

Endowment Fund: धर्मार्थ निधि A fund which is created for the use of endowment.

Energy: उर्जा It is a Dr. Ranganathan recognised facet to arrange action characteristics of any class.

Energy Facet: उर्जा पक्ष *See* Energy.

Energy Isolate: उर्जा एकल *See* Energy.

Encoding: कूट बनाना To associate a specific code with each letter of an alphabet (ISI).

Enlarged Edition: विस्तृत संस्करण *See* Revised Edition.

Entity: सत्ता Any existing thing or idea.

Entry: प्रविष्टि Unit record of information in a catalogue or in documentation list.

Entry Element: प्रविष्टि तत्त्व The blocks of information such as author, title, publisher, year, series, note etc.

Entry Word: प्रविष्टि शब्द A word used to arrange the entry.

Enumerated Array-Isolate: परिगणनात्मक पंक्ति एकल Array isolate of an array got by enumeration device.

Enumerated Common Isolate: परिगणनात्मक साधारण एकल Common isolate got by enumeration device.

Enumerated Special Isolate: परिगणनात्मक विशिष्ट एकल Special isolate got by enumeration device.

Enumeration: परिगणना Listing of subjects of past, present and anticipated future.

Enumerative Classification: परिगणनात्मक वर्गीकरण A classification which identify all possible classes and lists them after assigning notation.

Enumeration Device: परिगणनात्मक युक्ति Device of using successive digits for forming the classes or the isolates in facet or the array isolate in an array by directly enumerating them.

Entropy: असूच The unavailable information in a group of documents. The degree of disorganisation in an informational assemblage (ISI).

Ephemeral Material: अनावश्यक सामग्री/ग्रन्थ Document which becomes unimportant soon after these are seen.

Episode: घटना The term is used to represent incident.

Error: गलती The term is used for mistakes.

Estimates: अनुमान Calculation to project future requirements.

Evaluation: मूल्याकंन Technique used to estimate standards of various documents produced in different disciplines in a given time. *See also* Review/ Critical Review.

Even Page: समपृष्ठ Page allotted an even number.

Exchange: विनिमय An arrangement under which publications of any organisation are distributed in other organistions with the understanding that their publications will be made available in return. Even in case of periodical publications, price will not be claimed.

Executive: अधिशासी The person who admimisters an organisation. or A person who performs duties to satisfy the policies available to run the organisation.

Exhaust Edition: समाप्त संस्करण An edition which has become out of print.

Exibition: प्रदर्शनी *See* Book exhibition.

Exit: बाहर Halting in a operation of computer program.

Expansive Classification: व्यापक वर्गीकरण Scheme of classification designed by Charles Ammi cutter and published for the first time in 1893.

Expert Advice: विशेषज्ञ परामर्श Advice based on expertise.

Explosion of Information: सूचना की अधिकता Uncontrolled speedy growth of information.

Expressed Thought: अभिव्यक्त विचार Thought expossed in language, pictures or symbols or in any other medium and thereby made communicable (Ranganathan).

Extension Card: विस्तार पत्र *See* Continuation Card.

Extension Service: प्रसार सेवा Service extended to a number of points where users are available.

Extension Work: प्रसार कार्य When the existing equipment/service is extended to those who are not in direct service preview.

External Reader: बाहरी पाठक A person who is not a member of the library and makes use of library collections.

Extract: सार Selected part of a work issued as a separate work. *See also* Abstract.

Extrapolation: अन्तर्बेधन An act in which a new term in classification is assigned with an appropriate notation to put it in the end of the existing classes of an array.

Evaluation Acquisition Facet: मूल्यांकन खरीद पक्ष Part of the book number of a document, which is the evaluation acquision number.

Evaluation Number: मूल्यांकन संख्या Part of the book number of a document, which is an appreciation, criticism, evaluation or review of or a reply to a pseudo classic, attached after to part taken from the book number of the host pseudo classic (Ranganathan).

Evaluation Facet: मूल्यांकन पक्ष *See* Evaluation Acquisition Facet.

Every Book its Reader: प्रत्येक पुस्तक का पाठक It is third law which demands that every collection should be effective and in helpful sequence to put in intensive use.

Every Reader his/her Book: प्रत्येक पाठक की पुस्तक It is second law of library science cited by Dr. Ranganathan. The law demands that variety of books should be acquired to satisfy the various demands of the users.

F

Facet: पक्ष The totality of the isolates, each one of which can itself be attached to a specified basic class or a class derived from it, and which are enumerated together in a schedule as possible manifestation of a particular fundamental category in a specified level of a specific round, or generic name for a basic class or an isolate of a subject (Ranganathan), or group of divisions when a subject is divided on the basis of single characteristic.

Facet Analysis: पक्ष विश्लेषण Analysis of a subject into its facets according to the postulates and principles stated for the purpose (Ranganathan).

Facet Device (Idea Plane): पक्ष युक्ति (विचार तल) Device for sharpening a host focus in the form of a class by the addition of new facet (Ranganathan).

Facet Device (Notational Plane): पक्ष युक्ति (अंकन तल) Device of prefixing a connecting symbol to an isolate number with in a class number in order to implement the facet device of the idea plane. (Ranganathan).

Faceted Classification: पक्षात्मक वर्गीकरण A classification scheme based on fundamental concept of facet formula provided by Dr. Ranganathan.

Facet Formula: पक्ष सूत्र A formula used to group characteristics on a desired plan to achieve the sequence of various facets.

Facet Synthesis: पक्ष संश्लेषण Synthesis of the focal numbers of a subject into class numbers according to the postulates and principles stated for the purpose (Ranganathan).

Facet Telescoping Point: पक्ष दूरस्थ बिन्दु Stage in the enumeration of the isolates in a telescoped facet, where change of level of facet occurs.

Faculty Library: संकाय पुस्तकालय It is generally an extension library to the university library system.

Fair Copy: स्पष्ट प्रति Manuscript after corrections or copy emerged after seeing draft.

False Link: अनुपयुक्त कड़ी In a subject analysis in chain when notation is not able to spell out any concept/aspect.

False-drop: मिथ्या झुकाव A reference citation that does not pertain to the subject sought.

Family Name: परिवार नाम A name which is in use in family or represent its heredity. *See* Surname.

Fanciful Title: भ्रामक शीर्षक The title which does not reveal theme of the document.

Favoured Country: समर्थित देश Country about which the library has larger collection than other countries barring mother country (Ranganathan).

Favoured Focus Number: समर्थित मुख्य संख्या The digit representing a Favoured isolate number or a Favoured class number.

Favoured Language: समर्थित भाषा A language in which most of the collections are developed by a library.

Favoured System: समर्थित प्रणाली The system which is in use of a library.

Feasibility Study: सम्भावित अध्ययन A study to decide the area of work plan for a particular purpose.

Featured Space Isolate: गुण आधारित स्थान एकल Physiographical feature smaller than a continent or an ocean and man-made formations and population clusters (Ranganathan).

Feed-back: पुनर्निवेशन It is a process of arranging relevant information

Festschrift: अभिनन्दन ग्रन्थ A memorial volume issued in honour of someone. It may contain contributions of various people.

Field: स्थान In computer program format the space provided to keep a block of information/data/information group in a record. In cataloguing, a set of columns in a card fixed as to enter. The total area of the card available for information storage.

Field Chart: स्थान चित्र Layouts of the data showing the field program.

Field Data: स्थान-आँकडा Data generated from the field to plot.

Fiction: उपन्यास Narrative prose writing.

Fictitious Name: अवास्तविक नाम An assumed name.

File: फाइल It is an organised named collection of information for some particular purpose, or a collection of related records as one unit.

File Index: फाइल अनुक्रमाणिका A table, or list of files.

File Management System: फाइल प्रशासन प्रणाली A system used to control the files available in any database, or computer software to define data in specified records and files to make use on demand.

File Processing: फाइल संसाधन Updating of the file.

Filiatory Sequence: वंशानुक्रम Sequence of subject on the basis of their relationship.

Filing: क्रम व्यवस्था/फाइलिंग Arrangement of related items.

Filing Cabinet: फाइल मंजूषा A steel or wooden cabinet used to hold files in some helpful arrangement.

Film: चलचित्र A thin transparent sheet coated with a light sensitive emulsion.

Film Strip: फिल्म स्ट्रिप A record of illustrations and text on a single length film.

Film Library: फिल्म चलचित्र पुस्तकालय Library which keeps film collections.

Film Projector: चलचित्र प्रदर्शक A mechanical device which arranges visual of the recorded information.

Film Reader: चलचित्र पाठक A mechanical device through which film records can be used.

Final Proof: अन्तिम जाँच Last proof before printing a document.

Finance: वित्त Money affairs.

Financial Estimate: वित्त अनुमान Estimate or tentative financial requirement to continue library service.

Financial Management: वित्त प्रशासन Management which deals with collection and utilisation of funds.

Financial Record: वित्त अभिलेख Document keeping record of financial distribution and receipt etc.

Financial Resources: वित्तीय साधन Resources through which money is collected to run a library.

Financial Statement: वित्त विवरण Detials of the finance distribution.

Fine: दण्ड Penalty for over due documents which is calculated on the basis of number of days it is retained.

Finite Universe: सीमित ज्ञान जगत् Universe with a finite number of entities.

First Edition: प्रथम संस्करण The whole lot of the document published at the same time or a document published first time or a new edition.

First Indentation: प्रथम दण्ड Left edge line in a catalogue card.

First Link: प्रथम कड़ी The link of the lowest order contained in a chain (Ranganathan).

First Name: प्रथम नाम A name which appears first among group of authors on a document.

First Proof: प्रथम जाँच When draft of the text is put to print and corrections are incorporated first time.

First Vertical: प्रथम उर्ध्वस्थ The leftmost vertical line of a catalogue card which is used as heading line.

Five Laws of Library Science: पुस्तकालय विज्ञान के पाँच नियम The five laws are: Books are for use; Every reader his/her book; Every book its reader; Save the time of the reader and Library is a growing organism.

These were formulated by Dr. S R. Ranganathan.

Fixed Location: निश्चित स्थिति Arrangement of documents in terms of their fixed position on the shelves.

Flexible Notation: लचीला अकंन A notation which accommodates other symbol to represent new subjects in a classification scheme without disturbing the existing sequence.

Flexibility: लचीलापन Classification permitting the insertion of any new class and its notation being capable of expansion to mark that insertion without dislocating the rest of the notation (Ranganathan).

Floppy Disk: फ्लोपी डिस्क Computer used magnetic flexible disk for digital memory.

Floppy Disk Drive: फ्लोपी डिस्क ड्राइव A device in computer which handles floppy dish to use.

Flow Chart: विन्यास चित्र A graphical representation of the program.

Focus: केन्द्र Generic term to denote an isolate idea/basic class/compound class/complex class.

Foolscap: फुल स्कैप A standard size of the paper.

Footnote: संदर्भ टिप्पणी A note supplementary to the main text. Which is generally written in the bottom area.

Foreign Information Centres: विदेशी सूचना केन्द्र The information centres of the foreign agencies to disseminate information about their socio-cultural developments. In such centres American and British are available in metropolitan cities of India.

Foreign Publication: विदेशी प्रकाशन The publications of the countries other than mother country.

Fore Name: अग्रनाम It is the part of the name which indivisualises to a person.

Foreword: प्राक्थन An introductory statement in a book which speaks about the objectives and initiatives of the work.

Formal Education: औपचारिक शिक्षा Curricula based education in which registration in required in some institution to study a fixed curricula and to undergo with an examination on expiry of proscribed period. On completion of the whole process a degree/diploma is awarded.

Format: आकार The term used to demote physical space and size of document or structuring of information record in predetermined arrangement.

Format Control: आकार अनुशासन In computer, format control protects data block.

Format Storage: आकार संग्रह A system in which storage is done on a fixed available format.

Format of a record: अभिलेख आकार *See* Origination of Data.

Form Class: रूप वर्ग The class in which documents are grouped in their forms like poetry, drama, fiction and so on.

Form Division: रूप विभाजन These are the enumerated divisions listed in a scheme of classification to denote various forms of documents.

Forms of Catalogue: सूची रूप There are various type of catalogues identified on the basis if inner and outer forms.

Forwarding: अग्रसरण Process of pushing a subject/information for next action.

FORTRAN: फोरट्रान Computer used programming language developed by IBM corporation and widely accepted for commercial mathematical computations.

Form Facet: रूप पक्ष Part of the book number of a document, which represents its form.

Form Number: रूप संख्या Ordinal number which is the translation of the name of the form of arrangement or of exposition or again the physical form of the document

(Ranganathan).

Formula: सूत्र Fixed guideline.

Free Access System: मुफ्त प्रवेश प्रणाली A system which permits users unrestricted accesss to the library collections. *See also* Open Access.

Free hand: स्वतंत्र Without any reservation.

Frequency: आवृत्ति The number of occurrences of a publication as in case of periodicals some are weekly, monthly and quarterly etc.

Front Cover: बाह्य आवरण It is a first cover.

Full Cloth Binding: सम्पूर्ण कपड़ा जिल्द When for protection hard board cover is covered fully by cloth.

Full Leather Binding: सम्पूर्ण चमड़ा जिल्द The whole of the hard cover is covered with leather to ensure safty for longer period.

Full Name: पूर्ण नाम A mane consisting all parts like forename and surname.

Full Point: पूर्ण बिन्दु The punchuation mark used to end the sentence. Also known as full stop.

Full Title: पूर्ण शीर्षक *See* Main Title.

Functions of the Catalogue: सूची कार्य Catalogue is a key to know the presence of document on a given subject, author, title with its location on shelves.

Fund: कोष *See* Book Fund.

Fundamental Category: मूलभूत श्रेणी According to Ranganathan, there are five and only five fundamental categories — personality, matter, energy, space and time each facet of a subject is regarded as manifestation of one or other of these categories. These are arranged in order of PMEST in their decreasing concreteness.

Furniture: साज सामान It may be of plastic, wood or steel used to keep collection and also to arrange services.

Fused Link: नष्ट कड़ी Link whose end isolate number is a fused number because of its being got by subject device.

G

Galleries: दीर्घा The area used to keep exhibits in library.

Galley Proof: गेली प्रूफ Stage of the proof where author can make changes easily.

Gap Device: अन्तर युक्ति Device of leaving a finit gap between the numbers representing two array isolate ideas appearing to be consecutive at the time of the enumeration, in order to accommulate new isolates, as and when they arise, claiming their filatory places within that gap (Ranganathan).

Gate Register: द्वार पंजी *See* Visitor Register.

Gazetteers: गजेटियर These are reference documents which are especially designed to keep information about Nation, Cities, Districts. etc. with details of social, cultural and economic conditions. These also give geographical details.

General Book: सामान्य पुस्तक When a book gives general exposition of a subject.

General Catalogue: सामान्य सूची *See* Main Catalogue.

General Computer: सामान्य कम्प्यूटर See Micro-computer.

General Entry: सामान्य प्रविष्टि Entry not mentioning a specific objective.

General Relation: सामान्य सम्बन्ध Phase relation of a more or less comprehensive or non descriptive kind between the two phases (Ranganathan).

General Relation Phase: सामान्य सम्बन्ध पक्ष Second phase of a complex class or of a complex isolate or of a complex array isolate as the case may be, in which the phase relation in a general phase relation (Ranganathan).

General Library: सामान्य पुस्तकालय A library which is not limited to a special subject or a special user, and which is a main library of any Institution.

General Reader: साधारण पाठक A user who has no special requirement.

General Subject: सामान्य विषय Subject which is of common interest.

General Title: सामान्य शीर्षक *See* Collective Title.

Generalia Class: साधारण वर्ग A class in which the documents of general nature are kept.

Geographical Area: भौगोलिक क्षेत्र An area showing country, region, district and so on.

Geographical Device: भौगोलिक युक्ति A method of adding a notation to a class number to represent geographical area.

Ghost Writer: अदृश्य लेखक One who writes in the name of well-known person, without disclosing his name.

Gift Book Register: दानप्राप्त पुस्तक पंजी A register in which books received as gift are listed.

Glossary: शब्दकोश An alphabetical list of terms with description. It may be only for selected terms.

Good Office Committee: गुड आफिस समिति A committee of the representatives of book trade, librarians and government representative to recommend conversion rate and discount rate for Indian Book market. The committee has office in Delhi.

Government Document: सरकारी अभिलेख The publication brought out by government agency.

Government Library: सरकारी

पुस्तकालय The library maintained by the Government funds and functions under the government policies.

Government Publication: सरकारी प्रकाशन *See* Government Documents.

Gramophone Library: ग्रामोफोन पुस्तकालय A library keeps gramophones as its collections.

Grapheme: आलेखित A written or machine code representing a single semantenic, pictographs, ideographs, hieroglyphs are special forms of graphemes (Ranganathan).

Graphic: आलेख Any symbol/mark made on a flat surface or on paper.

Graphic Display: आलेख प्रदर्शन Data display in the various forms and drawings.

Graphic Package: आलेख पैकेज Software that converts data into visual form.

Grant: अनुदान Financial allocation based on some policy.

Group: समूह Any sub-aggregate of the entities formed by the division of the entities of a universe (Ranganathan), or unit composed of characters.

Group Notation Device: समूह अंकन युक्ति Device of using ordinal decimal fraction numbers of two or more digits to represent the numbers of coordinate isolate or array isolates, when they are too many to be represented economically by sector device alone (Ranganathan).

Guarantor: जमानती A person who takes responsibility of the new registered member.

Guide Book: निदेशक पुस्तक A book which deals either preliminaries or have operating formula of the subject to which it belongs.

Guide Card: सलाहकार पत्र Indicator card used in catalogue to point out separating points.

H

Half Binding: अर्द्ध जिल्द It is a style of binding in which back and corner of the hard cover are covered by the different material like cloth, leather etc. than the other material covers the whole of the hard cover.

Half Cloth Binding: अर्द्ध कपड़ा जिल्द Spine and corner of the document cover are protected by cloth rest of the portion by paper etc.

Half Leather Binding: अर्द्ध चमड़ा जिल्द Where spine and corner of the document cover are protected by leather and rest of the portion by other material.

Half Title: अर्द्ध शीर्षक A title which represents a section of the work.

Half Title Page: अर्द्ध शीर्षक पृष्ठ The page bearing the half title, sometimes it is resulted by extension of title page.

Half-yearly: अर्द्ध वार्षिक A periodical which comes at six monthly intervals may also be called semi-annual.

Hand Book: लघु पुस्तिका A small size book which contains concise information. *See also* Manual.

Hand-made Paper: हाथ का बना कागज The paper prepared manually which is generally used to develop very high class documents.

Hanging Indentation: लटकता दण्ड It is an imaginary indentation from the left side edge of the catalogue card. Which is parallel to other indentations. It is used to start a new paragraph of record.

Hard Board: दफ्ती Thick paper used to prepare bindings.

Hard Bound: पक्की जिल्द A book which is published in stiff cover. May also be called `Library Edition'.

Hard Copy: अंकित प्रति A printout of the visual display or a printed publication. Printed or filmed out put form of information.

Hard Disk: हार्ड डिस्क Storage disk coated with magnetic material and used in computer.

Hardware Compatibility: हार्डवेयर समानता The quality of computer by which one computer accepts data stored by another computer with out code modification.

Heading: शीर्षक Word or group of words appearing on the top of the entry and used as access point. It represents the entire work. *See also* Title.

Headline: शीर्ष पंक्ति A line of the front page or top of the page focusing subject. Usually the title or the heading of the chapter is used as headline.

Headquarters: मुख्यालय Main controlling office.

Health Science Library: चिकित्सा विज्ञान पुस्तकालय Library attached to the institution imparting instructions in health science education.

Hegel Classification: हीगल वर्गीकरण Scheme of classes implied in the logic (1812) of Hegel (Ranganathan).

Helpful Order: सहयोगी क्रम Order in a classification which provides all related information close to each other.

Helpful Sequence: सहयोगी सारणी Sequence of classes in a classification which groups classes according to the requirement of the user. Thus like things and unlike things are grouped in separate sequences.

Hierarchical Notation: पदानुक्रम अंकन A notation designed to show that two terms are in the same array, or the same chain. (Ranganthan)

Hierarchy: वंशानुक्रम The order of the terms showing their relation with each other in a scheme of classification.

High Speed Printer : उच्च गति मुद्रक A printer which operates to cope with on line operation of data with a high speed.

Holdings: सम्पत्ति संग्रह The collections of a library. *See also* Library Holdings.

Holiday: अवकाश A day when library remains closed.

Holiday Guide: अवकाश निदर्शिका A publication which contains information about the holidays to be observed by the organisation.

Home Delivery Service: गृह वितरण सेवा A service which makes possible reading material at the door of the user.

Home Library: घरेलू पुस्तकालय *See* Personal Collections.

Homogeneous Computer Network: सजातीय कम्प्यूटर तंत्र A network of similar computers or of particular model.

Homonym: समध्वनीय भिन्नार्थक शब्द A word which is similar in spelling and used in different meaning.

Hospital Library: अस्पताल पुस्तकालय A library developed for the use of hospital staff and patients.

Hospitality in Array: पक्ति में समायोजन Flexibility in co-ordinate classes to accommodate a new coordinate class.

Hospitality in Chain: शृंखला में समायेजन Flexibility in subordinate classes to provide appropriate place to a new class in chain.

Hospitality in Notation: अंकन स्वीकृति क्षमता It is the quality of the notation to accommodate new classes. Also called flexibility

Host Book : मूल पुस्तक A book on which another book is written.

Host Computer: मूल कम्प्यूटर A main control computer in the computer system or network.

Host Document: मूल अभिलेख *See* Host Book.

House Journal: गृह पत्रिका A journal for disseminating current activities of any origination, which has more concern within the department.

House Organ: मुख पत्र *See* House Journal.

Hybrid Computer: हाई ब्रिड कम्प्यूटर The combination of digital and analog computers. These are specially designed computers by combining the advantage of analog and digital computers.

Hyphen: हाइफन A mark used to join two words.

I

Idea Plane: विचारतल अथवा वैचारिक परिवेश The plane of concepts viewed by themselves, that is independently of the term denoting them and the number representing them, in other words independently or their expansion in a natural language or their representation in an artificial language of ordinal numbers (Ranganathan).

Identification Card: पहचान पत्र *See* Borrower's Card.

Ideograph: भाव-चित्र A specific scatch formed by notation.

Illustrations: चित्र The photographs, charts, maps etc. appeared in a book/document.

Illustrator: चित्रकार A person who draws the charts and pictures of a document.

Immediate Access: निकट पहुँच Which is in easy reach.

Immediate Universe: समीपस्थ ज्ञान जगत् The class of order next higher to that of a class or an array, when viewed relative to that class or array (Ranganathan).

Import of Books: पुस्तक आयात The books purchased from the foreign publishers.

Imprint: पहचान The cataloguing statement about the name of the publisher, place and year.

Incharge: प्रभारी *See* Librarian.

Incomplete Title: अपूर्ण शीर्षक The title which do not speak properly about the subject represented. It may be complete from the point of view of writer and publisher.

Indentation : दण्ड The distance from the left-edge or top edge of the catalogue card to plot information on fixed layout to make a new paragraph.

Index: अनुक्रमणिका An alphabetical list of terms, topics, names places, etc. which is used to operate the text or relative position of entries in a file/record.

Index Entry: अनुक्रमाणिका प्रविष्टि An entry which is formulated to develop an index.

Indexing : अनुक्रमणीकरण An art/technique of preparing an index.

Indexing Periodical: अनुक्रमणिका पत्रिका A periodical similar to an abstracting periodical but without giving abstract/annotations for the entires listed in it; or a periodical listing only the bibliographical details of articles, books and other collections on a subject in systematic order.

Index Number: अनुक्रमाणिका संख्या The number in a specific entry representing its document or the number in a class index entry representing its heading.

Index Number Section: अनुक्रमाणिका संख्या अनुभाग The section of an entry giving an index number, if any.

Index to Classification: वर्गीकरण अनुक्रमाणिका Dictionary giving class numbers representing a term in natural language or the jargon of a profession or a trade; in other words, helpful in finding the meaning of such a term, in terms of the ordinal names used in a classificatory language

(Ranganathan).

Indian Association of Special Libraries and Information Centres (IASLIC): विशिष्ट पुस्तकालय तथा सूचना केन्द्रों का संघ It is a registered society, with its office at Calcutta. It is to contribute for special libraries and information centres of the country. It has IASLIC News letter and Indian Library Science Abstract as an annual publication.

Indian Library Association: भारतीय पुस्तकालय संघ It was founded in 1933 as a national body. It is a registered society of library professionals and scholars. Its office is elected from the members by postal ballet system for two `years' term. It organises seminar, conference and workshop to debate on the issues of library science and services. It has publications like ILA News letter and ILA Bulletin to exchange the views of the contributors.

Indian National Scientific Documentation Centre (INSDOC) भारतीय राष्ट्रीय वैज्ञानिक प्रलेखन केन्द्र INSDOC is established to serve scientific community with bibliographical information support. It searches information and arranges photocopies on demand, subject bibliographies on various scientific aspects are developed. Translation facility is available in 18 languages. A number of serial publications are brought out to disseminate information.

Indian Publications: भारतीय प्रकाशन The publications broughtout by Indian publishers.

Indicative Abstract: सांकेतिक सार An abstract which only indicates about text features. This type of abstract does not give full information about the subject.

Indicator: संकेतक A device used in computer to visualise display place.

Indicator Digit: सांकेतिक अंक A symbol used to differenciate highlight the used digits

Indic Names : भारतीय नाम The names which reflects Indian origin.

Individualisation: प्रथक्करण Separation of an entity in a universe into a unitary class by the process of assortment (Ranganathan).

Individualizing Element: प्रथक्करण तत्त्व Term added to a name in a heading to resolve a homonym so as to individualise the entity intended to be denoted (ISI).

Indo-Arabic Numerals: भारोबीय संख्या The numerals used in arithmetic.

Infinite Universe: असीमित ज्ञान Universe with an infinite number of entities.

Influencing Phase: प्रभावी पक्ष Phase 2 of a complex class or of a complex isolate or of a complex array-isolate as the case may be, in which the phase relation is influencing relation (Ranganathan).

Informal Education: अनौपचारिक शिक्षा Education for which no school is required and education can be achieved without any registration.

Informatics: सूचना-विज्ञान The science of processing information/data.

Information: सूचना When a piece of knowledge/data is processed, interpreted and presented in an acceptable form or gets relation with existing relation, becomes information itself or it is data which is used to generate knowledge or in computer use that property of a signal/message whereby it conveys something unpredictable by and meaningful to the recipient, usually measured in BITS (DDPT).

Information Bits: सूचना बिट्स In telecommunications, the bits that are generated by the data source solely as a function of the input information, and not those used by the system for purposes of synchronization and error control (DDPT).

Information Centre: सूचना केन्द्र An orgnisation which collects and organises information for dissemination among specialised users. *See also* Documentation Centre.

Information Desk: सूचना डैस्क *See* Reference Desk.

Information Element: सूचना तत्त्व See Data Element.

Information Explosion: सूचना अधिक्य Enormous growth of information in each discipline.

Information Feedback System: सूचनादायक प्रणाली An information transmission system that varifies accuracy of transmission by means of an echo check. (DDPT)

Information Handling: सूचना संचालन The activities concerning collection, processing and retrieval of information/data.

Information Librarian: सूचना पुस्तकाध्यक्ष *See* Reference Librarian.

Information Library: सूचना पुस्तकालय *See* Reference Library.

Information Officer: सूचना अधिकारी One who works for providing information. *See also* Reference Librarian.

Information Policy: सूचना नीति Set of rules/guidelines to carry out effective use of information, framed by the Government/Government Agency.

Information Processing: सूचना संसाधन *See* Data Processing.

Information Retrieval: सूचना प्राप्ति Search of the desired information from the collection. The technique can be exercised manually or by machine application.

Information Retrieval System: सूचना प्राप्ति प्रणाली A set of instructions/programme used to retrieve information in desired manner.

Information Science: सूचना विज्ञान The study of the development and organisation of information.

Information Scientist: सूचना विज्ञानी A person who deals with information.

Information Society: सूचना समाज A society which is well informed about the latest developments taking place in its surroundings.

Information System: सूचना प्रणाली Data processing system operations and procedures.

Information Technology: सूचना तकनीक Technique of using machine for information processing and transmission to achieve efficiency and speed.

Information Work: सूचना कार्य The works developed as the result of various organised sets of information.

Informative Abstract: सूचना प्रद सार An abstract which gives important information about the main text. The information helps in deciding that the main text is required to see or not.

INFOTAL (on line service centre): इनफोटल (सीधी सूचना सेवा) INFOTAL is a fully equipped reliable service centre. Through a personal computer plugged to a telephone connected to GPSS and one can go around the computer data bases of the world to get on line service. The centre has trained search specialists with technical background who offers access to available major database of the world.

In House Service: आन्तरिक सेवा Service for the use of the employees within a unit.

Input: संग्रह Information stored into the internal memory of the computer (Ranganathan); or the information, data, signal, or the like supplied to a system of device (DDPT).

Input Area: संग्रह क्षेत्र In a storage, a section that has been reserved for input data. (DDPT)

Input Devices: संग्रह युक्ति In computer keyboard is most visible device used for input. Thus it is a meachanical unit which brings data into a computer for processing. *See also* Input Equipment.

Input Equipment: संग्रह साज-समान The equipment used for transferring data into a data processing system.

In Service Training: सेवअवधि प्रशिक्षण Training while working.

Instalment: अंश/किस्त Payment in parts.

Institution: संस्था An independent or autonomous corporate body other than Government. It may be created by a Government, or constituted under a law, or formed voluntarily either formally or informally. It has continued existence and functions beyond that of merely convening a conference (Ranganathan).

Institutional Library: संस्थागत पुस्तकालय A library run by the institution.

Institutional Membership: संस्था सदस्यता Extension of right to participate in the activities of the institution.

Instruction: आदेश Information when coded and fed as a unit into a digital computer, causes it to perform a sequence of manipulations (Ranganathan); or command forming a part of program and a set of identifying characters.

Interdisciplinary Work: अन्तरविषयी रचना A work which deals with more than one discipline.

Integral Treatment: आन्तरिक उपचार Treatment of a subject in a work in such a way that the treatment of its subdivisions are not separable from one another or from the whole work. (ISI)

Intermediate Service: मध्यवर्तीय सेवा Service at any stage in its progress towards ultimate service (Ranganathan).

Inter Library Loan: अन्तर पुस्तकालय उधार Loan between the libraries to share collections.

Inter-Class Phase Device (Idea Plane): अन्तर्वर्ग पक्ष युक्ति (विचार तल) Device for sharpening a host class by addition of another class as an additional phase.

Inter-Class Phase Device (Notational Plane): अन्तर्वर्ग पक्ष युक्ति (अंकन तल) Device of prefixing a connecting symbol to a digit representing a phase relation in the idea plane.

Internal Administration: आन्तरिक व्यवस्था Supervision of the various sections of the library.

Internal Memory: आन्तरिक स्मृति It is a total memory which is automatically accessible or data retaining capacity of the computer.

International Federation for Documentation and Information (FID): प्रलेखन तथा सूचना अन्तर्राष्ट्रीय फेडरेशन A non-Governmental organisation engaged in promotion and coordination of documentation and information activities through-out the world.

International Federation of Library Associations and Institutions (IFLA) : पुस्तकालय संघों तथा संस्थाओं का अन्तर्राष्ट्रीय संघ It is an International Association of Library Science and Librarian's Associations of the world. The organisation is to promote library and information science in the world. It was founded in 1927 and has 124 countries as members. It consists two type units - professional groups comprising 32 sections and 11 round tables and five core programmes.

International Standard Book Number (ISBN): अन्तर्राष्ट्रीय मानक पुस्तक संख्या It is a number assigned to a document before its publication which translates publisher, edition and volume number etc.

International Standard Serial Number (ISSN) : अन्तर्राष्ट्रीय मानक क्रम संख्या A number given to each serial title to identify a serial on international code number of periodicals.

Interpolated Number : समाहित संख्या A number consisting of an emptying digit preceded by another digit.

Interpolation Device: समाहन युक्ति Device of interpolating another digit between two consecutive digits.

Interrelation: अन्तर्सम्बन्ध Analysis of the information sought into facets alongwith their relation, and expression of it in the machine language (Ranganathan).

Inter Array Phase Relation: अन्तर पंक्ति पक्ष संबंध Relation between the component array isolates of a complex array isolate.

Intra-Facet Phase Relation: अन्तर पक्ष सम्बन्ध Relation between the component isolates of an complex isolate.

Internal Notation: आन्तरिक अंकन Notation which indicates the order of location of individual books, or other bibliographic items, within the class severally. (Ranganathan)

Interpreter: व्याख्याता A programme used to translate data in computer; or a person who reads line by line to link up relevant information with the planned objectives.

Introduction : भूमिका Preliminary writing in work to introduce the subject, method and sources used.

Invoice: प्रस्तावित बिल List of proposed items together with price to be charged.

Isolate: एकल Generic term used to denote idea/isolate number. These are of two type-common and special. *See also* Isolate Idea.

Isolate Idea: एकल विचार Thought unit, which is usually a manifestation of one of the five fundamental categories or is enumerated as such and which is not a subject itself, but yields, when added to a basic or compound class a subject or smaller extension than the host class (Ranganathan).

Issue: निर्गम/अंक Loaning of library documents or a part of the periodical publication.

Issue counter: निर्गम स्थान *See* Circulation Counter.

Issue Register: निर्गम पुंजी *See* Borrwer's Record.

Inventory: सम्पति सूची Checking of the holdings of the library.

Inverted Comma: संकेत चिन्ह Punctuation mark used to specify the word/clause. Some time single/sometimes double comma's are used.

Irregular Paging: विषम पृष्ठांकन Page numbering which is not in order.

Italics: तिरछा टाइप It is a sloping type style of writing/printing.

Item: वस्तु A recognised unit.

J

Jacket: जाकेट/पुस्तक आवरण *See* Book Jacket.

Job: कार्य A set of tasks proscribed for execution.

Job Press: छोटा छापाखाना A press which deals in small commercial work.

Joint-Author: संयुक्त लेखक A person or a corporate body sharing responsibility with another/other for the thought and expression contained in a work, the part of which each of the author is responsible being neither specified nor separable (ISI).

Joint Author Entry: संयुक्त लेखक प्रविष्टि When leading section is used to record the name of joint author. It is always an added entry.

Joint Catalogue : संयुक्त सूची Catalogue of two or more libraries.

Joint Committee: संयुक्त समिति A committee composed of representatives of various committees or various libraries.

Joint Consultative Committee: संयुक्त सलाहाकार समिति *See* Joint Committee.

Joint Editor: सह-सम्पादक Editor who associated with another editor.

Joint Entry: संयुक्त प्रविष्टि Entry which is made for associated document.

Joint Index Entry: संयुक्त अनुक्रमाणिका प्रविष्टि Index entry generated by merging one or more indices.

Journal: पत्रिका It is a serial publication and an important source for disseminating primary information of any subject. It may contribute on one or more subjects.

Journalism: पत्रकारिता The profession of compiling, writing and editing of information for the use of publication in periodicals.

Journalist : पत्रकार One who contributes for publication of periodicals and news papers.

Junior Assistant: कनिष्ठ सहायक A professional who works under the supervision of senior professional.

Junior Book: कनिष्ठ पुस्तक *See* Basic Book.

K

Kent Classification: कैन्ट वर्गीकरण Scheme of classes implied in the entique of purc reason (1781) of Immanuel Kent (Ranganathan).

Kernel Title: सार शीर्षक A title comprising only focal terms.

The term is used in colon classification scheme while analysing the title.

Key: **की** Mechanical device to enter data in computer.

Keyboard: **की-बोर्ड** A board keeping a number of keys associated with the code linked with electric switches.

Keying: **की-करना** It is a process of converting information into electrical signals.

Key-word: **मुख्य शब्द** Significant words or the words representing certain important concepts in any document.

Key Word in Context (KWIC): **की वर्ड इन कॉनटेक्सट** A method of achieving index with the help of keywords.

Key Word Out of Context (KWOC): **की-वर्ड आउड ऑफ कॉनटेक्सट** Key words are separated from the title to act as subject heading in index.

Knowledge: **ज्ञान** It is the result of assimilation process of the information. The volume of information can not be used until one knows the elements of analysis, selection of information and also use of it in adequate manner. *See also* Information.

Knowledge Class: **ज्ञान वर्ग** Subject ranked along other subjects of the universe of knowledge in a scheme of classification.

Knowledge Classification: **ज्ञान वर्गीकरण** Classification which is used for any branch of knowledge.

Known Document: **व्यक्त अभिलेख** A document about which user has some knowledge like writer, title, publisher and publication year and so on.

L

Label: **लेबल/संकेत पत्र** In computer process one or more characters associated with or attached to an item of data for purpose of identification (DDPT); or a small paper piece pasted on spine or at bottom end of front page to record class number as identifier to the record/document.

Label Field: **संकेत क्षेत्र** A field used to provide memory addresses.

Lalit Kala Akademy: **ललित कला अकादमी** It is a national organisation established to encourage and promote various activities pertaining to the advancement of arts.

Lamination: **स्तरण** Cover of a thin transparent layer on the reading papers for providing protection or combination of more then one formulation of a compound class.

Language: **भाषा** In computer, any set of symbols and rules governing interrelations between the symbols, which can be used to convey or represent information (DDPT) or a set of characters/rules used for meaningful communication.

Language Classification: भाषा वर्गीकरण When the documents are scheduled according to their language characteristic.

Language Facet: भाषा पक्ष Part of the book number of a document, which is its language number (Ranganathan).

Language Number: भाषा संख्या An ordinal number in which language is translated.

Language Processor: भाषा प्रक्रम A program or software that translates, interprets and performs other functions required for processing a particular programming language, requirements specification language, design language, etc.

Language Sub-division: भाषा उप-विभाजन Sub-division of a subject according to the language recorded in schedule of scheme.

Last Link: अन्तिम कड़ी The link of the highest order contained in a chain (Ranganathan).

Law: नियम A rule of action established by authority.

Law Library: विधि पुस्तकालय Specialised library for practising lawyers, teachers and research scholars working in the law field. The collection includes judicial decision, administrative orders, notifications and amendments appeared on rules etc.

Law Reports: न्यायिक प्रतिवेदन Publication containing case decisions of court.

Laws of Library Science: पुस्तकालय विज्ञान नियम *See* Five Laws of Library Science.

Layout: प्रदर्शन An structure showing main criteria.

Leading Line: अग्र पंक्ति The topmost horizontal line on a catalogue card which is generally used in recording headings.

Leading Section: अग्र अनुभाग The first section of the entry. It may be represented by class number or by search words on leading line.

Leaf: पत्र One page.

Leaflet: पत्रक/पुस्तिका Small booklet.

Learned Society: विद्वत समाज A society of educated people.

Ledger System: पंजी प्रणाली *See* Register System.

Lending Department: आदान-प्रदान विभाग *See* Circulation Department.

Lending Library: आदान-प्रदान पुस्तकालय *See* Library.

Letter by Letter Filing: अक्षर क्रम संयोजन Filing is done in alphabetical order and total heading is regarded as one unit.

Lexical: शब्द विषयक A word, with a meaning.

Lexicography: कोश रचना

Librarian: पुस्तकाध्यक्ष A person who is responsible to arrange library services.

Librarianship: पुस्तकालयध्यक्षता The profession of the librarian.

Library: पुस्तकालय Library is the keeper of our history and culture. In modern sense it is an information dissemination centre or a service institution.

Library Accounts: पुस्तकालय लेखा Accounts maintained for library funds.

Library Act: पुस्तकालय अधिनियम An act prepared to create library services in systematic order.

Library Activities: पुस्तकालय कार्यकलाप Various operations carried out to arrange services.

Library Administration: पुस्तकालय प्रशासन A method of supervision by which aims and objectives of a library are fulfilled or routine works of library carried out.

Library Advisory Committee: पुस्तकालय सलाहाकार समिति Committee to advise in library matters. It may have members from professionals, users, scholars and policy makers. *See also* Library Committee.

Library Agency: पुस्तकालय संस्था Agency which works for library.

Library Associations: पुस्तकालय संघ A common forum for library professionals to exchange their views/experiences to solve their professional problems, these may be of regional, national and international level.

Library Attendent: पुस्तकालय अनुचर A person who attends duty at library circulation desk or keeps library shelf arrangement.

Library Authority: पुस्तकालय अधिकारी An authority who is responsible to implement the library policies.

Library Automation: पुस्तकालय स्वचालन Library automation is an application of computers in library and also utilisation of computer products and services for various library service operations.

Library Binding: पुस्तकालय जिल्द The binding specially prepared with hard board.

Library Broucher: पुस्तकालय विवरणिका A small publication describing about the library.

Library Budget: पुस्तकालय बजट Allocations of money made available to a library for arranging library services.

Library Building and Furniture: पुस्तकालय भवन तथा साज समान The building and furniture used by the library.

Library Card: पुस्तकालय पत्र *See* Borrower's Card.

Library Catalogue: पुस्तकालय सूची It is a record of holdings of a library arranged in some definite order. *See also* Catalogue.

Library Cess: पुस्तकालय उपकार Provision under act to generate funds to provide essential library services.

Library Classification: पुस्तकालय वर्गीकरण It is translation of the subject in to a preferred artificial language of ordinal numbers, or the library classification is an arrangement of collections on shelves to make effective use. *See* Classification.

Library Clerk: पुस्तकालय लिपिक A clerk working in library for clerical operations.

Library Collection: पुस्तकालय संचय *See* Collection.

Library Committee: पुस्तकालय समिति *See* Library Advisory Committee.

Library of Congress (LC) : लाइब्रेरी ऑफ कॉंग्रेस Library of Congress, D.C. is national library of United States of America. Under copyright act it is a depository with 19 million collections and has become the world's largest information collection. About 6,000 trained staff are engaged.

Library of Congress Classification: लाइब्रेरी आफ काँग्रेस वर्गीकरण Scheme of classification designed at the library of Congress of the United States of America and published for the first time in 1904. (ISI)

Library Consultant: पुस्तकालय सलाहकार An advisor in the library matters.

Library Co-operation: पुस्तकालय सहयोग The entire or some specific resources of the number of libraries are pooled for sharing with the idea that individual library cannot afford to arrange that much resources.

Library Discount: पुस्तकालय छूट Discount allowed on the printed price of the document when purchased for library.

Library Document: पुस्तकालय अभिलेख A document owned by a library. *See also* Document.

Library Edition: पुस्तकालय संस्करण An edition specially brought out to use in libraries on a good paper and in hard binding.

Library Economy: पुस्तकालय अर्थव्यवस्था All aspects which has concern with library finances.

Library Equipment: पुस्तकालय उपकरण The Equipment used in library.

Library Expenditure: पुस्तकालय व्यय Expenditure incurred by a library.

Library Extension: पुस्तकालय प्रसार Expansion of library services to new points.

Library Fees: पुस्तकालय अंश A subscription amount to make user participative in arrangement of library services.

Library Finance: पुस्तकालय वित्त *See* Finance.

Library Funds: पुस्तकालय कोश *See* Finance.

Library Function: पुस्तकालय कार्य Main job of the library is collection organisation and dissemination of information to its users.

Library Hand : पुस्तकालय लेखन प्रकार Particular style of writing adopted to prepare catalogue cards etc.

Library Hours: पुस्तकालय समय The period during which library remains open.

Library Holdings: पुस्तकालय संचय *See* Library Collections.

Library Information: पुस्तकालय सूचना *See* Library Collection.

Library Location: पुस्तकालय स्थिति The place where it is situated.

Library is a Growing Organism: पुस्तकालय एक विकासशील संस्था है Library is a live institution in which all entities like reader, books, staff, building and furniture continuously added to meet the needs of present and anticipated future.

Library Materials: पुस्तकालय सामग्री *See* Stores.

Library Network: पुस्तकालय तंत्र When a group of libraries are connected with a communication link. *See also* Network.

Library Organistion: पुस्तकालय व्यवस्था The structure/layout of library resources.

Library Planning: पुस्तकालय नियोजन A plan through which library services are arranged.

Library Policy: पुस्तकालय नीति A policy formulated to develop library services in various sectors.

Library Records: पुस्तकालय अभिलेख Certain library records are kept in libraries such as accession record, issue record etc.

Library Repositories: पुस्तकालय संग्रह Storing place of library documents.

Library Resources: पुस्तकालय संसाधन The resources such as finance, collection and manpower etc. are required to maintain library services.

Library Rules and Regulations: पुस्तकालय नियम तथा अधिनियम Guiding rules used by the library professionals and users as well.

Library Science: पुस्तकालय विज्ञान Science in which systematic study of library services and education are covered.

Library Service: पुस्तकालय सेवा The efforts/facilities extended for using library collection.

Library Software: पुस्तकालय सोफ्टवेयर A computer program designed for handling library operations.

Library School: पुस्तकालय स्कूल A school where library science education is imparted.

Library Stack: पुस्तकालय संग्रह *See* Stack.

Library Staff: पुस्तकालय कर्मचारी The staff engaged to perform various activities carried out by a library.

Library Stamp: पुस्तकालय मुहर A stamp bearing the name of the library. It is fixed to indicate ownership.

Library Ticket: पुस्तकालय पत्र Membership card which can be used to borrow library books even outside the library pre mises. *See also* Borrower Card.

Library Visitor: पुस्तकालय प्रवेशी *See* User/Reader.

Library Worker: पुस्तकालय कर्मचारी *See* Library Staff.

Link: कड़ी Communication path or a class derived in a chain.

List: सूची Collection of information in some order.

List of Additions: संग्रह सूची A list of acquisitions of library for a defined period in a particular order.

Literature Guide: साहित्य सहायक A publication which helps in knowing the literature on a particular subject. It may be a reference document.

Literature Search: साहित्य खोज Systematic and intensive search for desired information on a given subject.

Literate: शिक्षित A person who can read, write and understand well.

Literary Title: साहित्यिक शीर्षक In library classification literary titles are translated to their actual theme. These are the title which do not speak about subject directly.

Literary Warrant: साहित्यिक आवृत्ति An amount of literature published or to be published on any subject.

Literary Work: साहित्यिक कार्य Creative work in the form of poetry, drama fiction, prose etc. of which the outstanding qualities are taken to be beauty of form and emotional appeal, and which is of instinctively or trans intellectual origin. (ISI)

Like Entities: ग्राह्य अस्तित्व Entities sharing a given attribute equally in measure, intensity, extent or any other basis, the likeliness being with reference to the said attribute (Ranganathan).

Line Printer: पंक्ति छपाई-मशीन A device that prints an entire line of characters simultaneously. (DDPT)

Loan Book: उधार पंजी It is a register in which entries are made for the loan received or given to any agency/person.

Loan Period: उधार अवधि The period allowed to keep library document away from library.

Loan System: उधार प्रणाली *See* Circulation System

Local Access: स्थानीय पहुँच Access to the information stored on number of computers for their own use; or use of the local database directly.

Local Area Network: स्थानीय क्षेत्र तंत्र A network of communication links/computers available in a particular compact area.

Local Collection: क्षेत्रीय संचय Collections of specific locality, local language, local history and culture etc.

Location Section: अवस्थिति

अनुभाग The section of an entry of a document forming a part of another document, specifying the name of the host document and the position of the document within the host document.

Loose assembly: अवरुद्ध एकत्रण

Loose Chain: मुक्त कड़ी Chain with a unitary class as its last link (Ranganathan).

Loose leaf Form Catalogue: मुक्त पत्र प्रकार सूची In this form, catalogue entries are prepared on loose leaves and are arranged in a binder for use.

Loss of books: पुस्तक हानि *See* Write off Books.

Lower link: निम्न कड़ी As between two links in a chain engaging attention the link occurring lower then the other one. (Ranganathan)

M

MARC: मार्क Abbreviation for Machine Readable Catalogue project. It was a pilot project started by Library of Congress in 1965.

Mark: चिन्ह A character used to identify data.

MS DOS: एम एस डोस Micro-soft disc operating system.

Machine Search: मशीन द्वारा सूचना प्राप्ति Search of information with the help of machine.

Machine Language: मशीनी भाषा Code language in non-graphic physical symbols suited to the machine for handling them in accordance with prescribed programme. (ISI) *See also* Binary Language.

Machine Readable: मशीन पठनीय That can be sensed by machenical device such as disk, tap, cassettes etc.

Machine Readable Catalogue: मशीन द्वारा पठनीय सूची When a library catalogue produced through computer in the form of tape, disk, floppy, CD-ROM etc.

Machine Readable Database: मशीन द्वारा पठनीय सूचना Information/data stored on electronic device to use the same by machine.

Machine Word: मशीनी शब्द Unit of information involving the standard number of distinct or primary code digits, which a computer regularly handles in each operation. (ISI)

Macro Document: पूर्ण अभिलेख Document embodying macro thought. Document elaborated to discuss concept in detail. *See also* Macro Thought.

Magazine: पत्रिका A periodical publication which appears after a fixed interval.

Magazine Rack: पत्रिका रैक *See* Periodical Display Rack.

Magazine Room: पत्रिका कक्ष *See* Periodical Room.

Magnetic Disk: मैगनेटिक डिस्क Computer device used to store data. In it combination of a number of flat circular plates of magnetic electronic readable are put together to enhance storing capacity.

Magnetic Storage: चुम्बकीय संग्रह Any form of storage device whose operation depends on the properties of a magnetic material (DDPT).

Magnetic Tape: चुम्बकीय पट्टी Plastic tape coated with magnetic material on which information can be recorded/located by mechanical device.

Main Card: मुख्य पत्र A catalogue card having the main entry for a work. It is also regarded as basic card/unit card.

Main Catalogue: मुख्य सूची Central catalogue which consist entries for total holdings of a library.

Main Catalogue Entry: मुख्य सूची प्रविष्टि It is the entry in which all relevant information is traced to develop other added entries. *See also* Main Entry.

Main Class: मुख्य वर्ग Class enumerated in the array of order in a scheme of classification for the universe of knowledge. (Ranganathan). *See also* Basic Class.

Main Entry: मुख्य प्रविष्टि An entry giving maximum information about a document. (Ranganathan)

Mainframe Computer: मुख्य आधार कम्प्यूटर The basic/essential portion of an assembly of computer hardware which has the capacity to support many powerful peripheral devices.

It may have multi user facilities and a network of terminals.

Main Heading: मुख्य शीर्षक The first heading among multiple headings.

Main Library : मुख्य पुस्तकालय *See* Central Library.

Main Store: मुख्य संग्रह Principle Store.

Main Subject: मुख्य विषय The subject which has number of established branches and accepted aspects.

Maintenance: रख-रखाव An activity of keeping a system operating.

Main Title: मुख्य शीर्षक The title which precedes with the subtitle/alternative title. *See also* Main Heading.

Main Title Page: मुख्य शीर्षक पृष्ठ A page which provides information about title and other details traced for catalogue.

Management: प्रशासन/प्रबन्ध Management is a combined process of planning, organising and controlling to accomplish objectives. *See also* Library Administration.

Management Information System: प्रबन्ध सूचना प्रणाली Computer based management in which automatic data processing is used by the users of the program.

Manual: पुस्तिका A helping book or guideline on the subject for which it has been prepared. *See also* Handbook.

Manual input: मनुष्य द्वारा निवेश Entering of data through manpower.

Manual operation: मनुष्यकृत क्रिया An operation in which the use of the machine and other devices is controlled by the person.

Manuscript: हस्तलिखित ग्रन्थ A document written by hand.

Manuscript Catalogue: हस्तलिखित ग्रन्थ सूची A catalogue based on the entries prepared exclusively for manuscripts.

Manuscript Librarian: हस्तलिखित ग्रन्थ पुस्तकाध्यक्ष A librarian who deals with handwritten books.

Manuscript Library: हस्तलिखित ग्रन्थ पुस्तकालय Library which has the collections of hand written books on various discipline.

Manuscriptology: हस्तलिखित ग्रन्थ विज्ञान Science/study of manuscripts.

Maps : मानचित्र Maps are the projection of a part or whole of the surface of the earth, traced on a plane surface.

Margin: हाशिया Blank space on a page both sides of the written text.

Master Card: मुख्य पत्र A card usually the first in its group and contains information about other associated cards.

Master File: मुख्य फाइल A file containing permanent data.

Material: सामग्री It includes all items which are in possession. The term is also used for literature in libraries.

Medium of Education: शिक्षा का माध्यम Language in which instructions are imparted.

Member: सदस्य One who fulfils the conditions laid down for participation.

Membership Record: सदस्यता अभिलेख A record which contains the names and address etc. of the members of the library.

Matter: पदार्थ Fundamental category to select the matter as characteristic of classification.

Media: मीडिया It includes various communication information dissemination methods like Radio, TV, News-papers etc.

Media Centre: मीडिया केन्द्र A centre in which audio-visual aids and media tachniques are used.

Media Programme: मीडिया कार्यक्रम The programme carried out to popularise media.

Medical Bibliography: चिकित्सा ग्रन्थ-सूची Bibliography for the documents available in the field of medical and allied sciences.

Medical Library: चिकित्सा पुस्तकालय *See* Health Library.

Medical Literature Analysis and Retrieval System (MEDLARS): मैडलर National Library of Medicine, USA has created computer database in the field of medicine to provide a comprehensive bibliography of medical literature.

Mediline: मैडीलाइन A computerised international service to search current medical literature.

Melvil Dewey: मैलविल ड्यूवे An American library scientist who is regarded as father of library science, contributed DDC.

Membership: सदस्यता Permission for using the library.

Membership List: सदस्यता सूची A list consisting names of the members of a library.

Memory: स्मृति It is a capacity of machine to store the information. The capacity once fixed cannot be increased. It is an essential part of the computer. *See also* Storage.

Menu: सूचक Set of instructions/messages required to handle operations.

Merrill Book Number: मैरिल पुस्तक संख्या A book number from a scheme devised by W.S. Merrill for arranging material in alphabetical order by means of numbers or in chronological order by means of data abbreviations. (ISI)

Message: संदेश An unit of the information. Length of which is not fixed and designed to communicate information.

Meta Language: मैटा भाषा Language used as a medium of exposition in the study, description and development of object language. (Ranganathan)

Microcomputer: छोटा कम्प्यूटर These are the smallest, cheapest and commonly used computer machines in modern age.

Micro Computer Functions: छोटे कम्प्यूटर के कार्य These computers have four basic units: central processing unit (CPU), control, memory, and input/output.

Micro-document : छोटा अभिलेख Document embodying micro thought (Ranganathan).

Micro-film: माइक्रो फिल्म A film containing information in reduced size as compared with paper form.

Microfiche: माइक्रोफिश A flat sheet of standard pictographic film used to record information. The record may be in rows and columns.

Microform: माइक्रोफॉर्म The document's hard copy when reduced/transferred to photographic sheet for making its use with mechanical device to achieve efficiency and also to reduce bulk. This includes role film and microfiche.

Micro-form Reading Room: माइक्रो फोर्म पठन कक्ष A specially designed room equipped with electronic gadgets.

Microprocessor: माइक्रोप्रोसेसर It is one of the principal components which consists of the arithmetic logic unit and the control logic unit etc.

Micro Thought: सूक्ष्म विचार A subject of great intention and small extension (Ranganathan). Deliberations on specialised topics, generally appears in periodicals/ newspapers.

Mini Computer: छोटा कम्प्यूटर It is a type of computer which has comparatively less memory.

Misleading Title: भ्रामक शीर्षक The title which does not represent the subject.

Missing Isolate: लुप्त एकल The isolate missing in chain-with gap. (Ranganathan)

Missing link: लुप्त कड़ी A link in a chain with gap, corresponding to a missing isolate in the chain. (Ranganathan)

Mixed Notation: मिश्रित अंकन When a scheme of classification uses more then one type of digits as notation.

Mnemonics: स्मृति सहायक An effort of replacing all the terms use for one concept in entire text by one term, symbol or synonym to aid memory or in computer it is an art of improving the efficiency of the memory.

Mnemonics Device: स्मृति सहाय युक्ति Device in which same digit is used to represent the same concept wherever it occurs.

Mobile Library: चल पुस्तकालय Library on wheels and which reaches door to door to give service.

Model : प्रतिरूप A pictorial representation of any equipment.

Model Library Act: आदर्श पुस्तकालय अधिनियम It is a legislative provision for setting up a library.

Modernisation: आधुनिकता Application of achievements of the present.

Modular: माड्यूलर Refers to the standardization of computer system components to allow for combinations and large variety of compatible units.(MD)

Modulation: नियंत्रण The process of encoding information on a carrier wave by altering some characteristics of the wave. (MD)

Module: मोड्यूल A programme unit that is separate and distinctly identifiable with respect to operations such as compilations, assembly, loading and combination with other such units (DDPT).

MODEM: मोडम The device which accepts digital wave form for transmission over an analog channel to develop a telecommunication channel.

Monograph: मोनोग्राफ A scholarly contribution on any subject.

Monthly Magazine: मासिक पत्रिका A periodical which comes after every month.

Monthly Progress Report: मासिक प्रगति प्रतिवेदन A report which contains the progress for the working of the origination during a month time.

Monitor: प्रबोधक It is display electronic device which may be in black and white or in colour.

It is a part of computer hardware.

Most Popular Language: **अधिकाधिक प्रिय भाषा** Language in which a library have more documents.

Mother Country: **अपना देश** The country to which the library belongs.

Multiple Class: **एकाधिक वर्ग** Class containing two or more entities.

Multiple Copies: **एकाधिक प्रतियाँ** The document of which more than one copy is available.

Multiple Group: **एकाधिक समूह** Group consisting of many entities.

Multiple Heading: **एकाधिक शीर्षक** Heading consisting many blocks, usually separated by a punchuation mark, such as a comma.

Multi-Focal Work: **एकाधिक-केन्द्र कार्य** Work treating several collateral subjects not having a common universe of the first remove according to the preferred scheme of classes. (Ranganathan)

Multi-Volumed Book : **बहुखण्डी पुस्तक** A book which contains many volumes, giving a continuous exposition of the subject, treating all the volumes in separable set. The total set may have a general title and continued pagination even.

Municipal Library: **नगर पालिका पुस्तकालय** It is a public library functioning in urban/municipal area.

Music Library: **संगीत पुस्तकालय** The collection comprises of music records etc.

Museum: **संग्रहालय** It is a place where all items reflecting culture and history of the nation are preserved.

Museum Library : **संग्रहालय पुस्तकाल** A special collection of rare documents representing history and culture is maintained to facilitate the users.

N

NICNET: **निकनेट** It is a computer network developed by the National Informatic Centre, New Delhi.

Name: **नाम** Identification of the entity.

Name Catalogue: **नाम सूची** A catalogue in which name entries are arranged in alphabetical order.

Naming of Entry: **प्रविष्टि नामकरण** After entering the words on leading line the entry is named as Author entry, Joint Author entry, subject entry and so on.

Name Heading: **नाम शीर्षक** A heading which refers a name of person, place, corporate body etc.

Name Reference: **नाम संदर्भ** A reference used in catalogue to indicate the more then one name used by the author.

Nascent Document: **नव अभिलेख** Coming article or other material thing offering latest information.

National Bibliography: राष्ट्रीय ग्रन्थ सूची It is a list of published documents in a country, about a country, in all the forms and languages of the country.

National Gallery: राष्ट्रीय कलाभवन A place where various arts of the nation gets florished.

Number : अंक Digits having certain defined properties. or A single issue of a periodical.

Number Entry: संख्या प्रविष्टि An entry begins with class/call number.

National Book Trust (NBT): राष्ट्रीय पुस्तक न्यास National Book Trust of India is an autonomous organisation set up in 1957 to foster book mindedness among the people of different ages and walks of life. It works to produce books in Hindi and English along with other eleven regional Indian languages, besides, it organises international, national and regional book fairs.

National Educational Research Centre: राष्ट्रीय शैक्षाणिक शोध केन्द्र One such centre, Raja Ram Mohan Roy Educational Resources Centre was established in 1972 with a view to promote writing and production of indigenous university level books.

National Informatic Centre: राष्ट्रीय सूचना केन्द्र Centre is situated in Delhi. It has a computer communication network with district headquarter's to create database.

National Information Centre: राष्ट्रीय सूचना केन्द्र The UGC has estabilished three such centres one each at Bombay, Baroda and Bangalore. Bangalore Centre is exclusively dealing in science discipline whereas social science and humanity subjects are distributed among these two SNDT, Bombay and MS University, Baroda centre.

National Information Centre for Chemistry and Chemical Technology (NICHEM): रसायन शास्त्र या रसायन प्रोद्योगिकी का राष्ट्रीय सूचना केन्द्र NICHEM is an information centre developed under National Information System for Science and Technology (NISSAT), functional from 1986. The centre is operational with library and documentation services of national chemical libaratory (NCL), Pune.

The centre has comprehensive collection in chemistry and chemical technology on mechanical retrieval system.

National Information System: राष्ट्रीय सूचना प्रणाली An information system evolved to disseminate information at national network.

National Information Systems for Science and Technology (NISSAT): विज्ञान तथा तकनीकी राष्ट्रीय सूचना प्रणाली

NISSAT was set up to coordinate the resources of science and technology library so that the wasteful expenditure is avoided.

National Library: राष्ट्रीय पुस्तकालय It has been established under article 62 of the VII Schedule of the Union List, at Calcutta. It is working under the Ministry of Human Resources Development. It has acquired 19 lachs of publications and 800 staff is engaged to complete various jobs.

National Social Science Documentation Centre (NASS DOC): राष्ट्रीय समाज विज्ञान प्रलेखन केन्द्र The centre is working in New Delhi under Indian Council of Social Science Research (ICSSR). It is generating publications based on current information acquired in the field of social sciences.

Natural Characteristic: प्राकृतिक गुण A quality or complex of qualities in the things classified in-herent and inseparable from the things and without which they could not be the things they are (Ranganathan).

Natural Language: प्राकृतिक भाषा Human spoken language such as Hindi, Gujarati, Marathi etc.

Natural Material: प्राकृतिक सम्पदा Concrete entity found in and extracted from nature (Ranganathan).

Net Price: वास्तविक मूल्य The price after deducting discount if any.

Network: तन्त्र A set of interconnected communication channels through which information can be transferred to all connected computers.

Networking: तन्त्रकरण Method of interlinking number of computers.

New Additions: नव संग्रह Acquisitions of a particular library.

New Books: नव ग्रंथ The books published recently or added to a library recently.

New Edition: नव संस्करण A reprint with additions and corrections or an edition which is different from the existing one.

News: समाचार Piece of current information/new information/ fresh event.

News Bulletin: समाचार पत्रिका A digest of current news which is to be generalised.

News Clipping: समाचार कतरन Paper piece taken form news papers for shorting current reported events.

News Letter: समाचार संदेश A report of current happenings issued regularly with some fixed interval. The news covered in such publication remains very brief and first hand generally.

News-Paper: समाचार पत्र A carrier of news of most current events.

News-Paper Stand: समाचार पत्र प्रदर्शक A stand used to display newspapers.

Node: **नोड** It is a point of function of the link or a control point in a network.

Noise: **व्यवधान** An undesirable signal which disturbs the desired signal in a communication network.

Noise Factor: **व्यवधान कारक** Ratio of the irrelevant documents among the selected documents to the total number of documents selected (Ranganathan).

Non-Book Material: **पुस्तक के अतिरिक्त पठन सामग्री** The information records which are not traditional and are in audio-visual form.

Non-conventional Zone: **अपारम्परिक क्षेत्र** Division of the surface of the earth or of a geographical area, based on any diameter other than the polar axis any other diameter orthogonal or oblique to it. (ISI)

Non-documentary Source of Information: **सूचना के अभिलेखीय स्रोत** Information sources such as oral, technology based database etc.

Non-formal Education: **अनऔपचारिक शिक्षा** An education achieved through self study or formal; no registration is required in any institution.

Non-Plan Grants: **नियमित अनुदान** Regular Budget allocation outside the plan.

Non Print Material: **अप्रकाशित सामग्री** *See* Audio-visual.

Non Recurring Expenditure: **योजना व्यय** *See* Plan Expenditure.

Notation: **अंकन** The system of ordinal numbers representing the classes in a scheme of classification, (Ranganathan) or it is a set of symbols used to represent classes in a classification.

Notation Plane: **अंकन तल** The plane of numbers representing concepts.

Note Area: **टिप्पण क्षेत्र** An area which consists the notes in the catalogue entry such as series and other documents relation etc.

Note Section: **टिप्पण अनुभाग** *See* Note Area.

Novel: **उपन्यास** It is a form of literary writing.

Numbcr: **संख्या** Any numerical digit.

O

OCLC : **ओ सी एल सी** It stands for Ohio College Library Centre and for on line computer library centre.

OPAC: **ओ पी ए सी** It is a abbreviation for on-line public access catalogue.

Object Language: **अभीष्ट भाषा** Language studied, described or developed (Ranganathan).

Octave Device: **अन्तिम अंक युक्ति** A device evolved by Dr. Ranganathan for accommodating successive co-ordinate numbers beyond the used available notation's digits without indicating subordination.

Official Gazette: अधिकृत राजपत्र A special authentic periodical publication containing Government notifications either used on behalf of the Government or by Government itself.

Official Catalogue: अधिकृत सूची A catalogue exclusively for the use of staff.

Official Publication: अधिकृत प्रकाशन A publication brought out by the Government/a Government agency Management.

Official Organ: अधिकृत प्रकाशन A publication circulated by any office to report its activities.

Off-line: आफ लाइन In computer information retrieval system, when equipment is not directly linked with central processing unit, it is known as off-line.

Off line System: आफ लाइन प्रणाली In teleprocessing, a system that requires human intervention between the original recording functions and the ultimate data processing function, such intervention being necessary in conversion functions as well as in the loading and unloading operations associated with the use of point to point or data gathering system. It may also be known as batch processing. (DDPT)

Omission Factor: निष्कासन कारक Ratio of the number of relevant documents not selected to the total number of relevant documents for the machine had been fed with entries. (Ranganathan)

On approval: स्वीकृत पर When documents are called from the market to get evaluated before purchase.

Online: सीधे संपर्क आनलाइन In computer information search when equipment is directly linked with central processing unit through communication line to connect available database.

Online Access: सीधी पहुँच Access to the number of database through a telecommunication network.

On-line Database: सीधा संचय A continuous up dated database on any subject which can be used through communication links directly.

Online Operation: सीधी कार्यवाही When computer CPU works under mechanical control to transfer data without manual interference.

On-line Tresaurus: सीधा विश्वकोश A list of synonyms culled with the help of the software program.

On-line Search Service: सीधे सूचना प्राप्ति सेवा *See* On-line Access.

On-line Storage: सीधा संचय Storage under the direct control of a computer system.

On-line System: सीधी प्रणाली A system in which data enters directly and also output data printed directly without human intervention.

Open Access: खुला प्रवेश When a library allows users to move around the shelves to get their information/documents.

Open Array: खुली पंक्ति An array of classes, admitting of extrapolation.

Open Entry: खुली प्रविष्टि An entry which can accept more information such as entries of periodicals are kept open to record new issues.

Open Purchase: खुली खरीद When the purchase orders can be placed to any book distributor at any place.

Opcration: कार्यवाही Generally refers to the action/job performed by a computer.

Operation Manual: कार्यवाही पुस्तिका The manual which contains instructions and specifications for a given application. (MD)

Operator: कार्यवाहक A person who operates/performs various machine jobs.

Optical Disk: आप्टिकल डिस्क It is a mechanical storage medium in which after writing only reading is possible.

Order: क्रय-आदेश A letter which contains instructions to supply items demanded.

Order Card: क्रय-पत्र *See* Order.

Order Form: क्रय-प्रपत्र It is a form used to place orders.

Order List: क्रय-सूची List of orders which are placed with the suppliers or a list of items which are to be purchased.

Order of an Array: पंक्ति का क्रम The number of successive characteristic on the basis of which the classes in the array are derived from a universe.(Ranganathan)

Order of a Chain: शृंखला का क्रम The order of the first link of the chain. (Ranganathan)

Order of a Class: वर्ग का क्रम The number of successive characteristic on the basis of which it is derived form a universe (Ranganathan).

Order of Complex Array Isolate: मिश्रित पंक्ति एकल का क्रम Number of Array isolates combined to form it.

Order of the Complex Class: मिश्रित वर्ग का क्रय Number of basic or compound classes combined to form it. (Ranganathan)

Order of Complex Isolate: मिश्रित एकल का क्रम Number of isolate combined to form it. (Ranganathan)

Order of a Compound Class: यौगिक वर्ग का क्रम Number of isolate facets in a class.

Order of a Link: कड़ी का क्रम Order of the class to which it represents.

Ordinal Name: क्रमबोधक नाम Class number of a class in a scheme of classification. (Ranganathan)

Ordinal Number: क्रमबोधक संख्या A number assigned to a document on the basis of its characteristic to fix up its position relation to other available documents in the same class on library shelves.

Ordinal Symbol: क्रमबोधक संकेत A symbol used in classification to fix-up the relationship of document.

Ordinary Composite Book: सामान्य संयुक्त पुस्तक A composite book with a single genetic title to denote all the contributions collectively. (ISI)

Ordinary Letter: सामान्य पत्र A letter of routine nature.

Ordinary Publication: सामान्य प्रकाशन A publication on traditional pattern.

Organ: मुख पत्र A official publication of current nature.

Organisation: व्यवस्था Grouping of activities in desired manner.

Orientation Division: विकास-विभाग Division of the surface of the earth or of a geographical area based on orientation as characteristics. (Ranganathan)

Original Edition: मूल संस्करण First edition.

Original Works: मौलिक रचनायें The work which refers as contribution of the author.

Outline : रेखाचित्र Overview on any subject.

Out of Print: समाप्त प्रकाशन When all printed copies are exhausted and printer is not printing more copies. The copies are not available for market.

Out of Stock: संग्रह समाप्त Not available with stockist and publisher, may be in press.

Output: उत्पादन The information collected through internal or external storage or information transferred from the internal memory of the computer to the outside in the form suited to the human mind. (Ranganathan)

Output Device: उत्पादन युक्ति The devices like printer, monitor etc used to get the information as desired by human mind.

Output Record: उत्पादन अभिलेख Record generated by an output device.

Outside User: बाहरी प्रयोक्ता A person who is not a member of that library which he wants to use.

Overdue Book: विलम्बित पुस्तक A book outstanding more then the period it was allowed.

Overdue Charges: विलम्बित शुल्क The charges collected for the late returne of library documents.

Overdue Notice: विलम्बित सूचना A request to call back the library document on expiry of its permission period

Overflow: आगे निकलना Jumping from the capacity of the reserved area.

Overhead Projector: प्रक्षेपक It

is used to project the things in focused manner.

Oversize Book: असाधारण बड़ी पुस्तक A book of bigger format.

Ownership Mark: स्वामित्व चिन्ह It may be stamp or printed stationary pasted on document to ascertain ownership.

P

PMEST: Acronym order for Ranganathan Facet Formula personality, matter, energy, space and time to arrange these in their decreasing concreteness.

Packet Device: एकीकृत युक्ति Notational mechanism used in subject device so that the subject number concerned can be taken as fused and treated as if it were a single digit. (Ranganathan)

Packet Notation: एकीकृत अंकन When notation group is used as it is a single digit. *See also* Packet Device.

Page: पृष्ठ One side of the leaf in a book.

Pagination: पृष्ठांकन Assigning a number to each leaf of a document.

Painting: चित्र When the thoughts are presented with the help of colours.

Paleography: लिपि विज्ञान The study of the early forms of handwritings of manuscripts.

Pamphlet: पुस्तिका When few printed pages of immediate use information are formed small paper back publication. Generally developed to disseminate information of current interest.

Pamphlet Box: पुस्तिका बक्स A box used for holding pamphlet.

Paragraph: अनुच्छेद A piece of the contents.

Paper: कागज Thin sheet of fibrous material.

Paper Back: कागजी आवरण See Paper Bound.

Paper Bound: कागजी जिल्द Bound with paper cover.

Paper Sizes: कागज का आकार The size in which paper used.

Papyrus: पेपीरस An ancient paper like material made from the stem of a specific tree and was used in place of paper to record knowledge.

Parallel Title: समानान्तर शीर्षक A title appears in more than one language/script.

Parchment: पार्चमेन्ट Processed skin used for writing.

Parody: नकल Work in which other work is mimicked.

PASCAL: पासकल Computer used high level block structured programming language.

Password: पहचान शब्द A word that permits a user access to retracted storage. The unique set of digits are allocated for this use.

Patent: पेटेन्ट/संरक्षक अधिकार The publication containing investigation description granted to a new manufacturing process or improvement on existing process, which is also not available in this form elsewhere.

Patron: संरक्षक Classed users of the library.

Pedestrian Work: नीरस रचना Work which is not a sacred work, a classic or literary work, and is not made into a quasi class or quasi subject by the scheme of classification in use (ISI).

Penumbral: उपच्छाया Penumbral is an arrangement of either side of the umbral consisting successively of classes or isolate or array isolates of progressively decreasing interest to the reader at the moment. (Ranganathan)

Penumbral Region: उपच्छाया क्षेत्र *See* Penumbral.

Period: समय The time required for a job.

Perfect Size: उचित आकार A size which is commonly accepted and standardised.

Periodical: पत्रिका A publication which appears in parts with regular intervals, having distinctive features like periodicity and issue number to a volume etc.

Periodical Article: पत्रिका रचना An article which appears in any periodical.

Periodical Box: पत्रिका बक्स A box used to collect loose issues of the current periodicals. *See also* Pamphlet Box.

Periodical Bulletin: पत्रिका *See* Bulletin.

Periodical Display Rack: पत्रिका प्रदर्शक रैक An especially designed rack used to display new issues of the periodicals in a library.

Periodical Room: पत्रिका कक्ष A room which is used exclusively for keeping and reading the periodicals.

Periodical Stand: पत्रिका दर्शक A stand used to display periodicals.

Periodical Stock: पत्रिका भंडार A place where back issues of the periodicals are arranged.

Periodicity: नियतकाल Interval after which a periodical is brought out.

Peripheral: वाह्य परिधीय Outside the purview of a subject or any hardware device connected to a computer system.

Personal Author: व्यक्ति परक लेखक Person as author the responsibility for thought expression contained in the work resting solely on his private capacity and not on the capacity of any office he may hold within a corporate body, nor on the corporate body. (ISI)

Personal Catalogue: व्यक्तिगत सूची A catalogue consists entries of one's collection and of collections about him.

Personal Computer: परसनल कम्प्यूटर Low priced, more popular widely used computers.

Personal Service: वैयक्तिक सेवा Service when rendered directly person to person.

Personnel Staff: कर्मचारी सेवा A staff attached to work with specific officer.

Personality: व्यक्तित्व An image of the individual among others.

Personality Isolate: व्यक्तित्व एकल The residue arising in the analysis of a subject into the fundamental categories after time, space, energy, matter and anteriorising isolates are separated out. (Ranganathan)

Pertinency: उपयुक्त अथवा प्रांसगिक A quality of being related to a subject sought.

Pertinence Factor: उपादेयता कारण Ratio of the number of relevant document among the selected documents to the total number of document selected. (Ranganathan)

Phase: पक्ष A component of a complex class or a complex isolate or a complex array-isolate as the case may be. (Ranganathan)

Phase 1: पक्ष प्रथम It is primary exposition of a complex class.

Phase 2: पक्ष द्वितीय It is not the direct exposition but thereby affects the exposition of phase 1.

Phase Device (Idea Plane): पक्ष युक्ति (विचार तल) Device for sharpening a host focus by the addition of a focus of the same species as a second phase. (Ranganathan)

Phase Device (Notational Plane): पक्ष युक्ति (अंकन तल) Device of prefixing a connecting symbol to a digit representing a phase relation in the idea plane. (Ranganathan)

Phase Relation: पक्ष सम्बन्ध Relation between the phases of a complex class or of a complex isolate or of a complex array-isolate. (Ranganathan)

Photocopier: प्रतिलिपि कारक A photocopying machine.

Photocopy: छायाचित्र/प्रतिलिपि Photographic copy of the document or xerox copy.

Photographs: छाया चित्र Visual/pictorial representation of the information.

Plan: योजना See Scheme.

Plan Grants: योजना अनुदान Funds arranged to carry a project.

Planning: योजना Method to coordinate activities of an organisation and direct them towards set objectives.

Plane of work: कार्यतल Dr. Ranganathan suggested three plane of work for library classification. These are Idea Plane, Verbal Plane and Notational Plane.

Plate: चित्र पृष्ठ An illustration on full page.

Pocket: जेब/पॉकेट A small paper made pocket/bag which is pasted inside the cover of the document to hold a card carrying the details of the document. *See also* Book Pocket.

Pocket Edition: लघु संस्करण Small size edition of any work.

Policy: नीति Guide line to achieve the set goals.

Popular Book : लोकप्रिय पुस्तक A book which is required by a large number of readers.

Popular Name: लोकप्रिय नाम A name which is known by the large number of people or commonly known name.

Population Cluster Isolate: जनसंख्या क्षेत्र एकल An area with a high density of population and with certain community centres, such as vihars, temples, mosques, churches, gurdwaras, market places, meeting places and cultural centres (Ranganathan).

Portable: स्थानान्तर योग्य Which can be carried from one place to another.

Portrait: रूप चित्र/शब्द चित्र The picture of a real person or vivid description in words.

Postal Circulation: डाक द्वारा परिचालन When books are provided through postal service.

Poster: विज्ञापन पत्र A paper containing information which requires immediate publicity

Post Co-ordinate Indexing System: उत्तर सयोजन अनुक्रमाणिका प्रणाली An indexing system in which words are put in simple order so that users can combine to achieve compound subject out of it.

Posterionising Common Isolate: पश्चकारक सामान्य एकल Common isolate idea whose attachment to a host class makes the resulting class succeed the host class. (ISI)

Postulates: अभिधारणा Postulate is an assumption which is never put to test.

Postulate of Basic Facet: आधार पक्ष की अभिधारणा An assumption of basic aspect or view.

Postulate based Permuted Subject Index (POPSI): अभिधारण आधारित अनुमत विषय अनुक्रमाणिका It is an indigenous indexing technique designed by Ganesh Bhattacharya of DRTC.

Postulate of Concreteness: निश्चितता की अभिधारणा The five fundamental categories fall into PMEST sequence, arranged according to their decreasing concreteness.

Postulate of Fundamental Category: मूलभूत श्रेणी की अभिधारणा There are five and only five fundamental categories. (Ranganathan)

Postulate of Isolate Facet: एकल पक्ष की अभिधारणा A subject may have one or more isolate facets each one of which can be deemed to be a manifestation of one and only one of the five fundamental categories. (Ranganathan)

Postulate of Level: स्तर की अभिधारणा Personality may manifest itself in one and the same record in a subject more than once, that is in two or more levels. So also in the case of matter, space and time. (Ranganathan)

Postulates of Rounds for Energy: शक्ति चक्र की अभिधारणा Energy may manifest itself in one and the same subject more than once in succession, that is in more than one round. (Ranganathan)

Postulate of Rounds for Personality and Matter: व्यक्तितत्व तथा पदार्थ चक्र की धारणा It is possible for a manifestation of personality and matter to occur after every energy round. (Ranganathan)

Postulate of Sequence: क्रम की अभिधारणा The basic facet of the subject should be put first, and the other facets should be arranged thereafter in the sequence of the decreasing concreteness of the fundamental categories of which they are respectively taken to be manifestation in the case of their not being more than one manifestation of any fundamental category. (Ranganathan)

Postulate of Sequence within a Round : चक्र के अन्तर्गत क्रम की अभिधारणा The sequence of the isolate facets within a round should be the same as given by the postulate of sequence. (Ranganathan)

Postulate of Space and Time Facet: स्थान तथा समय पक्ष की अभिधारणा Ordinarily space and item should be put in last in the sequence in which they are mentioned here. (Ranganathan)

PRECIS: प्रेसीज Acronym for preserved context index entry.

Preamble : आमुख A statement recording objectives of the contribution.

Preface: प्रस्तावना Authors statement in a document about purpose/method used for its development.

Preface Date: प्रस्तावना दिनांक The date given at the end of the preface.

Preferred Order: वाँछित क्रम Order in which the classes of a classification scheme are kept.

Prefix: अग्रनियोजित Addition of word/clause in the beginning.

Pre-natal: प्रकाशन पूर्व The technical processing of a document before its publication, the idea was first coined by Dr. Ranganathan.

Pre-natal Cataloguing: *See* Cataloguing in Source.

Prepaid Publication: पूर्वदत्त मूल्य प्रकाशन A publication for which advance payment has been made.

Preparatory: तैयारी

Prescribed: निर्धारित Recommonded

Prescribed Curriculum: निर्धारित पाठ्यक्रम Recommended subject contents.

Presentation Copy: प्रस्तुतिकरण प्रति A copy generally autographed by the author and given with out charging any price.

Preservation: संरक्षण Arrangement of protection of items.

Press Clipping: प्रैस कतरन *See* Clipping.

Press Cutting: सूचना कतरन *See*

Clipping

Press Mark: प्रैस चिन्ह A symbol indicating the object fixed according to the requirement of press.

Press Release: विज्ञप्ति An official effort to get information published for wider dissemination.

Primary Chain: मूल शृंखला The chain with the original universe as the first link.

Primary Document: मूल अभिलेख A basic document containing first hand original information/basic information on a topic.

Primary Journal: प्राथमिक पत्रिका A periodical covers unpublished research reports/papers on recent thoughts.

Primary Periodical: मूल प्रकाशन *See* Primary Journal.

Primary School Library: प्राथमिक स्कूल पुस्तकालय The library which is maintained by the school to support studies of the students and also to develop interest of books in their future studies.

Primary Source: मूल स्रोत The reference used by a author in work/original manuscript.

Principle: सिद्धांत *See* Rules.

Principle of Alphabetical Sequence: सारणी का सिद्धांत The isolates having international accepted current names. They may be arranged alphabetically by those names. (Ranganathan)

Principle of Away from Position: स्थिति से दूर का सिद्धांत If the isolate in an array can be taken to start from a certain point and diverge away from it roughly along a line, they should be arranged from the starting point along the diverging line. (Ranganathan)

Principle of Bottom Upward: तलोपर गमनीयता का सिद्धांत If the isolate in an array can be taken to be those occurring regularly along with a vertical line, then they should be arranged from bottom upward. (Ranganathan)

Principle of Classification: वर्गीकरण के सिद्धांत *See* Canons of Classification.

Principle of Clockwise: घड़ी दिशा का सिद्धांत In the isolates in an array can be taken to those occurring roughly in a circle, they should be arranged in clockwise direction. (Ranganathan)

Principle of Commercial Sequence: अनुक्रम का सिद्धांत When the isolates in an array are traditionally mentioned in specific sequence.

Principle of Increasing Concreteness: वर्धमान मूर्तता का सिद्धांत If two classes X and Y are such that X can be said to be more abstract and less concrete than Y, X should preceded Y. (Ranganathan)

Principle of Increasing Complexity: बढ़ती जटिलता का सिद्धांत If the isolate in an array show different degrees of complexity, it is helpful to arrange them in the sequence of the increasing measure of their complexity (Ranganathan).

Principle of Increasing Quantity: **बढ़ती मात्रा का सिद्धांत** If the characteristic used as the basis of classification admits of quantitative measurement, the sequence of the isolate should be in the ascending sequence of the measures in which the characteristic is shared by the isolate. (Ranganathan)

Principle of Inversion: **प्रत्यावर्तन कास सिद्धांत** The facets in the facet formula of a basic class should be in the decreasing sequence of their concreteness in each of the rounds (Ranganathan)

Principle of Later in Evolution: **विकास क्रम में उत्तरता का सिद्धांत** If the isolates in an array belong to different stages of evolution, they should be arranged parallel to the course of evolution. (Ranganathan)

Principle of later-in-time: **कालक्रम में उत्तरता का सिद्धांत** If the isolates in an array have originated at different times. They may be arranged in parallel time-sequence. (Ranganathan)

Principle of Left to Right: **बाम उत्तर सिद्धांत** If the isolates in an array can be taken to be those occurring roughly along a horizontal line, they should be arranged from left to right.

Principle of Literary Warrant: **साहित्य माँग का सिद्धांत** The isolates in an array may be arranged in the decreasing sequence of literary warrant.

Principle of Special Contiguity: **देशीय समीपता का सिद्धांत** If the isolates in an array occur continuously in space, they should be arranged in a parallel spatial sequence. (Ranganathan)

Printed Book: **छपी पुस्तक** A book produced in printed form by a mechanical method.

Printed Catalogue: **छपी सूची** A catalogue printed and brought out in book form. *See* Book Catalogue

Print-Material: **छपी सामग्री** *See* Book/Journal.

Printed Book Form Catalogue: **छपी पुस्तक आकार सूची** It is a physical form of catalogue. To up date it supplementary catalogues are issued. *See also* Printed Catalogue.

Printer: **मुद्रक** One who provides printed copies, or a mechanical device to produce printed copy. Output device for producing hard copies.

Printing: **मुद्रण** Process of printing.

Printing and Publication: **मुद्रण एवं प्रकाशन** An agency which prints and publishes document.

Printout: **छपी प्रति** Hard copy produced by a machine or paper output.

Private Library: **निजी पुस्तकालय** The library developed by the scholar for his own use.

Private Time: **निजी समय**

Probation: **परख अवधि** Period taken in evaluation.

Processing: **संसाधन** Technical operations carried out by library. And also an act of collection and organisation of information for effective service.

Processor: **संसाधक** In hardware a device works as a data processor and in software a computer program to perform various functions.

Profession: **व्यवसाय**

Professional: **व्यवसायिक** The staff who has professional skill to perform jobs assigned.

Professional Assistant: **व्यवसायिक सहायक** An assistant who possess professional skill.

Profile: **रूपरेखा** A list of users with the areas of their interest.

Proforma Invoice: **उपचारार्थ देयक** An invoice used to place the document on approval.

Program: **कार्यक्रम** Sequence of instructions given to a computer or an arrangement of jobs to take up. It is also known as software/computer program.

Programmer: **कार्यक्रम बनाने वाला** A specialist who designs, writes, and maintains the computer programs.

Programming: **कार्यक्रम** An act of creating software.

Programming Language : **कार्यक्रम की भाषा** Language used to express program.

Projector: **प्रदर्शक** A device used to project image on screen.

Promotion: **तरक्की/बढ़ावा** *See* Advancement.

Promotion of Reading Habit: **पठनरुचि विकास** The library has program like exhibition, extension lecture, essay competitions etc. to create reading culture.

Proof Reader: **प्रूफ पाठक/वाचक** A person who removes errors before final print out is brought out of a document/ book.

Prospectus: **विवरणिका** A small publication containing announcement of current programmes associated generally with an application.

Pseudonym: **उपनाम** An adopted name to keep real name out of scene.

Pseudo-classic: **कृत्रिम स्ववर्गी ग्रंथ** A pedestrian work provoking other works, such as criticism, parodies of itself and other dependent works.

Pseudo-Entity: **कृत्रिम सत्ता** Any class arising in the course of the complete assortment of a universe, considered as an empty receptable for the array of the entities. That is the unitary classes and the multiple class derived from it as the immediate universe. (Ranganathan)

Pseudo-series: कृत्रिम ग्रन्थमाला A set of books not constituting a multi-volumed book.

Publication: प्रकाशन Published contribution. *See also* Document, Book, Periodical.

Publication Date: प्रकाशन तिथि Year in which the book has been published.

Publication Division: प्रकाशन विभाग It is one of the largest publishing and book selling enterprise of the Government of India. More then 6800 titles have been published by it up to 1991. Publications are in low price on various subjects.

Public Library: सार्वजनिक पुस्तकालय A library wholly or partly run by public funds and remains open for all without reservation of caste, creed, sex etc.

Public Library Act: सार्वजनिक पुस्तकालय अधिनियम An act passed to establish a chain of Public Libraries.

Public Library Law: सार्वजनिक पुस्तकालय नियम *See* Public Library Act.

Public Library Manifesto: सार्वजनिक पुस्तकालय घोषणा पत्र A document on the subject was first published by UNESCO in 1949. It includes guide lines for the future development of public libraries.

Public Library System: सार्वजनिक पुस्तकालय प्रणाली Public libraries with extensions.

Public Record: सार्वजनिक अभिलेख Records which are in access of the public.

Public Relation: सार्वजनिक सम्बन्ध Systematic promotion of mutual understanding between organisation and information user.

Published Price: प्रकाशित/अंकित मूल्य The retail price indicated on a book.

Publisher: प्रकाशक A person/firm/corporate body responsible for the publication of a document.

Publisher's catalogue: प्रकाशक सूची List of books brought out by a publisher for market use. It may be for his publications or for his collections.

Punch: छेद A small hole as appears on catalogue card.

Punched Card: छेदवाला पत्र A standard size catalogue card which have an aperture in middle bottom to get it fit in a rod and a box designed to hold it.

Pure Notation: शुद्ध अंकन Simple base notation in which one type digits are used to represent all classes.

Q

Qualification: शिक्षा The education.

Qualifier: विशेषक A unique name or a name which has distinguishing additions.

Quality: गुण Merit of any thing.

Quality Control: गुण नियन्त्रण Process of review to examine characteristies

Quantity : मात्रा/परिमाण Volume of any thing.

Quarterly Journal: त्रि-मासिक पत्रिका A publication brought out after three months or four issues in a year.

Quasi Class: सदृश अंक Work, such as a secret work, a classic, a literary work, or a periodical publication or a bibliography, treated in a scheme of a classification as if it were a class in the universe of knowledge. (ISI)

Quasi Digit: सदृश अंक Group of digit to be treated as if they together form a single digit.

Quasi Isolate Idea: सदृश एकल विचार A characteristic enumerated in an array as if it were an isolate idea. (Ranganathan)

Quick Reference Service: शीघ्र संदर्भ सेवा Reference service is given in least possible time. *See also* Ready Reference Service.

Quota: नियतांश Fixed allocation.

Quotation: उद्धरण The words/para used as it is to strengthen the statement.

Quotes: उद्धरण The inverted commas placed at the beginning and at the end on a selected word/clause to highlight.

R

Rack: रैक Shelf/stand used to keep library collections.

Rapid Selector: शीघ्र चुनाव कारक Machine designed to scene film reel at high speed.

Raja Ram Mohun Roy Library Foundation (RRRLF) It was established in May 1972 as an autonomous organisation under Deptt. of Culture of Government of India for promoting library services in India. It arranges assistance under various schemes to develop public libraries and improve reading habits.

Random Access: बेतरतीव प्रवेश Access to a database without predetermined rule that from where the next item is to be obtained.

Random Access Memory (RAM): बेतरतीव स्मृति Main memory of a personal computer. The data will not be retained in case light goes off.

Ranganathan S.R.: रंगनाथन, एस. आर. First Indian Library scientist who designed colon classification and also developed theory in various areas of the subject.

Ranking: पंक्तिक्रम Arranging the groups formed by the division of the entities of a universe, so as to arrive at an assortment of the entities of the universe. (Ranganathan)

Rare Books: दुर्लभ ग्रन्थ Document for which multiple copies are not available.

Raw Data: अपरिष्कृत आंकडा/सूचना Unprocessed data.

Raw Material: कच्चा माल Material used to prepare object, in library raw material is required to carry out binding work.

Raw Title: अपरिष्कृत शीर्षक The actual title of the document.

Read: पढना Refers to the instruction to copy data from one storage to another; or to transfer data from input device to memory of the computer.

Reader: पाठक Library user or in computer a device that accepts information in one form and converts it to another form.

Reader Area: पाठक क्षेत्र *See* Reading Room

Reader's Advisory Service: पाठक परामर्शदात्री सेवा Service arranged to aid the user.

Reader-Printer: पाठक-मुद्रक A auto-device to read and reproduce a print copy on demand.

Reader's Ticket/Reader's Card: पाठक-पत्र *See* Borrowers Card.

Reading: पढ़ना

Reading Room: अध्ययन कक्ष/पठन कक्ष A room in a library used by the readers to consult library collections.

Reading List: पठन सामग्री सूची/सूचना सूची A list of books which is required to study the given subject.

Reading Material: सूचना संग्रह *See* Reading List

Read only Memory (ROM): केवल स्मृति पठन The memory used to hold programme. The data entered is retained even in case of light goes off.

Ready Reference Service: शीघ्र संदर्भ सेवा A quick service based generally on reference documents.

Real Name: वास्तविक नाम A name which has family recognition and recognition of law as well.

Real Time: वास्तविक समय Actual time taken in a physical process.

Real Time Computer: निश्चित समय कम्प्यूटर The computer which gives instantaneous results/response in a given time interval.

Rebinding : पुनर्बन्धन Reconstruction of a book for further use.

Recall: आह्वान It is an effort of getting books back for further use.

Recall Factor: आह्वान कारक Ratio of the number of relevant documents selected to the total number of relevant document for which the machine had been fed with entries.

Recognition: मान्यता Acceptance/approval.

Recommended Curricula: स्वीकृत पाठ्यक्रम Curricula which is approved to award a particular certificate/degree.

Record: अभिलेख Document which has classified information for preserving it for future use or unit of information in computer; or a written statement of items of an organisation; or group of related field of information treated as a unit.

Record Office: अभिलेख कार्यालय An office where records are kept for future consultation.

Reduction : संक्षिप्तकरण Reduced reproduction of the document.

Reference: संदर्भ Directing users to the source of information.

Reference Assistant: संदर्भ सहायक An assistant who retreives references.

Reference Book: संदर्भ ग्रंथ The books which supply definite piece of information and are not required for thorough reading. Such books are generally not loaned for outside use and are kept in reading room for consultation.

Reference Collection: संदर्भ संग्रह Collection which consist of reference documents.

Reference Department : संदर्भ विभाग A section of the library in which reference service is arranged.

Reference Entry: संदर्भ प्रविष्टि An entry which refers to another entry by using the term. *See / See also*.

Reference Librarian: संदर्भ पुस्तकाध्यक्ष A librarian who is incharge of reference desk to answer queries.

Reference Library: संदर्भ पुस्तकालय The library which has exclusive collections and which are also not available commonly in other libraries. These collections are not loaned.

Reference Room: संदर्भ कक्ष *See* Reading Room.

Reference Service: संदर्भ सेवा Service vide which reply is arranged for the query.

Reference Source: संदर्भ स्त्रोत Any document/individual used to obtain information.

Reference Work: संदर्भ कार्य Work created to meet reference service requirement.

References: संदर्भ A list of quoted documents, usually placed as supplement to the contribution.

Regional Library: क्षेत्रीय पुस्तकालय A library which is catering the needs of a region.

Register: पंजी/रजिस्टर A bound folder of papers used to record specific information.

Register Form Catalogue: पंजी आकार सूची In this form of catalogue, entries are written by hand in a bound register. The entries are made in the order of their receipt.

Register Issue System: पंजी आदान-प्रदान प्रणाली It is the earliest system in which page/ pages in a register are allotted to a user and at the time of issue details of document traced on the page marked to him.

Registration: पंजीयन/पंजीकरण An act of allowing library membership.

Registration Form: पंजीकरण प्रपत्र A form used to register the user in a library.

Registration Card: पंजीकरण पत्र A card which keeps identification of the user.

Registration Record: पंजीकरण अभिलेख Record of membership in library which is used to give clearance certificate/attendance certificates as and when required.

Regulation: नियम *See* Principle Rules/Guidelines.

Re-issue: नवीनीकरण Extension of loan period of the document which is already in possession.

Rejection-Slip: निरस्थ पर्ची Cancelled demand slip/requisition slip for which action is not required.

Relative Index: सापेक्ष अनुक्रमाणिका An alphabetical index to a classification scheme.

Relative Location: सापेक्ष स्थान Arrangement of document in relation to another.

Recurring Expenditure: निरन्तर खर्चा The expenditure which is of regular nature and repeats with every budget allocation.

Redundant Words in the title: शीर्षक में अनावश्यक शब्द Support words used in the title.

Remainder: अवशेष The remainders are constituted by the multiple titles which are unsold in Western market and collected by Indian market on low price to make money. Most of these are in paper back.

Reminder: स्मरण पत्र Letter or verbal effort to call over due library document.

Renewal: नवीनीकरण Extension of the existing arrangement.

Renewal of Book: पुनः निर्गम Reissue of library book to the same borrower.

Renewal of Subscription: पत्रिका खरीद आदेश नवीनीकरण The subscription of the same periodical is paid in advance to the same party which has arranged it for previous year.

Reply: उत्तर Response to a query.

Report: प्रतिवेदन A published primary source to know the activities of the organisation.

Reporting: सूचित करना Keeping informed about progress and achievements.

Repository: भंडार Store of a library or group of libraries.

Reprint: पुनर्मुद्रण Reproduction of an edition of a work without an alteration (ISI).

Reprography: प्रतिलिपिकरण An art of reproduction of the documents.

Reprography Service: प्रतिलिपिकरण सेवा Service which provides photocopy of the document.

Re-registration: पुन: पंजीकरण Registration of a member on expiry of his membership period.

Requisition Card: माँग पत्र A card which is used to place demand.

Research and Reference Library: शोध एवम् संदर्भ पुस्तकालय *See* Research Library.

Research Library: शोध पुस्तकालय The library which has selected material on the subject and useful for in-depth studies. It has sufficient number of journals/reference book.

Research Monograph: शोध मोनोग्राफ These are published research reports.

Reserve: आरक्षण Priority order among the chain of users.

Reserve Card: आरक्षण पत्र A card which is required to enter particulars of the document to be reserved.

Reserve Collection: आरक्षित संग्रह The collections which are not within the reach of every one or which are not for general circulation.

Resource Centre: स्त्रोत केन्द्र *See* Information Centre.

Resource Sharing: संसाधन अंश ग्रहण Sharing of collections and services of group of libraries to achieve economy.

Resolving Power: निश्चयकारक शक्ति The power of recognising the sub-classes appropriate to the array of the first order of an immediate universe. (ISI)

Resolution Factor: निश्चयकारक कारण Ratio of the number of selected documents to the total number of documents searched (Ranganathan).

Restricted Book: प्रतिबाधित पुस्तक The book of which circulation is permitted to selected users only.

Restricted Circulation: प्रतिबाधित निर्गम When loan period and number of books limit condition is imposed at the time of issue.

Restricted Publication: प्रतिबाधित प्रकाशन Publication of which circulation is stopped.

Retrieval: पुन: प्राप्ति An act or finding information.

Retrospective Bibliography: प्रारम्भिक ग्रन्थ सूची A bibliography which has current documents alongwith documents published in previous years as well.

Return Desk: निर्गम डैस्क *See* Circulation Desk.

Review: समीक्षा Critical article or method of introducing contents of document.

Review Copy: समीक्षा प्रति A copy of the publication used for preparing review.

Reviewing Periodical: समीक्षा पत्रिका A periodical giving, narrative form, an account of the contribution bearing on a stated subject and appearing in the fascicles of periodicals and the books published during its period of coverage.

(Ranganathan) or a periodical provides review on a particular subject.

Revised Edition: संशोधित संस्करण Corrected and enlarged edition based on previous work.

Rider's International Classification: राइडर का अन्तर्राष्ट्रीय वर्गीकरण Scheme of a classification designed by Fremont Rider and published for the first time in 1961.

Right Classification: अनम्य वर्गीकरण Classification which is not according to some scheme.

Rounds: स्तर More than once occurrence of the facet.

Routine: निरन्तर General use of instructions.

Routing of Documents: ग्रन्थों का संचरण Circulation of documents within users to inform about their presence and use.

Rules: नियम Set of guidelines put to practice.

Rules of Classification: वर्गीकरण के नियम Set of rules framed to guide classifier.

Running Title: चलता शीर्षक A secondary/subordinate title printed on the top line of each page of work.

S

Sacred Book: धार्मिक पुस्तक *See* Sacred Work.

Sacred Work: धार्मिक कार्य Basic work of a religion, generally accepted as such among its followers. (ISI)

Sample Page: नमूना पृष्ठ A selected page to project the document.

Sarada Ranganathan Endowment for Library Science: पुस्ताकलय विज्ञान के लिए शारदा रंगनाथनन्यास It was founded in 1961 by the late Dr. S.R. Ranganathan and his family with the objective of furthering the cause of library science and services.

Save: सुरक्षित An instruction in computer to retain record/data for future use.

Save the time of the Reader: पाठक का समय बचाओ It is fourth law of library science which is to improve/achieve accuracy in library services.

Scale of Popularity of Language: भाषा प्रियता मापक Descending scale of popularity of the languages, maintained by a library on the basis of their respective users as the medium in the exposition of its documents. (Ranganathan)

Scan: अवलोक To examine every reference as a part of retrieval. *See also* Sort.

Scanner: अवलोकन करने वाला Equipment/instrument used to do scanning of stored information.

Scanning: अवलोकन An act of searching records.

Schedule: सारणी A written statement of classes in a scheme of classification. *See also*

Schedule of Classification.

Schedule of Classification: वर्गीकरण की सारणी Dictionary helpful in finding the meaning of each class number or ordinal name, as expressed in a natural language or a jargon of profession or a trade. (Ranganathan) or Series of notations used to represent subject and their subbranches in a scheme of classification.

Scheme: योजना Complete description of a plan.

Scheme of Assortment: चुनाव योजना Method of shorting entitles of a universe.

Scheme of Classes: वर्ग विधि Statement showing the filiatory sequence of the classes. (Ranganathan)

Scheme of Classification: वर्गीकरण विधि *See* Schedule of Classification.

School Edition: स्कूल संस्करण An edition of a document especially designed for school use and provided on cheaper price. Which is generally in paper back. May be called student edition.

School Library: स्कूल पुस्तकालय A library maintained to achieve the ideals of the school and school education. It is mainly for the use of the staff and pupils of the schools.

Scientific Management: वैज्ञानिक प्रशासन *See* Modern Management.

Scientific Terms: वैज्ञानिक शब्दावली Terms which are used in science education.

Screen: चित्र परदा A specially prepared surface on which an image is projected.

Script: लिपि A term used to recognise hand-writing.

Search : ढूंढ़ना खोज An effort to locate the selected piece of information.

Search Aid: खोज सहायता Devices which are used to perform a search.

Search Method: खोज का तरीका The technique used to perform search.

Search Point: खोज बिन्दु *See* Access Point.

Search Service: खोज सेवा Service involved in retrieving information.

Search Term: खोज शब्द A term used as an approach point. *See also* key Word.

Secondary Document: सहायक अभिलेख The publication generated to know the flow of primary documents.

Secondary Elements: उप तत्त्व Word added after entry element. (ISI)

Secondary Journal: सहायक पत्रिका A journal based on published information like published articles, abstracts and reviews etc.

Secondary Periodical: सहायक पत्रिका *See* Secondary Journal

Secondary School Library: माध्यमिक स्कूल पुस्तकालय These libraries are maintained to support the curricula run by school and to update young children's about their surroundings.

Secondary Sources: उप स्रोत A compilation consists reference of primary sources.

Second Hand Book: पुनः खरीद पुस्तक A book sold after use.

Second Indentation: द्वितीय दण्ड The allotted space line form the left edge of catalogue card which is used to design information.

Section: अनुभाग *See* Part/Unit of the organisation.

Sector: खण्ड A set of isolate achieved on the basis of a single characteristic. (ISI)

Sector Device: क्षेत्र युक्ति Device of using a sectorising digit, that is, to form another sector or stretch of co-ordinate digits by adding to it the successive digits of the species and deeming the resulting double digit numbers as diffused into a single digit, and repeating this process to form successive sectors. (Ranganathan)

Sector Notation: क्षेत्रीय अंकन *See* Sector Device.

See: देखिए A direction note to shift subject search under another term.

See also: देखिए और A direction note to refer the same subject available under another term.

Select Bibliography: चयित ग्रन्थ सूची Bibliogrophy which lists only selective documents on a subject.

Selective Dissemination of Information (SDI) : चयित सूचना सम्प्रेषण Library service through which registered users are informed about the additions and information in the field of their interest.

Selection: चुनाव A process of arranging wanted items.

Semantic Rich Digit: अर्थ समृद्ध अंक A digit with ordinal value and representing a focal idea in conformity to the canon of seminal mnemonics. (ISI)

Semantic Value: अर्थ मूल्य The ordinal value which fixes the place of a subject relative to other subjects in a scheme of classification.

Seminal Isolate Idea: प्रारम्भिक एकल विचार Isolate idea that can be attached to several host classes and represented by the same isolate number, whatever be the host class but denoted by different isolate terms in the context of the host classes concerned. (ISI)

Seminar Room: सभा कक्ष A room in which special collections on any subject are kept for the use of the special user or a room where debates are organised.

Semi Professional: अर्ध व्यवसायिक A person with minimum basic qualification and preliminary professional skill.

Semi-weekly: अर्द्ध साप्ताहिक Publication which is brought out twice a week.

Serial: क्रमिक प्रकाशन A periodical publication in which each volume or each periodical group of volumes embodise more or less similar information mainly relating to its year of coverage. (ISI)

Serial Catalogue: क्रमिक-प्रकाशन सूची Catalogue formed for serials.

Serial Control: क्रमिक प्रकाशन नियन्त्रण A proper control on the collection of serial publications.

Serial Publication: क्रमिक प्रकाशन *See* Serial.

Serial Number: क्रमिक संख्या The successive number which fixes the position of number among other numbers of the volume of the publication.

Series: ग्रन्थमाला When publications are brought out under a collective title followed an independent title allotted with an individualising number.

Series Entry: ग्रन्थमाला प्रविष्टि An added entry is made to provide search through series approach.

Series Note: ग्रन्थमाला टिप्पण A note in catalogue entry to record name, number and editor of series to which document belongs.

Series Number: ग्रन्थमाला संख्या A number assigned to each of the volume of the series.

Series Statement: ग्रन्थमाला विवरण *See* Series Note.

Series Title: ग्रन्थमाला शीर्षक A Title allotted to a series.

Sequel : शेष Work continuing to another work.

Sequence : क्रम Progressive order of items.

Sequential Control: क्रमिक नियन्त्रण Digital computer operation in which the instructions are set up in sequence and fed to the computer consecutively during the solution for a problem. (MD)

Sequential File: क्रमिक फाइल The data file whose storage is accessible only in ascending order.

Service: सेवा An act of disseminating information.

Setelitte Communication: सेटेलाइट सम्प्रेषण It is a result of modern scientific and technological advancement. The communication links are established with the help of space and communication technology.

Shared Cataloguing: साझा सूचीकरण A group of libraries when share cataloguing work to achieve uniformity and efficiency.

Sharing: सहयोग Co-operative utilisation of all resources such as collections, technical know-how etc.

Sheaf: शीफ/पत्र Slip of paper.

Sheaf Form Catalogue: पत्र

आकार सूची *See* Loose Leaf Form Catalogue.

Shelf: शैल्फ An equipment of holding library collections.

Shelf Capacity: शैल्फ क्षमता Capacity of holding of number of volumes on a shelf.

Shelf Guide: शैल्फ दर्शक An indicator that documents belonging to the indicated class are only available on that particular shelf.

Shelf List: शैल्फ सूची A catalogue of library holdings arranged in order as these are available on shelves. For each document one entry with full details is arranged and used only by library staff.

Shelf Mark: शैल्फ चिन्ह A symbol showing the location of a shelf.

Shelf Number: शैल्फ संख्या A number assigned to a shelf to fix its location.

Shelf Rectificaton: शैल्फ संशोधन The process of restoring order of the scheduled documents.

Shelving: क्रमकरण An activity of putting document in their classes.

Short Time Loan: कम समय उधार Loan of a document for a restricted period.

Short Title: लघु शीर्षक *See* Abbreviated Title.

Signal: संकेत Any electrical pulse which is used to represent bits in computer operation.

Signed Edition: हस्ताक्षारित संस्करण *See* Autographed Edition.

Signed Page: हस्ताक्षरित पृष्ठ *See* Autographed Page.

Simple Base: सरल आधार A base consisting only one conventional set of digits.

Simple Book: सरल पुस्तक A book which is not a composite and which embodise continuous exposition of the subject matter.

Simple Heading: सरल शीर्षक Heading consisting of a single block.

Simplified Cataloguing: सरलीकृत सूची A catalogue in which entries are modified and only selected information is recorded.

Single Volumed Book: एक खण्डीय पुस्तक A book which is in one volume only.

Size: आकार Physical look of any thing.

Slip: पर्ची A piece of paper.

Software: सॉफ्टवेयर A computer program (set of instructions) or set of programs for performing specific job in one or more computers.

Source: स्रोत Main point/starting point.

Source Book: आधार ग्रन्थ A book which is helping or guide book to the subject.

Source Document: स्रोत अभिलेख Original document.

Source Material: स्रोत सामग्री *See* Primary Source.

Souvenir Volume: स्मारक खण्ड A

volume brought out on a special occasion.

Sought Link: **आँछित कड़ी** Link which is neither false nor part of a fused link nor an unsought link. (Ranganathan)

Space: **स्थान** Gap inbetween two letters. In classification the term is used to represent geographical area.

Space Isolate: **स्थान एकल** Conventional division of the inside and outside surface of the earth.

Special Classification: **विशेष वर्गीकरण** A classification developed for a particular purpose.

Special Collection: **विशेष संग्रह** A collection based on principles.

Special Edition: **विशेष संस्करण** An edition brought out to fulfil certain identified objectives.

Special Issue: **विशेष अंक** *See* Special Number.

Special Isolate Idea: **विशेष एकल विचार** Isolate idea special to a basic class or to an isolate idea or to an array—isolate idea—or to a small group of basic classes, isolate ideas and array isolate ideas as the case may be.

Special Library: **विशेष पुस्तकालय** The libraries developed by the various departments to achieve the special objectives. The collections and services of these libraries are designed according to the specific purpose.

Special List: **विशेष सूची** A list prepared to meet some definite purpose.

Special Number: **विशेष संख्या** A special issue of the periodical brought out to meet the special occasion/purpose.

Spine: **पश्च** *See* Back.

Specific Entry: **विशिष्ट प्रविष्टि** Entry mentioning a specific approach

Specific Information: **विशिष्ट सूचना** A selected information.

Specification: **मानक** *See* Standards.

Spensor Classification: **सैन्सर वर्गीकरण** Scheme of classes given in the classification of science (1864) of Herbart Spnsor.

Stacks: **पुस्तक भंडार** An area where book collections are kept.

Stack Guides: **भंडार दर्शक** The guides used to indicate location of the collections in a stack.

Stack Room: **पुस्तक भंडार** *See* Stack.

Staff: **कर्मचारी** Group of people working in a library.

Staff Manual: **कर्मचारी पुस्तिका** A guide book for day to day service of the staff.

Staff Room: **कर्मचारी कक्ष** A room reserved for the common use of the staff.

Standard: **मानक** The publications which provide specifications/standards to achieve uniformity.

Standard Book: **मानक पुस्तक** The

contributions of which are of permanent value.

Standard Copy: मानक प्रति A copy evolved after observing guidelines available on the subject.

Standard Format: मानक आकार Organisation of information on accepted guidelines.

Standard Size Card: मानक आकार पत्र A card of commonly accepted size like catalogue card usually of 5" × 3" used in all the libraries.

Standard Subdivision: मानक उपविभाजन Subdivision which are used to attech the form characteristic of the document.

Standard Work: मानक रचना *See* Standard Book

Standing Committee: स्थायी समिति The committee which assists in continuing functions. The committee can also be regarded as permanent committee.

Standing Order: स्थायी आदेश An order with understanding that a new publication/new edition should be supplied on its publication.

Starter: प्रारम्भक Curve symbol inserted at the beginning of a subject device or any other number which should be treated as if it were a single digit and should always be taken along with that digit symbol (Ranganathan)

State Central Library: राज्य केन्द्रीय पुस्तकालय It is a repository of the publications developed to serve from the state central place it may also serve to provide information about the state.

Statement: विवरण Enunciation in a standard form of the information for which the entries should be located.

Statistical Data: सांख्यिकीय आँकड़ा Information in numerical form.

Steps in Classification: वर्गीकरण के चरण Keeping in view the complex nature of classification Dr. Ranganathan suggested following eight steps.

Deriving of expensive title from raw title

Kernel title from raw title

Analysed title

Transformed title

Standard terms replaced

Facet numbers

Class number

Facet analysis of class number.

Stock: भण्डार In library book collections available.

Stock Book: भण्डार पुस्तक *See* Accession Register.

Stock Checking/Stock Taking: भंडार निरीक्षण *See* Stock Verification.

Stock Number: भण्डार संख्या A number assigned to item on the basis of the stock entry.

Stock Register: भण्डार पंजी A register in which entries are made for those items which are in possession of the organisation.

Stock Verification: मंडार जाँच Physical check up of library documents/holdings.

Storage: मण्डारण Device to keep information for future use, *See also* Memory.

Storage Capacity: मण्डारण क्षमता In computer it is memory capacity or in case of store it is a holding capacity of collections.

Student's Card: विद्यार्थी पत्र *See* Borrower Card.

Sub-committee: उप-समिति A committee constituted to supplement the work of the main committee. It may name members from outside or from the main committee.

Sub-class: उप-वर्ग Part of the class.

Sub-division: उप-विभाजन A further division achieved on the basis of certain characteristics.

Sub-heading: उप-शीर्षक Heading which is subordinate to main heading.

Subject: विषय The theme/matter discussed in a document.

Subject Arrangement: विषय व्यवस्था Arrangement of books in-their subject order.

Subject Analytical: विषय विश्लेषिक Specific added entry in dictionary catalogue, referring form the name of a subject forming a part of a document, to the host document and giving the place of occurrence of the subject in the host document. (ISI)

Subject Bibliography: विषय ग्रन्थ-सूची Bibliography which consists entries on the subject for which it is developed.

Subject Catalogue: विषय सूची When catalogue cards forming subject entries are strictly arranged in alphabetical order under subject headings.

Subject Classification: विषय वर्गीकरण Scheme of classification designed by James Duff Brown and published for the first time in 1906. (Ranganathan)

Subject Device: विषय युक्ति When a class number is used as an isolate number by enclosing it within circular brackets.,

Subject Entry: विषय प्रविष्टि An added entry referring the subject of the document.

Subject Heading: विषय शीर्षक The terms reflecting the main aspects of the text. Thus these are the words or group of words which are used as search point.

Subject Reference: विषय संदर्भ An entry which referes to other subject entry.

Subject Specialist: विषय विशेषज्ञ One who knows subject in detail.

Subordinate: अधीनस्थ One who works on guidance.

Subscription: शुल्क The price at which periodical literature is received.

Substantive Digit: सारगर्भित अंक A digit with ordinal value and representing a specific focal idea (ISI)

Sub-series: उप-ग्रन्थमाला A series within a series.

Sub-system: उप-प्रणाली A system applicable within a system.

Sub-title: उप-शीर्षक An explanatory secondary title.

Summary: सारांश Brief account culled form detailed text.

Superannuation: सेवा निवृत्ति Completion of the service period under the rules available for the purpose.

Super Computer: उच्च कम्प्यूटर Powerful and expensive computer machine which is used for large database and complex calculations with very high speed.

Super Imposition Device: अध्यारोपण युक्ति When a portion of an isolate falling within the range of another co-ordinate isolate.

Supervisor: निरीक्षक A person who coordinates to direct the work among the staff working in an organisation.

Supplement: परिशिष्ट/पूरक Volume forming a part of the work.

Supplement Facet: पूरक पक्ष Part of the book number of a document, which is its supplement number. (ISI)

Supplement Number: पूरक संख्या Number assigned to a supplement to individualise it from the document it belongs.

Supplement to Author Statement: लेखक विवरण पूरक Statement of the year of birth and of the alternative name, if any of each person mentioned in author statement. (ISI)

Supplement to a Periodical: पत्रिका पूरक An issue brought out on special occasion.

Supporting Staff: सहयोगी कर्मचारी The staff posted to assist professional or supervisory staff is known as supporting staff.

Surname: कुल नाम A family name which is used first in catalogue to bring all documents together created by the person concerned.

Survey: सर्वेक्षण Collection of data/information for conducting authentic studies.

Suspended Publication: प्रतिबाधित प्रकाशन Document of which publication is detained.

Switch Board: स्विच बोर्ड A panel or arrangement of panels bearing switches for connecting and disconnecting electric circuits. (DDPT)

Symbol: चिन्ह, प्रतीक Any thing that can represent something other than itself. The value of which is generally defined.

Symbolic Meta-language: A meta-language made of defined symbols (Ranganathan).

Synonyms: पर्यायवाची The words/names used for the similar meaning.

Synthesised Title: संश्लेषित शीर्षक Title abridged after using eight steps of classification process.

System: प्रणाली It can be a machine system/for collection of instructions which forms operating system or an organised grouping of people, methods, machines and materials collected together to perform specific objectives.

System Analysis: प्रणाली विश्लेषण Step by step investigation for doing the things in best way or an act of evaluation for working of a system.

System Analyist: प्रणाली विश्लेषक One who studies the activities, methods, procedures and techniques to make best use of the system.

Systematic Isolate Idea: व्यवस्थित एकल विचार Isolate idea whose isolate number is determined in conformity to a principle.

System Library/Library system: पुस्तकालय प्रणाली A library which has number of extensions.

Systematic Rich Digit: सुनियोजित समृद्ध अंक A digit with ordinal value and representing a focal idea in conformity to the canon of systematic mnemonics. (ISI)

T

Table: तालिका A layout of written numerical statement or words.

Table of Contents: तालिका-सूची List of the table headings with page number. In case of a periodical, it is a list of titles of contributions along with the name of contributors and page number.

Tablet: टिकिया An ancient writing material which is made of claystone etc.

Tabular Work: संख्यात्मक कार्य Figure arranged vertically in columns.

Tag : टैग In computer, a set of characters affixed to data item for identification.

In general, it is a piece of paper or cloth used for putting class number of a library documents.

Tape: टेप A transparent chemical coated thin material used to keep document intact or magnetic coated electronic media equipment on which information is stored.

Technical and Management Education: तकनीकी तथा प्रशासनिक शिक्षा The education imparted to develop technical know how and knowledge of management techniques.

Technical Journal: तकनीकी पत्रिका A journal devoted to a branch of technology. Also known as technical periodical.

Technical Library : तकनीकी पुस्तकालय A library which has most of the collections on technical subjects.

Technical Report: तकनीकी प्रतिवेदन A report presenting scientific result.

Technical Service: तकनीकी सेवा Service like cataloguing classification through which information is processed for use.

Technical Qualification: तकनीकी योग्यता Qualification of specialised nature to do technical work of libraries and information service centres.

Technical Term: तकनीकी शब्द The terms used in technical disciplines.

Telecommunication Service: दूर संचार सम्प्रेषण सेवा Service in which the copy of the document selected is read out and made available/visible to the reader at the distant place or is typed out at the consumer's end. (ISI)

Tele Reference: दूर संदर्भ A method for consulting catalogues from a remote location, consisting of a closed circuit television system or viewing the mechanical handling equipment for moving the catalogue cards or page about. (Ranganathan)

Telescoped Array: अन्तर्बेधित पंक्ति Array of isolates in a schedule of classification, made of co-ordinate or subordinate isolates, is viewed from idea plane, but whose isolate numbers appear to be co-ordinate, as viewed from the notational plane. (Ranganathan)

Telescoped Facet: अन्तर्बेधित पक्ष *See* Telescoped Array

Telex: टेलेक्स System of international teleprinter communication over public telegraphy links.

Term: शब्द Word in a natural language.

Terminal : त्रैमासिक Which is brought out after three months. *See also* Quarterly.

Terminal: टर्मिनल Computer equipment/peripheral like input and display devices which may also be known as data terminal.

Terminology : शब्दावली Set of terms

Testing: परीक्षण An art of checking

Text: विषय The main part of the document.

Text Book: पाठ्य पुस्तक The book developed on a fixed curricula to support teaching programme or a standard contribution which helps in understanding a specific branch of knowledge.

Text Book Library: पाठ्य पुस्तक पुस्तकालय A library which holds text books only.

Theme: विषय Topic

Theory: लिखित Written statement.

Thesauri: कोश *See* Thesaurus

Thesaurus: विश्व कोश A book of words that shows explicitly the relationship among the words it contains. It is an introduction to indexing system to control vocabulary in mechanised way.

Thesis: शोध प्रबन्ध *See* Dissertation.

Third Indentation: तृतीय दण्ड Imaginary distance parallel to the second indentation from the left edge of the catalogue card.

Thought: विचार A subject or a series of ideas.

Thought Content: विचार अंश The expressed thought embodied within a document or a volume of it. (ISI)

Time: समय Fundamental category in colon classification which speaks about period.

Time Table : समय सारणी A schedule of time to operate service.

Title: शीर्षक The word/group of words used as the name of the work.

Title Analytical: शीर्षक विश्लेषिक Specific added entry, referring from a title of a contribution forming a part of document to the host document and giving the place of occurrence of the contribution in the host document. (ISI)

Title Catalogue: शीर्षक सूची A catalogue in which all title entries are arranged strictly in alphabetical order.

Title Entry: शीर्षक प्रविष्टि Title entry is an added entry and prepared only for fanciful titles with proper noun or when the aspect is not represented by subject entry.

Title Cover: शीर्षक आवरण A cover on which title of the document is indicated.

Title-Heading: शीर्षक Heading consists of title.

Title in Facet Numbers: पक्ष संख्या शीर्षक A title comprises of facet numbers.

Title in Focal Numbers: मुख्य संख्या शीर्षक Title formed by replacing kernel terms by standard terms retaining with focal numbers with description symbols.

Title in Standard Terms: मानक-शब्द शीर्षक Title formed by standard terms used in a scheme of classification.

Title Page: शीर्षक पृष्ठ Page of the work containing title statement.

Title Section: शीर्षक अनुभाग The section of an entry, giving the title of the document, catalogued and the names of collaborator, if any, and the number or the name of the edition, if any. (ISI)

Title Statement: शीर्षक विवरण Record, in a document, of the title of the work, or of the title (name) given to the automatic record, forming the document. (ISI)

Tooling : अक्षर लेखन Impression on binding.

Track: मार्ग On a moving storage medium, the sequence of storage locations that is accessible from a given read head position. (DDPT)

Tracing : अभिलेखन It is a record of entries prepared for a document which is generally traced in one paragraph in accordance with cataloguing rules.

Tracing Section: अभिलेखन अनुभाग The section which keeps record of all the added entries.

Trade Catalogue: व्यापारिक सूची Catalogue of one or more publishers/distributors.

Trade Discount: व्यापारिक छूट Discount allowed on purchase of books to the distributors.

Trade Journal: व्यापारिक पत्रिका A journal which disseminates trade conditions and also used for publicity of initiatives in the field.

Trade Literature: व्यापारिक साहित्य The publicity literature used to popularise new publication.

Trainee: प्रशिक्षणार्थी An individual one who goes under training.

Trained: प्रशिक्षित An individual one who has taken training.

Training: प्रशिक्षण Programme of teaching for practical services.

Transfer: स्थानान्तरण When one is shifted from one operation to another.

Transformed Title: परिवर्तित शीर्षक Title drived from analyzed title by rearranging the kernel terms in accordance with the postulates and the principles stated for the purpose and retaining with each its own descriptive symbol. (Ranganathan)

Translation: अनुवाद Work forming the expression of another work in a language different from that of the original but not deserving to be deemed an independent work on the basis of the quality of its thought and expression.

Translation Service: अनुवाद सेवा A service which arranges information in the known languages of the user.

Translator: अनुवादक One who translates from one language to another.

Transmission: संचरण Transfer of information from one end to another.

Travel Guide: यात्री दर्शक A booklet consisting information on places, accommodation and transport facilities of tourist interest.

Travelling Library: चल पुस्तकालय *See* Mobile Library

Trustee: संरक्षक One who is member of the management board.

Type: प्रकार Kinds of the item.

Typescript: टंकित प्रति A typewritten form of a document or a typed manuscript.

U

Ultimate Class: अंतिम वर्ग The class of smallest extension accepted by a classification scheme.

Ultimate Commodity: अन्तिम वस्तु Natural or near natural material either directly consumable or processed beyond small limits and usually with the aid of technology and elaborate machinery and brought to the stage of being consumable as it is. (Ranganathan)

Ultimate Service: अन्तिम सेवा Service directly with the user.

Umbral: उपच्छाया Umbral is an arrangement consisting of the class or the isolate or the array-isolate of primary interest to the reader at the moment. (Ranganathan) or intimately relevant record.

Umbral Region: उपच्छाया प्रदेश *See* Umbral.

Unaccessioned Book: अपंजीकृत पुस्तक A book which is not entered in the library stock register.

Unauthorized Edition: अनाधिकृत संस्करण An edition which is published without the consent of the author.

Unbound: जिल्द रहित Loose publication.

Undated: तिथि रहित A document which does not have its date of publication.

Unesco Coupons: सूनैस्को कूपन International currency payment to meet assistance programmes.

Unlike Entities: अवांछित सत्ता Entities sharing a given attribute unequally in measure, intensity, extent, or on any other basis, the unlikeness being with reference to the said attribute. (Ranganathan)

Uniform Title: समान शीर्षक The common title used on all volumes and in their parts.

Union Catalogue: संयुक्त सूची A merged listing of the contents of two or more libraries (DDPT) or it is a record of holdings of a group of libraries, usually arranged in an alphabetical order, showing the name of the library where the document physically available

UNISIST: यूनिसिस्ट United Nations World Science Information System evolved by UNESCO around 1971 to share information.

Unit Card: इकाई पत्र *See* Main Card.

Unit Card System of Catalogue: सूची इकाई पत्र प्रणाली Catalogue in printed or near printed cards in which the main card is printed with the leading section vacant and copies of which are converted into specific entries by inserting the appropriate heading in the leading section.(ISI)

Unit Record : इकाई अभिलेख *See* Main Card.

Unitary Class: एकीय वर्ग Class containing one and only one entity. (Ranganathan)

Unitary Group: एकीय समूह Group consisting of one and only one entity (Ranganathan)

United Nations Educational Scientific and Cultural Organisation (UNESCO): यूनैस्को An intergovernmental agency, founded in 1946, since its inception, active in promotion, co-ordination and development of library, documentation and information services. It is arranging seminars and meetings to extend advisory services.

Uniterm: **एकात्मकता** In information retrieval, a word, symbol or number used to identify a particular item.(DDPT)

Universal Decimal Classification (UDC): **यूनीवर्सल डैसीमल वर्गीकरण** Scheme of classification sponsored by the international institute of bibliography and its successor body, the international federation for documentation published it for the first time in 1896. (ISI)

Universe of First Remove: **प्रथम विभाजन ज्ञान जगत** Immediate universe.

Universe of Knowledge: **ज्ञान जगत** Known World.

University: **विश्वविद्यालय** An autonomous educational body which imparts instructions in various disciplines to award diplomas/degrees.

University Grants Commission Grants: **विश्वविद्यालय अनुदान आयोग: अनुदान** Grants provided by the central autonomous body UGC for maintaining the standards of research, teaching and extension in universities/colleges.

University Library: **विश्वविद्यालय पुस्तकालय** The library maintained to support academic programmes of the university system.

University Library Committee: **विश्व विद्यालय पुस्तकालय समिति** *See* Advisory Committee for Library

Unpaged book: **पृष्ठ संख्या रहित पुस्तक** A book which has leaves without page number.

Unknown Document: **अज्ञात अभिलेख** When the document is not known to the user.

Unprocessed Book: **असंसाधित पुस्तक** A book which is not treated/classified/catalogued for use.

Unsought Link: **अवांछित कड़ी** Link which is not forming class number.

Update: **पूर्ण क्रिया** Incorporation of current/correct information in master file in accordance with the programme.

Upper Link: **ऊपरी कड़ी** Link other than the last link. (Ranganathan)

Upward Arrow: **उर्ध्वमुखी तीर** An arrow symbol used in Colon Classification Scheme.

User Friendly Program: **प्रयोक्ता सहयोगी कार्यक्रम** A program which is simple and without computer background even one can use it.

User: **प्रयोक्ता** One who uses library holdings.

User profile: **प्रयोक्ता रूपरेखा** A record of users with their subject interest.

User Services: **प्रयोक्ता सेवा** The service provided to make use of the holdings of the library.

V

Variable: परिवर्तन Set of characteristics used to group the collections.

Vedic Classification: वैदिक वर्गीकरण Scheme of classes implied in the *Upanishad* and later adopted in the *Puranas*, the *Bhaghavat Gita* and the *Tantras*. (Ranganathan)

Vedio Disk: वीडियो डिस्क It is used to record audio-video information for repeated use with the help of machine.

Vedio Tape : वीडियो टेप A magnetic tape to record information in audio and visual form.

Vendor: बेचनेवाला A person who sells

Verbal Plane: विचारतल The plane of expression of a concept in a natural language. (Ranganathan) or a stage where thoughts are assigned suitable term before assigning it appropriate notation.

Verification: सत्यापन A process of checking the holdings.

Vertical File: उर्ध्वस्थ फाइल When documents are arranged/ listed in vertical order.

Visitor's Card: आगन्तुक पत्र Borrower's Card.

Visual Display Terminal: चाक्षुष दृश्य पथ A device capable of displaying keyed input as output on screen.

Visual Aids: चाक्षुष उपकरण Aids to project information on monitor.

Visitor Register: आगन्तुक पंजी A register maintained at enterence of the library to record the details of those who visit library.

Voice Mail: ध्वनि संचरण When mail is operational on sound communication that is through machine application

Volume: खण्ड A written or printed work or part of a work occupying in several sheets or leaves of paper to other substance fastened together so as to be opened at any particular sheet of leaf. The whole being protected by binding or cover of some kind (ISI). *See also* Book.

Volume Number : खण्ड संख्या Number within the book number of a volume of a multi-volumed book, individualize the said volume in the set. (Ranganathan)

Volume Facet: खण्ड पक्ष Part of the book number of a document which is its volume number (Ranganathan)

Voluminous Book: बहुखण्ड ग्रन्थ Book in bigger size or many Volumes.

Voucher: खर्च पत्र Written statement of payment/expenditure.

W

Waiting List: प्रतीक्षा सूची A list prepared to fix up priority for a document in circulation.

Wall picture-Principle: भित्ति चित्र सिद्धांत If two facets A and B of a subject are such that the concept behind B will not be operative unless the concept behind 'A' is conceded. Even as a mural picture is not possible unless the wall exists to draw upon, then the facet 'A' should precede facet B. (Ranganathan)

Weeding Out: निष्कासन Process of removing obsolete and mutilated collections from the library.

Weekly: साप्ताहिक Publication which is brought out once in a week.

Whole-organ-Principle: सम्पूर्ण अंग सिद्धांत If a subject facet B is an organ, that is an organic part, then A should precede 'B'. (Ranganathan)

Who's who/who was who: कौन है कौन/कौन था कौन *See* Biography.

Window: गवाक्ष A portion of the visual display screen generally used to show the current status of the activity of the program on screen.

Withdrawal: निष्कासन The process of removing entries form the accession register and books from shelves

Withdrawal Record: निष्कासन अभिलेख See Withdrawal Register

Withdrawals Register: निष्कासन पंजी A record for the documents withdrawn from the library collections.

Word: शब्द A group of letters which has some meaning and purpose. In computer group of characters occupying one storage location.

Word Book: शब्द पुस्तक *See* dictionary

Word by Word Entry: शब्द अनुक्रमाणिका Method of arranging entries strictly in alphabetical order.

Word Entry: शब्द प्रविष्टि Entry beginning with a word.

Word Group: शब्द समूह A set of consecutive words to be taken together. In a heading for intelligibility, and not separated by any punctuation mark other than a hyphen. (Ranganathan)

Word Length: शब्द विस्तार The number of characters/bits used to form a word.

Word Processing: शब्द संसाधन Computer program which is used for writing, editing, printing etc.

Work: रचना Expressed thought, that is a thought expressed in language, symbols or in any other mode and thus made communicable. (ISI)

Work Assignment: कार्य नियोजन When responsibility of carrying out the job is shifted to some one.

X

Xeroxed Book: प्रतिलिपिकृत पुस्तक

A copy of the book obtained by using photocopier.

Y

Yearly: वार्षिक Publication which appears once in a year.

Year Book: वार्षिकी *See* Annual

Year Facet: वर्ष पक्ष Part of the book number of a document, which is its year number. (Ranganathan)

Year Number: वर्ष संख्या Ordinal number which is the translation of the year of publication of the document. (Ranganathan)

Year of Publication: प्रकाशन वर्ष Year in which the work is published.

Z

Zone: क्षेत्र A portion of an array in which all the array-isolates are formed by one and the same device. Division of the surface of the earth.

Zonal Isolate: मण्डलीय एकल Subdivision of a physiographical feature based on some characteristic intrinsic to it. (Ranganathan)

CICIL LIST

CONCEPTS IN COMMUNICATION, INFORMATICS & LIBRARIANSHIP

(CICIL)

General Editor: **S.P. AGRAWAL**

CICIL-1 Development of Library Services in India: Social Science Information
S.P. Agrawal Rs. 150

CICIL-2 Development of Documentation in India: Social Science Information
S.P. Agrawal Rs. 250

CICIL-3 UNESCO and Social Sciences: Retrospect and Prospect
S.P. Agrawal and **J.C. Aggarwal** Rs. 250

CICIL-4 INDIANA : A Bibliography of Bibliographical Sources
M.K. Jain Rs. 200

CICIL-5 Dimensions of Library and Information Science: Kaula Festschrift
V. Venkatappaiah (Eds.) Rs. 600

CICIL-6 Book Numbers: Some Indian Methods
M.P. Satija and **S.P. Agrawal** Rs. 100

CICIL-7 National Policy for University Libraries in India: Problems and Perspectives
N.B. Inamdar and **L.S. Ramaiah** (Ed.) Rs. 250

CICIL-8 Media Utilisation for the Development of Women and Children
B.S. Thakur and **Binod C. Agrawal** Rs. 150

CICIL-9 Terrorism: An Annotated Bibliography
Susheela Bhan (Ed.) Rs. 275

CICIL-10 Transnational Library Relations: The Indo-American Experience
M.B. Konnur Rs. 175

CICIL-11 Geography of Marketing and Commercial Activities in India (Documentation on Research Information)
R.S. Dixit Rs. 130

CICIL-12 Information India 1988: Global View
S.P. Agrawal and **J.C. Aggarwal** Rs. 200

CICIL-13 Women's Education in India: Historical Review, Present Status and Perspective Plan
S.P. Agrawal and **J.C. Aggarwal** Rs. 360

CICIL-14 Cultural Communication in India: Role and Impact of Phonograms
J.M. Ojha Rs. 220

CICIL-15 Second Historical Survey of Educational Development in India: Select Documents 1985-1989
S.P. Agrawal and **J.C. Aggarwal** Rs. 490

CICIL-16 Documentation Encyclopaedia of UNESCO and Education
J.C. Aggarwal and **S.P. Agrawal** Rs. 800 (set of 2 parts)

CICIL-17 Attitude Towards Information: A Study of Post-Graduate Teachers and Researchers in Social Sciences
N.G. Satish (in press)

CICIL-18 Librarianship and Bureaucratic Organisation: A Study in the Sociology of Library Profession in India
P.K. Jayaswal Rs. 175

CICIL-19 Literature Search
K.A. Isaac Rs. 150

CICIL-20 Child Education in India: Index to Scholarly Writings in Indian Educational Journals and Newspapers since independence
S.P. Agrawal and **Naresh Kanta** Rs. 100

CICIL-21 Lok Sabha and Vidhan Sabha Elections in India 1989 & 1990: Process and Results with Comparative Study of Manifestos
S.P. Agrawal and **J.C. Aggarwal** Rs. 250

CICIL-22 Islamic Studies in India: A Survey of Human, Institutional and Documentary Sources
Mohamed Taher Rs. 180

CICIL-23 Panchayati Raj: An Annotated Bibliography
N.B. Inamdar, N.G. Satish and **Anil Takalkar** 290

CICIL-24 Information India 1989-90: Global View
S.P. Agrawal and **J.C. Aggarwal** Rs. 500

CICIL-25 First Handbook of Psychological and Social Instruments
Udai Pareek and **T. Venkateswara Rao** Rs. 500

CICIL-26 Educational and Social Uplift of Backward Classes: At What Cost and How? Mandal Commission and After
S.P. Agrawal and **J.C. Aggarwal** Rs. 275

CICIL-27 Mass Media and New Horizons: Impact of TV & Video an Urban Milieu
H.R. Trivedi Rs. 180

CICIL-28 Indian Writings on Education : An Indicator to Indian Educational Journals Grouped by Subject Deseriptors 1979 to 1986 (in two parts)
S.P. Agarwal Rs. 900 (per set)

CICIL-29 Nation in Crisis
S.P. Agrawal and **J.C. Aggarwal** Rs. 200

CICIL-30 Information India 1990-91: Global View
S.P. Agrawal and **J.C. Aggarwal** Rs. 500

CICIL-31 Development of University Libraries in India after Independence
O.P. Gupta Rs. 270

CICIL-32 Handbook on Child : With Historical Background
Pramila Pandit Barooah Rs. 320

CICIL-33 Weaker Section in Indian Society : Undiscovered Past, Uncertain Present and Unpredictable Future : Index to Writings in

Indian Scholarly Journals and 10 National Newspapers Classified under 1500 Descriptors 1886-1990
S.P. Agrawal and **Rajeev Kumar Sharma** Rs. 600

CICIL-34 Communication Informatics and Librarianship in India : An Introductory Guide to Publications Based on a Survey of Libraries in Capital City of India
S.P. Agrawal and **Pushpa Rani Sharma** Rs. 720

CICIL-35 Problems of Collection Development in Special Libraries
M.S. Sridhar Rs. 225

CICIL-36 National Information Resources for Social Sciences in India : Mobilisation, Dispersal and International Enhancement
S.P. Agrawal Rs. 225

CICIL-37 Modern History of Punjab : A Look Back into Ancient Peaceful Punjab Focusing Confrontation and Failures Leadingto Present Punjab Problem, and a Peep Ahead : Relevant Select Documents
J.C. Aggarwal and **S.P. Agrawal** Rs. 400

CICIL-38 India Information Sources : Economics and Business
Kyllikki Ruokonen and Manohar Lal Rs.

CICIL-39 Educational Planning in India : With a Slant to Educational Financing and Administration, Vol. 1, Reports of Committees and Commissions, Five Year Plans, Statistical Tables
J.C. Aggarwal and **S.P. Agrawal** Rs. 650

CICIL-40 Integrated Library System : Two Case Studies : Latin America and India
Maria Luiza Rigo Pasquarelli, Rosaly Favero Krzyanowski, Ines Maria M. Imperatriz and **S.P. Agrawal** Rs. 160

CICIL-41 Social Science Information in India: Effort towards Bibliographical Control
S.D. Vyas Rs. 300

CICIL-42 Higher Education in India Since Independence: U.G.C. and Its Approach
O.P. Gupta Rs. 360

CICIL-43 Government and Politics in India: A Bibliographical Study of Contemporary Scenario Chronicling Rajiv Gandhi Era
S.P. Agrawal and **Rajeev Kumar Sharma** Rs. 500

CICIL-44 Second Handbook of Psychological and Social Instruments
D.M. Pestonjee Rs. 300

CICIL-45 Development/Digression Diary of India; 3D Companion Volume to Information India: 1990-91
S.P. Agrawal Rs. 200

CICIL-46 Development/Digression Diary of India; 3D Companion Volume to Information India: 1991-92
S.P. Agrawal Rs. 300

CICIL-47 Information India 1991-92: Global View
S.P. Agrawal and **J.C. Aggarwal** Rs. 500

CICIL-48 Committees and Commissions in India 1974, A Concept's Project, Compiled by a team of professionals guided by Virender Kumar (Vol. 12) Rs. 450

CICIL-49 Committees and Commissions in India 1975, A Concept's Project, Compiled by a team of professionals guided by Virender Kumar (Vol. 13) Rs. 450

CICIL-50 Committees and Commissions in India 1976, A Concept's Project, Compiled by a team of professionals guided Virender Kumar (Vol. 14) Rs. 450

CICIL-51 Committees and Commissions in India 1977, A Concept's Project, Compiled by a team of professionals guided by Virender Kumar (Vol. 15) (in four parts) Rs. 450 each

CICIL-52 Committees and Commissions in India 1978, A Concept's Project, Compiled by a team of professionals guided by Virender Kumar (Vol. 16) (in two parts) Rs. 450 each

CICIL-53 Subject Guide to Communication, Informatics and Librarianship in India (Based on a Survey of Library Holdings in Capital City of India)
S.P. Agrawal and **Pushpa Rani Sharma** Rs. 400

CICIL-54 Restructurring of Library and Information Science Curriculum A. Tejomurty Rs. 250

CICIL-55 Committees and Commissions in India 1979, A Concept's Project, Compiled by a team of professionals guided by Virender Kumar (Vol. 17) (in two parts) Rs. 450 each

CICIL-56 Committees and Commissions in India 1980, A Concept's Project, Compiled by a team of professionals guided by Virender Kumar (Vol. 18) (in two parts) Rs. 450 each

CICIL-57 Third Historical Survey of Educational Development in India
S.P. Agrawal and **J.C. Aggarwal** Rs. 700

CICIL-58 Model Library Legislation
Velaga Venkatappaiah Rs. 400

CICIL-59 Indian Library and Information Science Literature (1990-91)
Sewa Singh Rs. 525

CICIL-60 Librarianship and Library Science in India
Mohamed Taher and **Donald Gordon Davis, Jr**. Rs. 350

CICIL-61 Comprehensive Glossary for Library & Information Science by
O.P. Gupta Rs.300

कॉन्सेप्ट्स इन कम्यूनिकेशन
इन्फॉरमेटिक्स एण्ड लाइब्रेरियनशिप - 61

सर्वीय सम्पादक : **एस. पी. अग्रवाल**

बृहत्
पुस्तकालय एवं सूचना विज्ञान शब्दावलि
द्विभाषिक
(हिन्दी-अंग्रेजी : अंग्रेजी-हिन्दी)

ओ. पी. गुप्ता
विश्वविद्यालय अनुदान आयोग
नई दिल्ली

कॉन्सेप्ट पब्लिशिंग कम्पनी, नई दिल्ली-110059

कॉन्सेप्ट्स इन कम्यूनिकेशन इन्फॉरमेटिक्स एण्ड लाइब्रेरियनशिप

इस श्रृंखला मे छपे हुये प्रकाशनों की सूची
कृपया अंग्रेजी-हिन्दी भाग के अंत में
पृष्ठ संख्या 133-136 पर देखें।

अ

अकादमी: Academy विद्वानों की उच्च स्तरीय शैक्षणिक संस्था जिसका उद्देश्य शैक्षणिक विकास तथा प्रसार की योजनाओं का कार्यान्वयन है।

अखबारी-कतरन *देखिये*: Press Cutting सूचना-कतरन/कतरन।

अग्र अनुभाग: Leading Section प्रविष्टि का प्रथम/मुख्य अनुभाग।

अग्रनाम: Fore Name नाम का भाग जो जाति/समूह को व्यक्त करता है।

अग्र नियोजित: Prefix मूल विषय के आगे जोड़ा गया अंश।

अग्र पंक्ति: Leading Line सूची-पत्र की प्रथम पंक्ति जिसका प्रयोग साधारणतः शीर्षक/आह्वान संख्या अंकित करने में होता है।

अग्रसरित: Forwarding विषय निदान के लिये प्रस्तुत करने की क्रिया।

अग्रिम प्रति: Advance Copy प्रति जिसको निर्धारित तिथि से पूर्व प्रस्तुत किया जाए।

अग्रिम-भुगतान: Advance Payment वस्तु प्राप्त करने से पहले की भुगतान व्यवस्था जिससे पुस्तकालय में पत्र पत्रिकाओं/सरकारी प्रलेखों की प्राप्त करने के लिये भुगतान किया जाता है।

अतिरिक्त प्रतियाँ: Added Copies पूर्व उपलब्ध प्रति के अतिरिक्त उसी ग्रन्थ की अन्य प्रतियाँ।

अतिरिक्त प्रविष्टि: Added Entry मुख्य प्रविष्टि से निर्मित अन्य सूची प्रविष्टि है। इनका शीर्षक मुख्य प्रविष्टि से अतिरिक्त सूचना व्यक्त करता है। तथा पाठक के सूचना पाने के अनेकानेक प्रयास जैसे लेखक, अनुवादक समीक्षक, शीर्षक, ग्रन्थमाला को जानने के प्रयास को पूरा करती है।

अतिरिक्त पुस्तकाध्यक्ष: Additional Librarian पुस्तकाध्य‌‌‌‌क्ष जो मुख्य पुस्तकाध्य के समानान्तर सहयोग के लिये उत्तरदायी होता है।

अतिरिक्त संस्करण: Added Edition पहले से उपलब्ध संस्करण के अतिरिक्त संस्करण।

अतिरिक्त शीर्षक प्रविष्टि: Added Title Entry इस प्रकार की प्रविष्टि में शीर्षक को प्रधानता के साथ सूची पत्र की प्रथम पंक्ति में अंकित किया जाता है।

अर्थ मूल्य: Semantic Value क्रम बोधक मूल्य जिसके आधार पर किसी वर्ग का अन्य वर्गों के मध्य स्थान नियत किया जाता है।

अर्थ पूर्ण अंक: Semantic Rich Digit अंक जिसका क्रमिक मूल्य तथा स्थान मूल्य क्रमिक स्मृति उपनियम के आधार पर निश्चित हो।

अर्ध कपड़ा जिल्द: Half Cloth Binding जिल्द जिस में पुस्तक आवरण का पीठ भाग तथा कोने कपड़े से शेष भाग कागज से ढका जाता है।

अर्ध चमड़ा जिल्द: Half Leather Binding इस प्रकार की जिल्द में पीठ तथा कोने में चमड़े के प्रयोग के साथ शेष भाग को किसी अन्य आवरण से बनाया जाता है।

अर्ध वार्षिक: Half Yearly पत्रिका जिसका प्रकाशन छः माह के अन्तर से होता है।

अर्ध विराम चिन्ह: Comma चिन्ह जिससे वाक्य के मध्य ठहराव लाया जाता है।

अर्ध शीर्षक: Half Title ग्रन्थ के विषय को आंशिक रूप से व्यक्त करने वाला सहयोगी शीर्षक।

अर्ध शीर्षक पृष्ठ: Half Title Page पृष्ठ जिस पर अर्ध शीर्षक का उल्लेख होता

है तथा शीर्षक पृष्ठ का विस्तार परिणाम भी हो सकता है।

अध्यारोपण युक्तिः Super Imposition Device एकल का अंश समानान्तर एकल में समाविष्ट हों।

उध्यारोपण एकल विचारः Super Imposed Isolate idea एकल विचार जब समानान्तर एकल परिधि में आ जायें।

अध्यायः Chapter रचना-अंश जो ग्रन्थ विषय के पूरक रूप में प्रयुक्त होते हैं।

अधिकार पत्रः Authority Card पत्र जिसका प्रयोग पहचान के लिए होता है।

अधिकार रेखाः Byline किसी रचना के ऊपर/नीचे की पंक्ति के साथ समानान्तर रेखा जो रचनाकार के अधिकार की संकेतक होती है।

अधिकार हस्तान्तरणः Delegation of Power अधिकार प्रयोग के लिए स्थानान्तरित कर दिये जायें।

अधिकाधिक प्रिय भाषाः Most Popular Language पुस्तकालय का सर्वाधिक सकंलन जिस भाषा में हो।

अधिकृत पुस्तकः Blue Book सरकारी प्रकाशनों के लिए प्रयुक्त नाम।

अधिकृत गजटः Official Gazette सरकारी घोषणा के लिये अधिकारिक प्रकाशन जो निश्चित खण्ड, उपखण्ड में वर्गीकृत आदेश व्यक्त करता है।

अधिकृत पुस्तकालय सूचीः Official Catalogue पुस्तकालय कर्मचारियों द्वारा प्रयुक्त सूची तथा इसका प्रयोग पाठक को सुलभ नहीं होता।

अधिग्रहणः Acquisition पुस्तकालय द्वारा ग्रन्थ प्राप्ति की निरन्तर क्रिया है जिसके अन्तर्गत खरीद/दान/अदल-बदल द्वारा ग्रन्थ प्राप्त किए जाते हैं।

अधिग्रहण कार्यः Acquisition Work कार्य जिससे ग्रन्थ चुनाव तथा प्राप्त करने की क्रिया का समावेश होता है।

अधिग्रहण अधिकारीः Acquisition Officer अधिकारी जिसका उत्तर दायित्व संग्रह का विकास करना होता है।

अधिग्रहण अभिलेखः Acquisition Record इस प्रकार के अभिलेख साधारणतः अवाप्ति पंजिका जी अवाप्ति पंजी के रूप में होते हैं। पुस्तकालय आवश्यकतानुसार 'खरीदे हुए अभिलेख और अन्य श्रोतों से प्राप्त अभिलेख' के लिए अलग-2 पंजी और *देखिये* अवाप्ति पंजिका।

अधिग्रहण विभागः Acquisition Department पुस्तकालय विभाग जिसका कार्य प्रलेख खरीदना तथा अन्य श्रोतों से प्राप्त करना है।

अधिग्रहण सख्ंयाः Acquisition Number *देखिये* अवाप्ति संख्या।

अधिग्रहण-सूचीः Additions List/Acquisition List पुस्तकालय द्वारा प्राप्त सभी सूचना प्रलेखों का व्यवस्थित विवरण होती है। जो निश्चित अन्तराल से उपलब्ध कराई जाती है।

अधिशासीः Executive व्यक्ति जो उद्देश्य प्राप्ति के लिये प्रशासनिक कार्य करता है।

अधीनस्थः Subordinate व्यक्ति जो निर्देश पालन करता है।

अधीनस्थ वर्गो का प्रनियमः Canon Of Subordinate Classes वर्ग के अधीनस्थ वर्ग चाहे वह किसी भी शृंखला में उत्पन्न हुए हो वह बिना किसी बाधा अथवा अन्य वर्ग को बीच में स्वीकार करते हुये अपने वर्ग के अनुगामी होने चाहिऐ।

अर्ध वार्षिकः Bi-annual प्रकाशन जिसकी आवृत्ति वर्ष में दो बार होती है।

अर्ध व्यवसायिकः Semi-Professional व्यक्ति जिसके पास साधारण

ज्ञान/आवश्यक शैक्षणिक योग्यता के साथ प्राथमिक व्यवसायिक योग्यता भी हो।

अर्ध साप्ताहिकः Bi-weekly पाक्षिक का समानार्थक है।

अन्तर-युक्तिः Gap Device यह युक्ति प्रयोग दो एकल पंक्ति विचारों के बीच स्थान छोड़ देती है। फलतः भविष्य में स्वीकृत बचे विषय को बिना किसी बाधा के उपयुक्त अंकन प्रदान किया जा सकता है।

अन्धों का पुस्तकालयः Braille Library पुस्तकालय जिसके संकलन विशेष रूप से अन्धों के प्रयोग के लिए अन्धें द्वारा प्रयुक्त लिपि में होते है।

अर्न्तपुस्तकालय उधारः Inter Library Loan पुस्तकालयों के मध्य ग्रन्थ उधार प्राप्त करने की प्रक्रिया।

अन्तर पंक्ति पक्ष सम्बन्धः Intra Array Phase Relation पंक्ति एकल/मिश्रित पंक्ति एकल के बीच का सम्बन्ध।

अन्तर वर्ग पक्ष युक्ति (अंकनतल): Inter Class Phase Device (Notational Plane) युक्ति जिसमें विचारतल पर प्राप्त चिन्ह अंकन के साथ प्रयोग कर पक्ष सम्बन्ध व्यक्त किया जाता है।

अन्तर वर्ग पक्ष युक्ति (विचारतल): Inter Class Phase Device (Idea Plane) युक्ति जिसमें एक वर्ग के साथ अन्य वर्ग का सम्बन्ध स्थापित कर मुखर किया जाए जिससे उसकी विशेष पहचान बन सके।

अन्तर मुख पक्ष सम्बन्धः Intra-Facet Phase Relation मिश्रित एकल/अंश एकल के बीच का सम्बन्ध।

अन्तर्राष्ट्रीय मानक क्रम संख्याः International Standard Serial Number (ISSN) अन्तर्राष्ट्रीय स्वीकृत संकेत संख्या है जिससे किसी पत्रिका की पहचान होती है। यह देश तथा स्थान का संख्यिकीय अनुवाद होता है।

अन्तर्राष्ट्रीय मानक ग्रन्थ संख्याः International Standard Book Number (ISBN) अन्तर्राष्ट्रीय स्वीकृत मानकों के आधार पर पुस्तक प्रकाशन के साथ ही प्रकाशक, शीर्षक, संस्करण, खण्ड आदि को संख्या अनुवाद रूप में प्रस्तुत किया जाता है।

अन्तिम वर्गः Ultimate Class वर्गीकरण प्रणाली द्वारा स्वीकृत लघुतम विस्तार वाला वर्ग।

अन्तिम वस्तुः Ultimate Commodity वास्तविक अथवा समकक्ष जिसको सीधे अथवा तकनीकी सहायता से उपयोग किया जा सके, पुस्तकालय के संदर्भ में सूचना।

अन्ततोगत्वा सेवाः Ultimate Service सेवा जो सीधे उपयोक्ता से सम्बन्धित हो।

अन्तर्निहित विचारः Embodied Thought अभिलेख के विषय जिनको एक स्थान से दूसरे स्थान पर ले जाया जा सके, जिनका कुछ आकार हो तथा दीर्घकाल तक सुरक्षित रखे जो सके।

अन्तिम अंक युक्तिः Octave Device इस युक्ति द्वारा उपलब्ध अंकन के अन्तिम अंक के विशेष प्रयोग से उत्पन्न समकक्ष वर्गों को बिना किसी अंकन सम्बन्ध अभिव्यक्ति के प्रयोग कर अंकन प्राप्त कराया जा सकता है।

अन्तिम कड़ीः Last Link श्रृखला क्रम की कढ़ी जिसके बाद और कड़ी प्राप्त करना सम्भव न हो।

अन्तिम प्रूफः Final Proof ग्रन्थ के छपने से पूर्व का अन्तिम त्रुटि रहित प्रूफ।

अन्तर्वेधित पंक्तिः Telescoped Array

अन्तर्वेधनः Extrapolation वर्गीकरण पद्धति में किसी वर्ग को उसका उपयुक्त स्थान प्रदान कराने की क्रिया जिसमें अन्य वर्गों का परिवर्तन न किया जाए।

अन्योन्य सम्बन्ध प्रविष्टिः Cross Reference Entry सांकेतिक प्रविष्टि जो दूसरी प्रविष्टि की ओर इंगित करती है।

अनऔपचारिक शिक्षाः Non-Formal Education शिक्षा ग्रहण विधि जिसमें किसी प्रकार के पाठ्यक्रम/पंजीकरण की आवश्यकता नहीं होती तथा शिक्षार्थी स्वयं शिक्षा ग्रहण करता है।

अनम्य वर्गीकरणः Rigid Classification वर्गीकरण जिसमें नये वर्गों को स्वीकारने की सुविधा नहीं होती है।

अनामक पुस्तकः Anonymous Book कृति जिसमें रचना कार सम्बन्धी सूचना निहित नहीं होती।

अनावश्यक शीर्षक शब्दः Redundant Words in Title शीर्षक में प्रयुक्त अतिशयोक्ति पूर्ण अनावश्यक शब्द।

अनाधिकृत संस्करणः Unauthorised Edition संस्करण जिसके प्रकाशन की अनुमति लेखक/प्रकाशक से न ली गई हो।

अनुच्छेदः Paragraph रचना अंश।

अनुक्रम का सिद्धान्तः Principle of Canonical Sequence

अनुक्रमणिकाः Index शब्द/विषय/स्थान/नाम आदि आवश्यक सूचना की वर्णनुक्रम सूची जिसका प्रयोग ग्रन्थ में संग्रहीत सूचना प्रयोग के लिए होता है।

अनुक्रमणिका पत्रिकाः Indexing Periodical सार पत्रिका के समान ही प्रविष्टि क्रम होता है परन्तु सार नहीं होता रचनाओं की सूची मात्र होती है और *देखिए* सार पत्रिका।

अनुक्रमणिका प्रविष्टिः Index Entry प्रविष्टि जिसका प्रयोग अनुक्रमणिका सृजन में होता है।

अनुक्रमणिका संख्याः Index Number प्रविष्टि संख्या जो अभिलेख का प्रतिनिधित्व करती है।

अनुक्रमणिका संख्या अनुभागः Index Number Section प्रविष्टि का अनुभाग जिसमें अनुक्रमणिका संख्या अंकित होती है।

अनुक्रमणीकरणः Indexing अनुक्रमणिका बनाने की प्रक्रिया।

अनुचरः Attendant *देखिए* पुस्तकालय अनुचर।

अनुदानः Grant आर्थिक नीति पर आवाण्टित धन का अंश।

अनुपयुक्त कड़ीः False Link कड़ी जो विचार अभिव्यक्त न कर सके।

अनुवादः Translation जब एक भाषा की रचना को दूसरी भाषा में परिवर्तित कर दिया जाए।

अनुवादकः Translator व्यक्ति जो अनुवाद का कार्य करता है।

अनुवाद सेवाः Translation Service भाषा सीमा की बाधा को दूर कर इच्छित भाषा में उपलब्ध रचना को प्राप्त कराया जाये।

अनुमानः Estimate भविष्य की आवश्यकताओं की काल्पनिक गणना।

अनुविम्बन का प्रनियमः Canon of Modulation ज्ञान जगत् से वर्गशृंखला सृजन उपयुक्त निर्णायक शक्ति प्रयोग से ही प्रत्येक स्तर पर होना चाहिए।

अनुशासनः Discipline *देखिए* पुस्तकालय अनुशासन।

अनुच्छेद चिन्हः Paragraph Mark चिन्ह जिसके प्रयोग से अनुच्छेद प्रारम्भ करने की ओर इंगित किया जाता हैं।

अनुशीर्षकः Caption *देखिए* शीर्षक।

अनुशीर्षकः Caption Title शीर्षक जो प्रत्येक पृष्ठ पर अंकित होता है।

अनुलिपि प्रविष्टिः Duplicate Entry एक प्रविष्टि के एक से अधिकबार आवृति को अनुलिपि प्रविष्टि जाना जाता है।

अप्रासंगिकः Alien विषय जो चुने गये विषय से असमंद्ध हो।

अपंजीकृत ग्रन्थः Unaccessioned Book अभिलेख जिसको पुस्तकालय पंजी में अंकित न किया गया हो।

अपूर्ण शीर्षकः Incomplete Title शीर्षक जो पूर्ण रूप से विषय का प्रतिनिधित्व नहीं करता अतः वर्गीकरणकार के अनुरूप नहीं होता।

अप्रकाशित सामग्रीः Non-Print Material *देखिए* श्रव्य-दृश्य।

अपेक्षित सार्मथ्यः Requisite Capacity.

अपदानुक्रम अकंन का प्रनियमः Canon of Non-Hierarchical Notation वर्ग निर्माण में प्रयुक्त प्रत्येक लक्षण को व्यक्त करने के लिए वर्ग संख्या में अंक होना आवश्यक नहीं है।

अपरिष्कृत शीर्षकः Raw Title शीर्षक का मूल रूप जो ग्रन्थ पर अंकित हों।

अपूपा व्यवस्थाः Apupa Arrangement डा0 रगंनाथन द्वारा सुझाई गई व्यवस्था जिसके अनुसार केन्द्र में मुख्य विषय तथा सामीप्य सम्बन्ध के आधार पर अन्य विषयों को स्थान दिया जाता है।

अवलोकनः Scanning कमप्यूटर प्रणाली की क्रिया जिससे सूचना का अवलोकन अथवा साधारण अर्थ में प्रत्येक कार्य/संदर्भ/प्रविष्टि की जाँच परख करना है।

अवांछित कड़ीः Unsought Link कड़ी जिससे वर्ग अभिव्यक्ति प्राप्त करने में विषय न पहचाना जा सके।

अवांछित सत्ताः Unlink Entities समान गुणों के आधार पर प्राप्त स्थितियों के बाद की शेष स्थितियाँ।

अवकाशः Holiday दिन जब पुस्तकालय सेवकों को कार्यालय कार्य के लिए नहीं आना होता तथा पुस्तकालय सेवा बन्द रहती है।

अवाप्ति पुस्तकः Accession Book *देखिए* अवाप्ति पंजी।

अवाप्ति क्रमः Accession Order प्रलेखों का उनकी प्राप्ति क्रम में रखा जाना अथवा अंकित अवाप्ति संख्या के क्रम में व्यवस्थित करना।

अवास्तविक नामः Fictitious Name कल्पित नाम।

अवाप्ति दिनाँकः Date of Accession दिनाँक जब कोई ग्रन्थ पुस्तकालय पंजी में सूची बद्ध होता है।

अवाप्ति संख्याः Accession Number अवाप्ति पंजी में अंकित क्रम संख्या जो पुस्तकालय में अधिग्रहीत प्रलेख में अंकित की जाती है पुस्तकालय प्राप्त संग्रह की क्रम संख्या होती है पुस्तक पर लगी लेखन सामग्री शीर्षक, पृष्ठ के पश्च भाग तथा गोपनीय पृष्ठ पर अंकित की जाती है।

अवाप्ति संख्या क्रमः Accession Arrangement पुस्तकालय प्रलेखों को उनके प्राप्तिक्रम में रखने का प्रकार।

अवरुद्ध अंकनः Closed Notation जब अंकन प्रणाली वर्ग अभिव्यक्ति के लिए नये अंक का प्रयोग नही करती।

अवरुद्ध पंक्तिः Closed Array वर्ग पंक्ति जिसमें अन्य विषयों को स्वीकार करने की सीमा समाप्त हो चुकी हो।

अवप्तिः Accession *देखिए* अवप्ति संख्या।

अवाप्ति अभिलेखः Accession Record *देखिए* अवप्ति पंजी।

अवाप्ति विभागः Accession Department विभाग जिसमें पुस्तकालय संग्रह को अधिकारिक अवप्ति पंजी में अंतिक किया जाता है।

अवाप्तिकरणः Accessioning क्रिया जिसके द्वारा निरीक्षण परीक्षण के बाद ग्रन्थों को अवान्ति पंजी में अंकित किया जाता है।

अवाप्ति संख्या अनुभागः Accession Number Section प्रविष्टि का अनुभाग जो कि प्रलेख की अवाप्ति संख्या व्यक्त करता है सूची पत्र पर यह स्थान सूची करण प्रणाली द्वारा निर्धारित किया जाता है।

अवाप्ति सूचीः Accession List अवाप्ति संख्या के क्रमशः संयोजन से सूची बनाई जाती है जो पुस्तकालय संग्रह सत्यापन जैसे कार्यो में प्रयोग होती है।

अवाप्ति पंजीः Accession Register यह पंजी पुस्तकालय का मुख्य अभिलेख हे जिसमें पुस्तकालय में प्राप्त प्रत्येक अभिलेख का पूर्ण विवरण क्रमशः अंकित होता है। अभिलेख के आने की तिथि, रचनाकार, शीर्षक, प्रकाशक, प्राप्ति स्थान तथा मूल्य आदि का उल्लेख प्रमुख रूप से मिलता है।

अवाप्ति संख्या मुहर/मुद्राः Accession Stamp मुद्रा जिससे प्रलेख पर अवाप्ति क्रम संख्या अंकित की जाती है।

अभिलेखः Record कम्प्यूटर प्रयोग में सूचना की इकाई अथवा किसी संस्था की गतिविधि का लिखित विवरण होता है अथवा सूचना संग्रह का अंकित विवरण है।

अभिलेखनः Tracing मुख्य प्रविष्टि के पीछे/प्रविष्टि के अन्त में सूचीकरण प्रविष्टियों का विवरण अनुच्छेद रूप में अंकित किया जाए।

अभिलेखन अनुभागः Tracing Section मुख्य प्रविष्टि का अनुभाग जिसमें अतिरिक्त प्रविष्टियों की सूची अंकित की जाती है जिससे स्पष्ट होता है कि कितने पत्र बनाये गये हैं।

अभिनन्दन ग्रन्थः Festschrift विशिष्टि व्यक्ति के सम्मान में प्रकाशित अनेक रचनाकारों की रचनाओं का सकंलन।

अभिनतः Bias आपसी सम्बन्ध अभिव्यक्ति।

अभिधारणाः Postulates अभिधारणा कल्पना अथवा स्वीकृति है। जिसका सत्यापन नहीं होता। डा0 रगांनाथन ने वर्गीकरण प्रणाली की पाँच मूल अभिधारणाओं की परिकल्पना की थी।

अभिधारणा आधारित अनुमत विषय अनुक्रमणिकाः Postulate Based Permuted Subject Index (POPSI) भारतीग अनुक्रमणिका तकनीक है जिसका विकास श्री गणेश भट्टाचार्य, डी0 आर0 टी0 सी0, बैंगेलौर द्वारा किया गया है।

अभिलेख प्रणालीः Ledger System *देखिए* पंजी प्रणाली।

अभिलेख सुरक्षाः Conservation of Documents अभिलेखों को नष्ट होने से बचाने के उपाय।

अभिव्यंजना का प्रनियमः Canon of Expressiveness वर्ग संख्या में प्रयुक्त अंक अलग अभिलक्षणों को व्यक्त करने में सक्षम हाने चाहिए।

अभिलक्षणः Characteristic गुण जिनके आधार पर विषयानुसार वर्गीकरण समभव

हो पाता है।

अभिलेखः Document सूचना का व्यक्त आकार परम्परात्मक रूप में पुस्तक/पत्रिका/मशीन प्रयुक्त डिस्क/फ्लापी/कैसेट आदि।

अभिव्यक्त विचारः Expressed Thought विचार का भाषा, चित्र, चिन्ह अथवा किसी इसी प्रकार के माध्यम से सम्प्रेषण प्रयास है।

अभिगम केन्द्रः Approach Point *देखिए* पहुँच केन्द्र।

अभिगम विषयः Approach Material विषय वस्तु जिसकी सहायता से विषय को अधिक स्पष्ट किया जा सकें।

अभिलेखागारः Archives प्राचीन दुर्लभ अभिलेखों का संरक्षण केन्द्र जहाँ आवश्यकता पड़ने पर इनको प्रयोग किया जा सके।

अभिलेखपालः Archivist व्यक्ति जिसका कार्य अभिलेखों को सुरक्षित/व्यवस्थित रखकर भविष्य के लिए उपयोगी बनाना है।

अभीष्ट भाषाः Object Language भाषा जिसको पढ़ा, विवेचित तथा विकसित किया जाय।

अमेरिकन पुस्तकालय संघः American Library Association यह संसार का प्राचीनतम एवम् विशाल पुस्तकालय संघ है जिसकी स्थापना 1876 में हुई थी। इसका कार्यालय शिकागो में है। अमेरिकी पुस्तकालय विज्ञान प्रचार प्रसार के साथ व्यवसायिक विकास के लिए कान्फ्रेन्स आदि का संयोजन करता हे इसके लिए 13 अनुभाग क्रियाशील है।

अल्प आयु ग्रन्थः Ephemeral Material प्रलेख जो देखने भर के बाद ही अनावश्यक होने लगते हैं।

अलग ग्रन्थः Separate Book प्रलेख का आंशिक प्रकाशन अथवा प्रतिलिपिकरण।

अवस्थिति अनुभागः Location Section प्रविष्टि का अनुभाग जिसमें आश्रय दाता प्रलेख में ग्रन्थ की स्थिति का उल्लेख होता है।

असहयोगी विषयः Alien Subject *देखिए* असहयोगी प्रदेश।

असहयोगी प्रदेशः Alien Region असम्बन्ध अन्य विषय जिनका मुख्य विषय से निकट का सम्बन्ध न हो तथा पाठक की तत्काल आवश्यकता न हो।

असामान्यः Abnormal साधारणतः अस्वीकृत।

असामान्य आकारः Abnormal Size ग्रन्थ का आकार जो साधारण प्रचलित आकार से बहुत बड़ा हो।

असंसाधित पुस्तकः Unprocessed Book प्रलेख जिसका वर्गीकरण/सूचीकरण न हुआ हो।

असीम ज्ञान जगतः Infinite Universe असीम सम्भावित स्थितियों से युक्त ज्ञान जगत।

असीमित ज्ञान संसारः Infinite Universe अपरिमित विशेषताओं से पूर्ण ज्ञान जगत्।

अक्षर क्रम संयोजनः Letter by Letter Filing संयोजन प्रकार जिसमें सम्पूर्ण शीर्षक को इकाई मानकर वर्णाक्षर क्रम में रखा जाए।

अक्षर लेखनः Tooling जिल्द पर लेखन।

अज्ञात अभिलेखः Unknown Document प्रयोक्ता को जिस प्रलेख प्रकाशन तथा उपलब्धतता का ज्ञान न हो।

अज्ञात रचनाः Anonymous Work रचना जिसके रचनाकार का पता न हो।

आ

आउटपुट उत्पादनः Output कमप्यूटर प्रयुक्त सूचना जो दृश्य पटल/प्रिन्टर/फ्लापी-डिस्क आदि के द्वारा प्रस्तुत की जाती है।

आउट पुट युक्तिः Output Device उत्पादन युक्ति जिससे मशीन द्वारा सूचना को स्थानान्तरित किया जाता है।

आकारः Format साधारणतः प्रलेख के बाह्य आकार-लम्बाई चौडाई तथा मोटाई को व्यक्त करता है तथा कमप्यूटर मे सूचना नियमन का द्योतक है।

आगन्तुक पंजीः Visitor Register पुस्तकालय मे प्रवेश करने वालों का विवरण रखने वाली पंजी।

आत्मकथाः Autobiography लेखक द्वारा अपने जीवन से सम्बन्धित घटनाओं की विवरणिका।

आदर्श पुस्तकालय अधिनियमः Model Library Act पुस्तकालय स्थापित करने सम्बन्धी कानून।

आदान-प्रदानः Circulation पुस्तकालय ग्रन्थों का प्रयोक्ताओं के बीच संचरण।

आदान-प्रदान अभिलेखः Circulation Record उधार प्रलेखों की आधिकारिक सूचना।

आदान-प्रदान कार्यः Circulation Work संचरण में प्रयुक्त प्रलेखों की व्यवस्था तथा आवश्यकता पर अन्य पुस्तकालय से प्रलेख प्रयोक्ता को उपलब्ध कराना।

आदान-प्रदान पुस्तकालयः Lending Library *देखिए* पुस्तकालय।

आदान-प्रदान नियन्त्रणः Circulation Control प्रलेख संचरण से सम्बधित सभी गति विधियों का नियमन।

आदान-प्रदान विभागः Circulation Department पुस्तकालय का विभाग जहाँ से प्रलेख पढ़ने के लिए प्रदान किए जाएं तथा लौटने पर प्राप्त किए जाएं।

आदान-प्रदान डैस्कः Circulation Desk *देखिये* आदान-प्रदान विभाग।

आदान-प्रदान सांख्यिकीः Circulation Statistics उधार प्रलेखों की गणितीय सूचना।

आदेशः Instruction कार्य करने के निर्देश।

आधारः Base वर्गीकरण प्रणाली के अंकन में प्रयुक्त सभी प्रकार के अंक।

आधार ग्रन्थः Source Book ग्रन्थ जिसमें मूल सूचनाओं-का समावेश होता है।

आधार पक्ष की अभिधारणाः Postulate of Basic Facet प्रत्येक विषय में एक आधार पक्ष होता है।

आधारभूत वर्गीकरण/मूल वर्गीकरणः Basic Classification साधारण प्रयोग के लिए किया गया प्राथमिक वर्गीकरण ।

आधार मुखः Basic Facet *देखिए* मुख्य वर्ग।

आधी जिल्दः Half Binding एक प्रकार की जिल्द जिसमें जिल्द के कोने तथा पीठ का भाग अलग प्रकार के आवरण से अधिक मजबूती देने के लिए बनाये जाते हैं।

आधुनिकताः Modernisation

आन्तरिक अंकनः Internal Notation वर्ग विशेष के अन्तर्गत प्रलेख की स्थिति व्यक्त करने वाला अंकन।

आन्तरिक उपचारः Integral Treatment किसी रचना में विषय का ऐसा उपचार जिससे उसके उपविभागों को पूरी रचना में अलग न किया जा सके।

आन्तरिक व्यवस्थाः Internal Administration संस्थागत प्रशासनिक व्यवस्था।

आन्तरिक सेवाः Inhouse Service संस्थागत सेवा।

आप्त क्रमः Canonical Order उप विभागों का क्रमिक संयोजन।

आप्त वर्गः Canonical Class ज्ञान जगत् से प्राप्त परम्परात्मक उपवर्ग है जिनको वर्गीकरण प्रणाली में पंक्तिबद्ध कर दिया

जाता है। अभिलक्षणों के आधार पर पहचानने की आवश्यकता नहीं होती।

आप्टिकल डिस्क: Optical Disk डिस्क आप्टिकल प्रकार की होती है जिसका सूचना संचय में उपयोग होता है सूचना को मात्र पढ़ा जा सकता है।

आवश्यकता/माँग: Requisition ग्रन्थ प्राप्ति प्रार्थना।

आवरण: Cover सुरक्षा प्रदायक।

आवरण शीर्षक: Cover Title सुरक्षा प्रदायक आवरण पर अंकित शीर्षक।

आवन्टन: Allocation निर्धारित नितियों के अन्तर्गत भविष्य की आवश्यकता पूर्ति के लिए धन निर्धारण। यह कार्य सरकारी संस्था/मूल संस्था जिसका पुस्तकालय है करती है, अथवा विषय की अन्य विषयों के साथ सापेक्ष स्थिति निर्धारण प्रक्रिया।

आवृत्ति: Frequency निश्चित अन्तर से पुनः प्रकाशन।

आवेदनपत्र: Application Form पुस्तकालय नियमानुसार पाठक/प्रयोक्ता को सदस्यता प्रदान करने का प्रपत्र।

आँकड़ाकरण: Datamation संचलित आंकड़ा संचरण।

आमुख: Preamble विषय के उद्देश्य का संक्षिप्त विवरण।

आरक्षण: Reserve शीघ्र आवश्यकता पूर्ति अथवा सीमित पुस्तकों का अधिकाधिक प्रयोग सुनिशिचित करने को उपभोक्ताओं का अधिक माँग के आधार पर पाठक वरीयता क्रम निश्चित करने की क्रिया है।

आरक्षित संग्रह: Reserve Collection विशेष संग्रह जिस तक प्रभोक्ता की सीधी पहुँच नहीं होती पुस्तकालय सेवक की सहायता से प्राप्त किया जा सकता है।

आरोह क्रम: Ascending Order विषय के विकास का क्रम।

आश्रित कार्य: Dependent Work किसी पूर्व रचना के आधार पर परिष्कृत/संयोजित रचना।

आह्वान संख्या: Call Number वर्ग संख्या तथा पुस्तक संख्या के योग से बनी संख्या। जिसकी सहायता से पुस्तकालय में पुस्तक की स्थिति सूची के क्रम में निर्धारित होती है तथा इस संख्या का संख्यात्मक मूल्य नहीं होता।

आह्वान संख्या अनुभाग: Call Number Section प्रविष्टि अनुभाग जिसमें आह्वान संख्या अंकित हो।

आह्वान संख्या प्रविष्टि: Call Number Entry प्रविष्टि की प्रथम पंक्ति पर आह्वान संख्या अंकित होती है तथा अनुक्रमणिका अथवा सूची में संख्या के क्रम में स्थान प्राप्त करती है।

ऑनलाइन: Online कम्प्यूटर मशीन के सीधे सम्पर्क अथवा दूरभाष संचार साधन प्रयोग से सूचना सम्प्रेषण हो तथा मानवश्रम का प्रयोग न किया जाये।

ऑफ लाइन: Off Line मशीन (कम्प्यूटर) प्रणाली जब केन्द्रीय संसाधन एकक (सी. पी. यू.) से अथवा अन्य मशीन से संचार मुक्त हो जाय।

इ

इकाई अभिलेख: Unit Record *देखिए* इकाई पत्र।

इकाई पत्र: Unit Card सूची पत्र जो मुख्य पत्र होता है तथा इसकी सहायता से प्रतिलिपि प्राप्त कर उपयुक्त शीर्षक योग से अतिरिक्त प्रविष्टि बनाई जाती है और *देखिए* मूल पत्र।

इतर प्रविष्टि: Added Entry *देखिए* अतिरिक्त प्रविष्टि।

इतर प्रति: Added Copy *देखिए* अतिरिक्त प्रति।

इतर संस्करणः Added Edition *देखिए* अतिरिक्त संस्करण।

इनफोटलः Infotal आधुनिक कमप्यूटर कृत अर्न्तराष्ट्रीय सूचना केन्द्र है जहाँ से चुने हुए सूचना केन्द्रों पर कम्प्यूटर की सहायता से सीधा सम्पर्क कर सूचना संग्रहों का प्रयोग सम्भव है।

इलैक्ट्रोनिक अभिलेख प्रदाय प्रणालीः Electronic Document Delivery System प्रणाली जिसमें मशीन की सहायता से सूचना सम्प्रेषण होता है तथा मशीन युक्ति से सूचना इलैक्ट्रोनिक माध्यम पर अंकित कर ली जाती है।

इलैक्ट्रोनिक खरीद आदेशः Electronic Ordering मशीनी व्यवस्था पर आधारित सीधी खरीद आदेश प्रणाली।

इलैक्ट्रोनिक पुस्तकालयः Electronic Library पुस्तकालय जहाँ आधुनिक उपकरण जैसे कम्प्यूटर आदि का प्रयोग सूचना संग्रह तथा प्राप्ति को हो।

इलैक्ट्रोनिक माध्यमः Electronic Media कम्प्यूटर अथवा तकनीकी साधनों का सूचना सम्प्रेषण में प्रयोग।

इलैक्ट्रोनिक मेलः Electronic Mail (E-Mail) सूचना सम्प्रेषण की मशीन आधारित तकनीकी व्यवस्था जिसमें कम्प्यूटरतन्त्र का प्रभावी प्रयोग किया जाता है।

उ

उत्पन्न पंक्ति एकलः Devised Array Isolate पंक्ति एकल जिसका सृजन क्रमिक, वर्णानुक्रम अथवा विषय युक्ति द्वारा किया जाये।

उत्पन्न साधारण एकलः Devised Common Isolate विषय युक्ति द्वारा प्राप्त किए जाते हैं तथा वर्गीकरण में प्रयुक्त होते हैं।

उतारनाः Down Loading शब्द का प्रयोग कम्प्यूटरीकृत सूचना को एक कम्प्यूटर से दूसरे में अथवा मूल कम्प्यूटर से उप केन्द्रों पर स्थानान्तरित करने के लिए किया जाता है।

उधार देना/निर्गमः Issue प्रक्रिया जिसमें प्रयोक्ता को इच्छित ग्रन्थ पुस्तकालय परिसर से बाहर ले जाने की अनुमति दी जाती है।

उन्नतिः Promotion *देखिए* विकास/वरीयता।

उच्च कम्प्यूटरः Super Computer विकसित तकनीक पर आधारित कम्प्यूटर जिसका प्रयोग सूचना एवं आंकड़ा संग्रह के लिए होता है।

उचित आकारः Perfect Size आकार जो सामान्यतः स्वीकृत तथा मानकीकृत हो।

उर्जाः Energy क्रियात्मकता पहचान का डा. रंगनाथन द्वारा वर्गीकरण के पाँच पक्षों में से एक पक्ष है।

उर्जा पक्षः Energy Facet *देखिए* उर्जा।

उर्जा एकलः Energy Isolate *देखिए* उर्जा।

उपकरः Cess *देखिए* कर।

उपतत्त्वः Secondary Element प्रविष्टि विवरण के बाद प्रयुक्त शब्द।

उपनियमः Bye-laws पुस्तकालय के प्रभावी प्रयोग के लिए स्वीकृत दिशा-निर्देश।

उपनामः By Name/Secondary Name नाम का अंश जो जाति/समूह को व्यक्त करता है।

उपच्छायाः Penumbral विषय के केन्द्रीय विचार के समीवस्थ वर्ग एकल/एकल पंक्ति समूह। जो तुरन्त प्रयोक्ता की उपयोगिता न हो।

उपच्छाया प्रदेशः Umbral Region *देखिए* उपच्छाया।

उपचारार्य देयकः Proforma Invoice

देयक जिसका प्रयोग प्रामाणिक रूप से ग्रन्थ की कीमत जानने के लिए होता है।

उप पुस्तकाध्यक्ष: Deputy Librarian पुस्तकाध्यक्ष का निकटतम सहयोगी तथा पुस्तकाध्यक्ष की अनुपस्थिति में प्रभारी के रूप में कार्य करने वाला व्यक्ति।

उपमाला: Sub-Series माला जो किसी माला के अन्तर्गत हो।

उप-प्रणाली: Sub-system प्रणाली जो किसी मूल प्रणाली का अंग हो।

उप-विभाजन: Sub-Division किसी विभाजन से प्राप्त लघु विभाजन शब्द वर्गीकरण प्रणाली में बहुप्रचालित है।

उपरी-प्रक्षेपण: Overhead Projector तकनीक जिससे सूचनाओं को दृश्य पटल पर इच्छित आकार में व्यक्त किया जाये।

उपरी कड़ी: Upper Link अन्तिम कड़ी/पूर्व की कड़ी।

उपस्रोत: Secondary Sources सूचना संचय जिनकों प्राथमिक सूचना स्त्रोत से बनाया जाता है इसका उद्देश्य सूचना की बढ़ती मात्रा का नियन्त्रण करना है।

उपस्थिति: Attendance कार्य में भागीदारी का प्रमाण।

उपसमिति: Sub Committee मुख्य समिति की सहायता के लिए मुख्य समिति के सदस्यों से अथवा अन्य सदस्यों से बनी विशेष विषय पर कार्य करती है।

उपवर्ग: Sub Class वर्ग जिसका सृजन उपलब्ध वर्ग से होता है।

उपशीर्षक: Sub Title विषय स्पष्टीकरण शीर्षक/सहयोगी शीर्षक/अतिरिक्त शीर्षक जाना जाता है।

उपयुक्त: Pertinency विषय के चुनाव से जुड़े अभिलक्षण।

उपादेयता कारण: Pertinence Factor कुल चुने हुए प्रलेखों में से पुनः उपयोगी प्रलेखों का प्रतिशत प्राप्त करने की क्रिया।

उद्धरण: Quotation/citation सूचना के मूल स्रोत को इंगित करने की व्यवस्था।

उद्धरण अनुक्रमणिका: Citation Index लेखों में प्रयुक्त संदर्भ अभिलेखों पर आधारित अनुक्रमाणिका।

उद्धरण क्रम: Citation Order क्रम जिसमें अभिलक्षण/उद्धरणों को संयोजित किया गया है।

उधार ग्रहणकर्ता संख्या: Borrower's Number प्रत्येक पुस्तकालय सदस्य की पंजीकरण/पहचान संख्या।

उधार ग्रहणकर्ता: Borrower पुस्तकालय का सदस्य जो पुस्तक प्राप्त कर सकता है।

उधार पुस्तक प्राप्त करने का पत्र: Borrower's Card सदस्यता पत्र जिसकी सहायता से पुस्तकालय पठन सामग्री प्राप्त की जा सके।

उधार ग्रही पंजी: Borrower's Register पंजी जिसमें प्रलेख उधार ग्रहण करने वालो का आवश्यक विवरण जैसे पता/व्यवसाय/विषय का उल्लेख रहता है।

उधार देना: Issue उधार सेवा।

उर्ध्वमुखी तीर: Upward Arrow चिन्ह जिसका प्रयोग द्वि बिन्दु वर्गीकरण प्रणाली में होता है।

उर्ध्वस्थ फाइल: Vertical File व्यवस्था जिसमें अभिलेखों को समानान्तर उर्वमुखी अवस्था में प्रयोग सुलभ रखा जाय।

ए

एक खण्डीय ग्रन्थ: Single Volumed Book ग्रन्थ जिसका प्रकाशन मात्र एक खण्ड में हो।

एक मुस्त युक्ति: Packet Device अंकन प्रयोग विधि जिसमें प्रयुक्त अंक समूह एक इकाई के रूप में जाना जाता है। उदाहरण

के रूप में विषय युक्ति प्रयुक्त अंकन।

एकल: Isolate शब्द से विचार अथवा वर्गीकृत संख्या की अभिव्यक्ति होती है। *और देखिए* एकल विचार।

एकल पक्ष-अभिधारणा: Postulate of Isolate Facet विषय में एक या एक से अधिक एकल पक्ष हो सकते हैं। परन्तु वह निश्चित रूप से किसी न किसी भूल-भूत श्रेणी रूप होते हैं।

एकल विचार: Isolate Idea विचार इकाई की अभिव्यक्ति है तथा अनेक एकल मिलकर विशेषतः पाँच मूलभूत श्रेणियों के क्रम में व्यक्त होकर वर्गीकरण प्रणाली में वर्ग स्थिति प्राप्त करते हैं।

एकात्मकता: Uniterm सूचना सम्प्रेषण में शब्द/चिन्ह जिनका प्रयोग किसी खास पहचान में किया जाए।

एकाधिक वर्ग: Multiple Class वर्ग जिसमें दो या उससे अधिक सत्ताओं का समावेश हो।

एकाधिक समूह: Multiple Group समूह जिसमें दो और दो से अधिक सत्ताओं का समावेश हो।

एकाधिक शीर्षक: Multiple Heading जब एक से अधिक शीर्षक प्रयुक्त हों। इनको अलग-2 व्यक्त करने को लघु विराम या अलग भाषा का प्रयोग हो सकता है।

एकीय वर्ग: Unitary Class वर्ग जिसमें मात्र एक ही स्थिति हो।

एकीय समूह: Unitary Group समूह जिसमें एक स्थिति हो।

एंग्लो-अमेरिकन सूची नियम: Anglo-American Cataloguing Rule सूचीकरण को नियमित करने के लिए एंग्लो-अमेरिकन नियमों की व्यवस्था है यह नियम निरन्तर परिष्कृत किये जा रहे हैं।

एंग्लो-अमेरिकन सूचीकरण संहिता: Anglo-American Cataloguing Code 1908 में अमेरिकन पुस्तकालय संघ तथा ब्रिटिश पुस्तकालय संघ के सहयोग से बने सूचीकरण सिद्धान्तों का संकलन है।

एगरिस: Agris कृषि, विज्ञान तथा तकनीकी विषयों के क्षेत्र में आधुनिकतम अन्तर्राष्ट्रीय सूचना सम्प्रेषण व्यवस्था है।

एनालोग कम्प्यूटर: Analog Computer कम्प्यूटर जो मूलतः आणविक तकनीक पर आधारित है।

एमपेरे वर्गीकरण: Ampere Classification वर्गीकरण प्रणाली 1834 में वैज्ञानिक दार्शनिक लेख के साथ प्रकाश में आई।

एफ आई डी: F.I.D अन्तर्राष्ट्रीय संस्था जो विश्व सूचना तथा प्रलेखन विकास के कार्य से जुड़ी है इसमें संस्थापक सदस्य प्रख्यात पुस्तकालय विज्ञानी पाल आटलैट तथा हेनरी ला फाउन्टेन रहे हैं। यह संस्थान सरकारी न होते हुए भी विश्व में अपने कार्यक्रम व्यापक रूप से चला रहा है।

एम एस डोस: MS DOS छोटी सोफ्ट डिस्क संचालन प्रणाली।

एसलिब: Aslib इस प्रमुख पुस्तकालय तथा सूचना विभागों के संघ की स्थापना 1926 में व्यापक सूचना प्रसार को लक्ष कर की गई थी इसका उद्देश्य सूचना का नियमित प्रयोग जनकार्यों, व्यवसायों तथा विज्ञान प्रयोगों में सुनिश्चित करना है।

ओ

ओ पी ए सी: OPAC कम्प्यूटर प्रयुक्त सीधे जन पहुँच पुस्तकालय सूची का परिवर्णी शब्द है।

ओ सी एल सी: OCLC 'ओहियो कालेज पुस्तकालय केन्द्र' अथवा 'सीधे कम्प्यूटर

पुस्तकालय केन्द्र' का परिवर्णी शब्द है।

औ

औचित्य क्रम का प्रनियम: Canon of Relevant Sequence विश्व ज्ञान जगत् के वर्गीकरण आधार में प्रयुक्त अभिलक्षणों का प्रयोग सारिणी में क्रमशः होना चाहिए जिससे कि वर्गीकरण प्रासंगिक हो।

औचित्य का प्रनियम: Canon of Relevance वर्गीकरण के आधार में प्रयुक्त गुण वर्गीकरण के उद्देश्य के अनुरूप हों।

औपचारिक शिक्षा: Formal Education शिक्षा निश्चित उद्देश्य, विषय अथवा संस्था से ग्रहण की जाए।

और देखो: See also सांकेतिक शब्द जिसका प्रयोग अनुक्रमणिका में सर्वाधिक होता है। विषय के अन्य नाम/शब्द की ओर इंगित करता है।

अं

अंकन: Notation चिन्ह जिसका वर्गांकन प्रणाली में प्रयोग किया जाये तथा निश्चित मूल्य हो।

अंकित प्रति: Typed Script प्रलेख का टंकित/मुद्रित मूलरूप।

अंक: Digit/Number प्रत्येक चिन्ह जिसका प्रयोग वर्गीकरण संख्या/आह्वान संख्या निर्माण में होता है अथवा पत्रिका का एक खण्ड।

अंकन का आधार: Base of a Notation वर्गीकरण प्रणाली में प्रयुक्त सम्पूर्ण अंकन की संख्या से अभिप्राय है।

अंकन तल: Notational Plane संख्याओं का तल जिससे विचारों को अभिव्यक्त किया जाता है।

अंकन की क्षमता: Capacity of Notation अंकन की क्षमता को उसके द्वारा व्यक्त वर्ग संख्या से जाना जा सकता है।

अंकन तल के प्रनियम: Canon of Notational Plane प्रनियम जिनकी सहायता से अंकन को नियमित किया जाता है।

अन्तर पुस्तकालय उधार: Inter Library Loan एक से अधिक पुस्तकालयों के मध्य प्रलेख आदान प्रदान सेवा।

अंश: Cell सूचना का वह भाग जो साधारणतः कम्प्यूटर प्रयुक्त शब्द अथवा एक करैक्टर होता है।

अंशदान: Contribution रचना जो ग्रन्थ/पत्रिका/प्रलेख आदि का भाग बनती है।

क

कतरन: Clipping पत्र/पत्रिका से काटकर अलग किया हुआ सूचना-अंश।

कतरन सेवा: Clipping Service सेवा जिसके द्वारा तत्कालिक सूचना संकलित कर वर्गीकृत क्रम में प्रयोक्ता को उपलब्ध कराई जाय।

कच्चा माल: Raw Material सामान जिसकी सहायता से वांछित वस्तु बनाई जा सके। पुस्तकालय में जिल्द साजी के लिए अलग-2 प्रकार का समान एकत्रित किया जाता है।

कटर संख्या: Cutter Number यह संख्या लेखक/पुस्तक संख्या भी जानी जाती है इसकी सहायता से समान वर्ग के प्रलेखों की अलग पहचान रखी जाती हैं।

कड़ी: Link कम्प्यूटर सूचना सम्प्रेषण मार्ग अथवा वर्गीकरण प्रणाली में शृंखला भाग।

कड़ी का क्रम: Order of a Link अभिव्यक्त वर्ग का क्रम ।

कम्पाइलर: Compiler जिसके द्वारा कम्प्यूटर प्रणाली में पूरा प्रोग्राम मशीन की भाषा में बदला जाता है तथा सम्बन्धित कमियों पर अंकुश रखा जाता है।

कम्प्यूटर प्रोग्राम: Computer Program कम्प्यूटर निर्देशों का संकलन जिसको आधार मानकर सूचना नियमित की जाती है।

कम्प्यूटर तन्त्र: Computer Network कम्प्यूटर को अन्य कमप्यूटर तथा अनेक टर्मिनल्स से जोड़ा जाता है।

कपड़ा जिल्द: Cloth Binding ग्रन्थ की दीर्घ आयु के लिए कपड़े का आवरण प्रदान किया जाता है।

कर्मचारीगण: Staff व्यक्ति जो सवैतनिक सेवा शर्तों में कार्य करते हैं।

कर्मचारी पुस्तिका: Staff Manual कर्मचारियों के दिन-प्रतिदिन के मार्ग निर्देशन की सहयोगी पुस्तिका।

कला भवन/कला दीर्घा: Art-gallery भवन का वह भाग जहाँ पर कला के विभिन्न रूप/चित्र/मूर्ति आदि को प्रदर्शित किया जाए।

कला पत्र: Art Paper विशेष प्रकार का चिकनी सतह वाला कागज़।

क्रम संख्या: Serial Number संख्या जिसके निश्चित मूल्य के आधार पर ग्रन्थ संयोजन में सुविधा होती है।

क्रमिक: Serial समसामयिक विषयों पर एक निश्चित अन्तराल से रचना प्रकाशन।

क्रमिक युक्ति: Chronological Device युक्ति जिसके समय को व्यक्त किया जाए।

कृषि शोध सूचना केन्द्र: Agricultural Research Information Centre कृषि सम्बन्धी शोध की सूचना को राष्ट्रीय स्तर पर एकत्रित कर यह केन्द्र अन्तर्राष्ट्रीय सूचना सम्प्रेषण केन्द्र 'एगरिस' को प्रदान करता है।

कृषि पुस्तकालय: Agricultural Library इस प्रकार के पुस्तकालय कृषि सम्बन्धी शोध परक सूचनाओं के सम्प्रेषण केन्द्र हैं इस श्रेणी में कृषि विश्वविद्यालय पुस्तकालय/कृषि अनुसंधानशाला पुस्तकालय अथवा इसी प्रकार के अन्य पुस्तकालय आते हैं।

क्रम की अभिधारणा: Postulate of Sequence इस सिद्धान्त के अनुसार प्रथम विषय का मुख्य पक्ष तदन्तर अन्य पक्ष उनके निश्चित घटते क्रम की अभिधारणा में व्यक्तस्थित होने चाहिए।

क्रम व्यवस्था: Filing सम्बद्ध सदर्भों को इच्छितक्रम में रखना।

कृत्रिम अंक: Artificial Digit अंक जिसका पूर्व निर्धारित मूल्य नहीं होता।

कृत्रिम अभिलक्षण: Artificial Characteristic समूह विशेष की पहचान की विशेषता जिसका प्रत्येक इकाई में होना आवश्यक नहीं।

कृत्रिम भाषा: Artificial Language मनचाहे प्रयोग की भाषा अथवा पुस्तकालय वर्गीकरण में प्रयुक्त सांकेतिक भाषा जिसके प्रयोग सम्बन्धी नियम इसके साथ प्राप्त कराये जाते हैं।

कृत्रिम संयुक्त पुस्तक: Artificial Composite Book एक से अधिक पुस्तकों को एक जिल्द में रखा जाये तथा रचनाओं की पहचान अलग-2 बनी रहे तथा कोई संयुक्त शीर्षक न हो।

कृत्रिम ज्ञान: Aritificial Intelligence तकनीकी प्रकार जिसके ज्ञान होने का आभास भर होता है।

कृत्रिम स्ववर्गी ग्रन्थ: Pseudo Classic स्ववर्गी ग्रन्थ जिससे सम्बन्धित आलोचना आदि रचना उपलब्ध हो।

कृत्रिम सत्ता: Pseudo Entity सम्पूर्ण चुनाव की प्रक्रिया में किसी सत्ता को स्वतन्त्र स्वीकार कर लिया जाये।

कृत्रिम ग्रन्थ मालाः Pseudo-Series ग्रन्थ माला न होने पर भी आभाष मात्र हो।

क्रय आदेशः Order खरीद सम्बन्धी आदेश।

क्रय आदेश पत्रः Order card पत्र जिससे क्रय आदेश दिया जाता है।

क्रय आदेश प्रपत्रः Order Form पत्र जिसका प्रयोग खरीद आदेश के रूप में होता है।

क्रय आदेश सूचीः Order List सूची जिसका प्रयोग खरीद पत्र के साथ होता है।

क्रमबोधक संख्याः Ordinal Number संख्या जिससे पुस्तकालय ग्रन्थ की क्रमिक स्थिति अन्य ग्रन्थों के मध्य निश्चित की जाती है।

क्रमबोधक संकेतः Ordinal Symbol वर्गीकरण में प्रयुक्त संकेत जिससे प्रलेख की क्रमिक स्थिति का बोध होता है।

कम समय उधारः Short Time Loan ग्रन्थ का अल्प अवधि तक के लिए उधार दिया जाना।

कागजः Paper तन्तु समायोजन से बनी पतली चादर जिसका प्रयोग लिखने में होता है।

कागजी आवरणः Paper Back/Wrapper *देखिए* कागजी जिल्द/जैकेट।

कागजी जिल्दः Paper Bound पुस्तक की सुरक्षा जिल्द कागज की बनी हो।

कागज आकारः Paper Size आवश्यकतानुसार कागज के विभिन्न आकार।

कार्यक्रमः Program कम्प्यूटर में कार्य प्रतिपादन के लिए दिये गये निर्देशन/विषय सम्बन्धी रूपरेखा।

कार्यक्रम बनानेवालाः Programmer व्यक्ति जो सूचना नियन्त्रण से सम्बन्धित निर्देश प्रणाली बनाता है।

कार्यः Job सेवाएं जिनको प्रतिपादित किया जाए।

कार्य नियोजनः Work Assignment कार्य का उत्तरदायित्व।

कार्य छापाखानाः Job Press छापाखाना जो आर्थिक उन्नति के लिए अन्य व्यवसायियों के छोटे-2 काम करता है।

कार्य धरातलः Plane of Work डा. रगांनाथन ने कार्य के तीन धरातल-विचार तल, मौखिक तल तथा अंकनतल व्यक्त किये हैं इन्हीं तीनों तलों से वर्गीकरण प्रणाली निकलती है।

कालक्रम में उत्तरता का सिद्धान्तः Principle of Later-in-Time यदि पंक्ति एकल विभिन्न समय में उत्पन्न हुए हैं तो उनको समानान्तर समय सारिणी में व्यक्त करना होगा।

कार्य सूचीः Agenda विषय विशेष पर चर्चा से पूर्व निर्धारित रूपरेखा जनित कार्यक्रम।

कालानुक्रमः Chronological Order काल/तारीख क्रम संयोजन।

कालानुक्रमिक युक्ति (विचारतल): Chronological Device (Idea Plane) कालक्रम/तिथि के अनुसार एकल संयोजन का विचार।

कालानुक्रमिक युक्ति (अंकनतल): Chronological Device (Notational Plane) युक्ति जिसमें कालानुक्रमिक संख्या को अभीष्ट एकल से जोड़ कर काल क्रम संख्या बनाई जाती है।

कालेज पुस्तकालयः College Library पुस्तकालय जिसका प्रयोग शिक्षा संस्थान के शिक्षक, विद्यार्थी तथा अन्य कर्मचारी करते हैं।

कारडैक्सः Cardex मानक आकार का स्टील का बना बक्सा होता है जिसमे प्रत्येक पत्रिका का विवरण रखने की अलग व्यवस्था होती है।

किताबी कीड़े: Book Worm कीड़े जो पुस्तकों में पाये जायें।

किस्त: Instalment भाग, अंश।

कुल नाम: Family Name/Surname नाम जो परिवार से सम्बन्ध व्यक्त करे अथवा जिसका प्रयोग केवल परिवार के निकट सम्बन्धी करे।

कूट बनाना: Encoding.

केन्द्र: Focus शब्द विशेष अर्थ के लिए मुख्यवर्ग, मिश्रित वर्ग तथा यौगिक वर्ग के अन्तर्भाव के लिए प्रयुक्त होता है।

केन्द्रीकृत् सूचीकरण: Centralised Cataloguing सूचीकरण में एकरूपता के साथ आर्थिक अपव्यय रोकने के लिए एक से अधिक पुस्तकालय ग्रन्थ सूची प्रविष्टि केन्द्रीय प्रणाली द्वारा बनाई जाय। कार्यक्रम से जुड़े पुस्तकालय/पुस्तकालय अनुभाग प्रविष्टि की प्रति लिपि प्राप्त कर लेते हैं।

केन्द्रीय सूची: Central Catalogue जब पुस्तकालय के अनेक विस्तार पुस्तकालयों की मिलाकर एक सूची हो तो केन्द्रीय सूची जानी जाती है।

केन्द्रीय पुस्तकालय: Central Library पुस्तकालय प्रणाली का मुख्य भाग जो मूल व्यवस्था, देख-रेख तथा नीति निर्धारण करता है।

केन्द्रीय संसाधन: Centralised Processing पुस्तकालय कार्य-खरीद, सूचीकरण, वर्गीकरण आदि एक रूपता तथा मितव्ययता प्राप्ति के लिए केन्द्रीय इकाई द्वारा किए जाते हैं।

केन्द्रीय संसाधन इकाई: Central Processing Unit (CPU) कम्प्यूटर प्रणाली का विशेष भाग जिसका कार्य सूचना संचय कर योजनानुसार व्यवस्थित करना है।

कैन्ट वर्गीकरण: Kent Classification ऐमेनुएनल कैन्ट द्वारा 1781 में सृजित वर्गीकरण प्रणाली।

कैशबुक/रोकड़बही: Cash Book पंजी/पुस्तिका जिसमें पुस्तकालय के दैनिक आय व्यय का विवरण होता है।

कोश: Dictionary किसी भाषा के शब्दों को वर्णानुक्रम में व्यवस्थित कर उनके प्रयोग के बारे में स्पष्टीकरण होता है।

कोष्टकान्तक: Arrester चिन्ह जिसकी सहायता से अंक समूह को इकाई रूप में प्रस्तुत किया जाता है तथा जो इस संख्या व्यवस्था का अनुगामी होता है।

कोबोल: Cobol कम्प्यूटर प्रयुक्त कार्यक्रम भाषा का परिवर्णी शब्द है।

कोलन वर्गीकरण/द्वि अंगी वर्गीकरण: Colon Classification यह स्वतन्त्र पक्ष विश्लेषित संश्लेषण वर्गीकरण प्रणाली है जिसका सृजन 1933 में भारतीय पुस्तकालय विज्ञानी, डा. रंगनाथन ने किया था। प्रणाली में व्यापक रूप से (कोलन) द्वि बिन्दु का प्रयोग सुविचारित नियम, उपनियम तथा सिद्धान्तों के साथ हुआ है।

कोलन पुस्तक संख्या: Colon Book Number कोलन पुस्तक संख्या एक अथवा उससे अधिक पक्षों के योग से बनती है पक्ष जैसे भाषा संख्या, प्रकार संख्या, वर्ष संख्या, खरीद संख्या अथवा खण्ड संख्या हो सकती हैं।

कौन है कौन/कौन था कौन: Who's who/who was who *देखिये* जीवनी।

ख

खण्ड: Sector/Volume/Block एक अभिलक्षण के आधार पर प्राप्त एकल समूह/लिखित अथवा मुद्रित रचना जिसका संयोजन अनेक उपखण्डों के योग से होता है तथा निश्चित उद्देश्य की पूरक होती है। अथवा शब्द, अभिलेख तथा लक्षण को जब

समूह रूप में प्रयुक्त किया जाए।

खण्ड पक्षः Volume Facet ग्रन्थ संख्या का भाग जिससे खण्ड की अभिव्यक्ति हो।

खण्ड विन्यासः Block Arrangement निश्चित प्रकार के प्रलेख रखने की निश्चित व्यवस्था।

खण्ड शीर्षकः Block in Heading शब्द समूह का पृथकता कारक चिन्हों के साथ शीर्षक में प्रयोग हो।

खण्ड संख्याः Volume Number संख्या जिसकी सहायता से प्रत्येक खण्ड की पहचान होती है।

खाली पृष्ठः Blank Page पृष्ठ जिस पर कुछ भी अंकित न हो। साधारणतः पुस्तक के प्रारम्भ तथा अन्त में कुछ खाली पृष्ठ रखे जाते हैं।

खुली खरीदः Open Purchase जब प्रलेख किसी भी स्थान तथा विक्रेता से प्राप्त किया जा सके।

खुली पंक्तिः Open Array वर्ग पंक्ति जिसमें नये विषयों को समाहित करने की व्यवस्था हो सके।

खुली प्रविष्टिः Open Entry प्रविष्टि जो पूर्ण नहीं हुई है। जिसमें सूचना परिवर्तन तथा प्रवेश सम्भव हैं। इस प्रकार की प्रविष्टि पत्रिकाओं के लिये बनाई जाती हैं।

खोज/ढूंढ़नाः Search वाँछित सूचना प्राप्त करने का प्रयास।

खोज का तरीकाः Search Method सूचना प्राप्त करने का प्रकार।

खोज बिन्दुः Search Point *देखिए* पहुँच बिन्दु।

खोज सेवाः Search Service.

खोज शब्दः Search Term शब्द जिसका प्रयोग पहुँच बिन्दु के रूप मे किया जाये।

खोज सहायतायेंः Search Aids.

ग

गवर्न्मैंनट लाइब्रेरियन्स एण्ड इनफॉरमेशन स्पेशलिस्ट संघः Association of Government Librarians and Information Specialists (AGRIS) यह संघ इससे पूर्व गवर्न्मैंनट ऑफ इण्डिया लाइब्रेरियन्स एसोसिऐसन के नाम से 1933 में स्थापित हुआ था। वर्तमान नाम 1977 में दिया गया। सम्पूर्ण भारत में इसके सदस्य हैं। संघ का कार्य पुस्तकालय तथा पुस्तकालय विज्ञान का विकास करना है। सम्पर्क सूत्र बनाये रखने को मासिक तथा त्रय मासिक पत्र प्रकाशित करता है तथा वार्षिक गोष्ठी का आयोजन करता है।

गजेटियर/भौगोलिक कोशः Gazetteers ये संदर्भ प्रलेख हैं जिनमें राष्ट्र, जिला, तहसील, शहर से सम्बन्धित, एतिहासिक, सांस्कृतिक, सामाजिक, भौगोलिक तथा आर्थिक सूचना रहती है।

गहन वर्गीकरणः Depth Classification लघुतम विचारों तक वर्गीकरण करने की पद्धति।

गलतीः Error.

ग्रन्थ अनुदानः Book Budget अनुदान जिसका प्रयोग पुस्तक तथा अन्य पठन सामग्री खरीदने में होता है।

ग्रन्थ आवरणः Book Cover ग्रन्थ सुरक्षा कवच।

ग्रन्थ पर्चीः Book Plate कागज की नियमित आकार की पर्ची जिस पर पुस्तकालय का नाम अंकित होता है तथा प्रत्येक पुस्तक आवरण के अन्दर चिपकाई जाती है।

ग्रन्थ का आकारः Body of the Book ग्रन्थ के बाह्य आकार से अभिप्राय है जिससे पुस्तक की लम्बाई, चौड़ाई तथा मोटाई को जाना जा सकता है।

ग्रन्थ प्रतिस्थापन्न: Book Replacement विशेष परिस्थिति में पुस्तकालय प्रलेख के स्थान पर प्रतिलिपि स्वीकार की जाए।

ग्रन्थ लेखा: Book Record किसी विषय तथा भाषा पर उपलब्ध ग्रन्थों की सूची अथवा प्रलेख संचरण का विवरण।

ग्रन्थ सूची: Bibliography ग्रन्थ विज्ञान सूची विज्ञान अथवा प्रक्रिया जिसमें नियम, उपनियमों के आधार पर ग्रन्थ-सूची बनाई जाती हैं। जिसका विस्तार पुस्तकालय विशेष या विषय विशेष के संकलनों तक ही सीमित नहीं होता।

ग्रन्थ वाहन: Book Van वाहन जिसका प्रयोग पुस्तक स्थानान्तरण में किया जाए।

ग्रन्थमाला: Series विषय विशेष के ग्रन्थों को एक सामान्य शीर्षक की पहचान ग्रन्थमाला देती है जो मुख्य शीर्षक से अलग होता है।

ग्रन्थमाला शीर्षक: Series Title शीर्षक जिससे ग्रन्थमाला व्यक्त होती है।

ग्रन्थमाला विवरण: Series Statement *देखिए* ग्रन्थमाला टिप्पणी।

ग्रन्थमाला संख्या: Series Number संख्या जो ग्रन्थमाला के प्रत्येक प्रलेख की पहचान स्वरूप दी जाती है।

ग्रन्थमाला टिप्पण: Series Note सूची प्रविष्टि में टिप्पण जहाँ ग्रन्थमाला का नाम तथा संख्या दी जाये।

ग्रन्थमाला प्रविष्टि: Series Entry अतिरिक्त प्रविष्टि प्रकार है जिसको मुख्य प्रविष्टि में प्राप्त ग्रन्थमाला सूचना के आधार पर बनाया जाता है।

ग्रन्थ सूचीकार: Bibliographer व्यक्ति जिसको ग्रन्थ सूची बनाने का तकनीकी ज्ञान हो।

ग्रन्थ संग्रह की उच्च अभिलाषा: Bibliomania पुस्तक संग्रह का निरन्तर उपक्रम।

ग्रन्थात्मक-अभिलेख: Bibliographic Record प्रलेख जिसमें ग्रन्थात्मक सूची सम्बन्धी सूचना अंकित होती है।

ग्रन्थात्मक अभिलेख का बाह्यकार: Bibliographic Record Format ग्रन्थात्मक सूचना प्रविष्टि विस्तार।

ग्रन्थात्मक केन्द्र: Bibliographic Centre स्थान जहाँ पर ग्रन्थात्मक सूचना संकलन तथा सम्प्रेषण का कार्य नियन्त्रित होता है।

ग्रन्थात्मक नियन्त्रण: Bibliographic Control अनुपूरक प्रकाशनों का नियन्त्रण।

ग्रन्थात्मक वर्गीकरण: Bibliographic Classification हेनेरी इबेलेन ब्लेस द्वारा प्रतिपादित वर्गीकरण प्रणाली जिसका प्रथम आर्विभाव 1935 में हुआ *और देखिए* सूक्ष्म वर्गीकरण।

ग्रन्थात्मक विवरण: Bibliographic Description प्रविष्टि में निहित लेखक, सहलेखक, सम्पादक, संस्करण, शीर्षक, प्रकाशक, प्रकाशन स्थान, प्रकाशन तिथि आदि सूचनाओं को ग्रन्थात्मक विवरण की संज्ञा दी जाती है।

ग्रन्थात्मक सूचना: Bibliographic Data, Bibliographic Information *देखिए* ग्रन्थात्मक विवरण।

ग्रन्थात्मक सूचना-संचय: Bibliographic Database कम्प्यूटर पर ग्रन्थात्मक सूचना का संचय।

ग्रन्थात्मक पत्रिका: Bibliographical Periodical पत्रिका जिसमें विषय से सम्बन्धित रचनाओं की ग्रन्थात्मक सूचना संकलित होती हैं।

ग्रन्थात्मक संख्यिकी: Bibliometrics विषय पर उपलब्ध ग्रन्थ सूचना का गणितीय

विश्लेषण।

ग्रन्थाश्रयः Book Rest उपादन जिसके सहयोग से पुस्तक प्रदर्शक पर स्थापित की जाती है।

ग्रन्थों की देखरेखः Care of Book व्यवस्था जिससे ग्रन्थों की धूल, धूआँ तथा आकस्मिक ऋतु परिवर्तन से रक्षा की जाती है।

गृह वितरण सेवाः Home Delivery Service पुस्तकालय सेवा जिसमें पाठक/प्रयोक्ता को सूचना/ग्रन्थ उसके घर पर ही प्राप्त कराये जाएं।

गृह-पत्रिकाः House Journal सीमित प्रसार पत्रिका जिसमें संस्थान की वर्तमान गतिविधियों का विवरण प्रस्तुत किया जाता है।

ग्राम पुस्तकालय सेवाः Rural Library Service पुस्तकालय सेवा जिसका प्रयोग ग्रामीण अंचल के प्रयोक्ता करते हैं।

ग्राह्य अस्तित्वः Like Entities गुणों की समान ग्राह्य विशेषताओं के अस्तित्व की स्वीकृति।

गुड आफिस कमैटी/गुड कार्यालय समितिः Good Office Committee पुस्तकाध्यक्ष/पुस्तक व्यवसायियों की समिति जो निश्चित अवधि के लिए विदेशी मुद्रा विनिमय दर तथा पुस्तकों की खरीद पर छूट दर निर्धारित करती है। इस का कार्यालय दिल्ली में है।

गुणः Quality वस्तु में समाहित विशेषतायें।

गोपनीय फाइलः Confidential File अति विशिष्टि पत्रों की फाइल जिसको सार्वजनिक नहीं किया जाता।

गो-वत्स सिद्धान्तः Cow-calf Principle एक ही वर्ग के पक्ष 'अ' और 'ब' को साथ ही साथ उनकी आवृति के क्रम में गाय-बछड़े के समान अलग-2 पहचान होते हुये भी साथ-2 रखा जाना चाहिए।

घ

घटना/प्रंसगः Episode प्रकरण।

घड़ी की दिशा का सिद्धान्तः Principle of Clock-wise यदि एकल को चक्राकार स्थिति में रखना हो तो घड़ी की सूइयों की गति दिशा में व्यवस्थित करना चाहिऐ।

च

चयित ग्रन्थ सूचीः Select Bibliography ग्रन्थ सूची जिसमें चुनी हुई प्रविष्टियों को स्थान मिलता है।

चयित सूचना सम्प्रेषणः Selective Dissemination of Information (SDI) सेवा जिससे प्रयोक्ता को उसके विशेष वांछित अध्ययन विषय से सम्बन्धित सूचना/ग्रन्थ की पुस्तकालय द्वारा प्राप्ति के बारे में सूचना दी जाती है।

चलचित्रः Film विषय का दृश्य तथा श्रव्य प्रकार।

चलचित्र प्रदर्शकः Film Projector तकनीकी उपादान जिसकी सहायता से दृश्य श्रव्य साधन प्रयोग होते है।

चलता शीर्षकः Running Title शीर्षक जो रचना के प्रत्येक पृष्ठ के ऊपरी सिरे में अंकित होता है।

चल पुस्तकालयः Travelling Library वाहन प्रयुक्त पुस्तकालय सेवा। इसमें चुनीं हुई पुस्तको, पत्रिकाओं को पाठक अथवा अन्य पुस्तकालय केन्द्रों पर वाहन द्वारा पहुँचाया जाता है।

चक्र के अन्तर्गत क्रम की अभिधारणाः Postulate of Sequence within a Round चक्र के अन्तर्गत एकल सारिणी उसी प्रकार होनी चाहिए जैसी कि अभिधारण में व्यक्त है।

चाक्षुष उपकरणः Visual Aids उपकरण

जिनकी सहायता से ग्रन्थों को चित्र पटल पर देखा/पढ़ा जा सके।

चिकित्सा ग्रन्थ सूची: Medical Bibliography सूची जिसमें चिकित्सा सम्बन्धी ग्रन्थ सम्मिलित होते हैं।

चिकित्सा पुस्तकालय: Medical Library/Hospital Library पुस्तकालय जिसका प्रयोग चिकित्सक तथा रोगी दोनों ही करते हैं।

चित्र पृष्ठ: Plate पृष्ठ जिसका पूर्ण या अंश आकार चित्र अथवा चित्र प्रकार हो

चित्र: Illustrations प्रलेख के बीच प्रयुक्त चित्र, चार्ट तथा ग्राफ आदि।

चित्र: Painting चित्रात्मक रचना

चिप: Chip सिलिकन का पतला चिप्पड़ जिस पर इलेक्ट्रोनिक परिपथ स्थापित किए जाते हैं।

चित्रकार: Illustrator व्यक्ति जो हर प्रकार के चित्र बनाता है।

चित्र परदा: Screen एक विशेष प्रकार का परदा जिस पर चित्र प्रक्षेपित किये जाते हैं।

चिन्ह: Mark आवश्यक अभिव्यक्ति के लिए अनुवादित किया जा सके।

चिन्हांकन: Coding मशीन की भाषा प्रयोग करने के लिए उपयुक्त संकेत प्रतिस्थापन।

चुनाव: Selection/Sorting गुण आधारित चुनाव

चुम्बकीय डिस्क: Magnetic Disk कम्प्यूटर प्रयुक्त डिस्क जिसका प्रयोग सूचना संचय के लिए किया जाता है डिस्क की बनावट में एक से अधिक चुम्बकीय पत्रों का योग होता है जिससे संकलन क्षमता बढ़ जाती है।

चुम्बकीय संकलन: Magnetic Storage.संग्रह युक्ति जिसके कार्य का आधार चुम्बकीय गुण हो।

चुम्बकीय टेप: Magnetic Tape प्लास्टिक की चुम्बकीय प्रभाव युक्त पट्टी सूचना संचय में प्रयोग होती है इसका प्रयोग मशीन की सहायता से हो सकता है।

चट्टोपाध्याय (डी.पी.) समिति : Chattopadhayay (D.P.) Committee समिति जिसको भारत सरकार ने पुस्तकालय कर्मचारियों के वेतनमान चतुर्थ वेनत आयोग के सुझाव पर निर्धारित करने के लिए नियुक्त किया।

छ

छद्म नाम: Pseudonym वास्तविक नाम के अतिरिक्त नाम जिसके उदाहरण साहित्य लेखकों में प्रायः प्राप्त हैं।

छपी पुस्तक आकार सूची: Printed Book Form Catalogue इस प्रकार की सूची को सम सामयिक बनाने के लिए पूरक निकालने पड़ते हैं। प्रविष्टियों का निश्चित क्रम में आवद्ध कर छपवा कर पुस्तक रूप दे दिया जाता है या फिर पंजी रुप में होती है।

छपी सामग्री: Printed Material देखिए पुस्तक/पत्रिका।

छाया चित्र: Photographs अभिलेख जिसकी विषय-वस्तु चित्रों में व्यक्त होती है। कभी आंशिक तो कभी पूरा ग्रन्थ ही इस प्रकार का होता है।

छोटा कम्प्यूटर: Micro Computer/Minicomputer यह कम स्मृति तथा कम कीमत वाला विकसित आधुनिक कम्प्यूटर है।

छूट: Discount छपी हुई/घोषित मूल्य से घटाया गया मूल्य।

छोटा शीर्षक: Short Title देखिए संक्षेपित शीर्षक।

छेद: Punch सूचीकरण पत्र के मध्य का कटा हुआ गोल भाग।

छेद वाला पत्र: Punched Card विशेष मानक पत्र निश्चित स्थान पर छेद दिया

जाता है। जिससे छेद अलग-2 स्थान पर अलग-2 विचार, मूल विषय, एकल तथा शब्द को व्यक्त करते हैं और मशीन के उपभोग से छाँटा जा सकता है।

छाँटने की विधि: Scheme of Assortment प्रणाली जिसके आधार पर सूचना को अलग-अलग किया जा सके।

ज

जमानती धन: Caution Money राशि संस्था द्वारा पुस्तकालय प्रलेख सुरक्षा के लिए धरोहर रूप में ली जाती है तथा सदस्यता समाप्ति पर लौटा दी जाती है।

जंतरी: Almanac पंचाग साधारणतः वार्षिक प्रकाशन होते है जो कि तिथि, राशि, ग्रह आदि से सम्बन्धित साम्प्रतिक सूचना रखते हैं।

जनसंख्या क्षेत्र एकल: Population Cluster Isolate क्षेत्र जिसमें जनसंख्या घनत्व अधिक हो तथा अनेक समाज केन्द्र हों।

जमानती: Guarantor व्यक्ति जो अपरिचित व्यक्ति की पुस्तकालय सदस्यता के लिए पहचान निश्चित करता है।

जातिबोध: Connotation अभिलक्षण जो किसी वर्ग में समाहित हो।

जिल्द: Binding प्रलेख का सुरक्षा आवरण।

जिल्द के साथ: Bound with शब्द का प्रयोग सूची करण में पुस्तक के अन्य पुस्तक के साथ होने को व्यक्त करने को किया जाता है।

जिल्द युक्त खण्ड: Bound Volume प्रलेख जिसकी जिल्द बना दी गई हो। साधारणतः सुरक्षा के लिए पुस्तकों/ पत्रिकाओं की जिल्द बाँध दी जाती है।

जिल्द पर्ची: Binding Slip कागज की पर्ची जिस पर प्रत्येक जिल्द बँधने वाले प्रलेख से सम्बन्धित सूचना जिल्द साज की उपयोगिता के लिए अंकित की जाय।

जिल्द अभिलेख: Binding Record जिल्द सम्बन्धी सूचना संचय।

जिल्द किनारा: Binding Edge प्रलेख आवरण पृष्ठ जोड़ने वाला पिछला भाग जो जिल्द से ग्रन्थ को जोड़ता है।

जिल्द साज: Book Binder व्यक्ति जिसका कार्य पुस्तकों की जिल्द बाँधना है।

जिल्द साजी केन्द्र: Bindery स्थान जहाँ जिल्द बन्दी की जाती है।

जिल्द साज शीर्षक: Binder's Title संक्षिप्त शीर्षक जिसको जिल्द की पीठ पर अंकित किया जाता है।

जिला पुस्तकालय: District Library जिला स्तर का पब्लिक पुस्तकालय हैं जो जिला केन्द्र पर कार्य करता है।

जिला केन्द्रीय पुस्तकालय: District Central Library *देखिए* जिला पुस्तकालय।

जीवनी: Biography किसी व्यक्ति के जीवन की विशेष घटनाओं का विवरण।

जीवनी कोश: Biographical Dictionary विभिन्न विषयों के चुने हुए विद्वानों की जीवन सम्बन्धी चुनी सूचनाओं का संचय होता है प्रत्येक प्रविष्टि में उनका जन्म स्थान, शिक्षा, जीवन की उपलब्धि तथा विशेष कार्य का उल्लेख होता है प्रविष्टियाँ वर्ण क्रम में होती है।

जीवनी लेखक: Biographer व्यक्ति जो जीवनी लिखता है।

जेब: Pocket प्रत्येक ग्रन्थ में पुस्तकालय उपचार के समय एक छोटी जेब पुस्तक पहचान पत्र रखने को लगा दी जाती है।

जैकेट: Jacket *देखिए* पुस्तक जाकेट।

ट

टर्मिनल/अन्तिम केन्द्र: Terminal केन्द्र जहाँ कम्प्यूटर तन्त्र में सूचना प्राप्त अथवा

प्रयोग करने का कार्य होता है।

टिकली/टेग: Tag कागज/कपड़ा इत्यादि का निश्चित आकार का छोड़ा टुकड़ा जिस पर पुस्तक आह्वान संख्या अंकित की जाती है।

टिप्पण क्षेत्र: Note Area प्रविष्टि का क्षेत्र जिसमें मूल सूचना के अतिरिक्त टिप्पण सम्बन्धी सूचना को अंकित किया जाता है।

टिप्पण अनुभाग: Note Section प्रविष्टि भाग जिसमें ग्रन्थ का अन्य ग्रन्थ से सम्बन्ध तथा ग्रन्थमाला आदि के बारे में उल्लेख होता है।

टेप: Tape सूचना संग्रह में प्रयुक्त चुम्बकीय शक्ति संयोजित साधन है अथवा विशेष प्रकार का रसायन युक्त टेप जो पृष्ठ जोड़ने के काम आता है।

टेले संदर्भ: Tele Reference मशीनी प्रक्रिया से सूची निरीक्षण क्रिया है।

ड

डमी/नमूना अंक: Dummy मूल का प्रतिरूप।

डाक परिचालन: Postal Circulation निर्गम/परिचालन सेवा के लिए डाक व्यवस्था का सहयोग लिया जाए।

डाइजैस्ट: Digest प्रकाशन जो किसी विषय और उसके समीपी विषय के ज्ञान की सामायिक सूचना देता है।

डायरी: Diary सामायिक क्रम में सूचना सम्प्रेषक पुस्तिका

डारमेटरी पुस्तकालय: Dormitory Library पुस्तकालय कार्य डारमेटरी मे सम्पादित हो

डिजिटल कम्प्यूटर: Digital Computer कम्प्यूटर जिसमें सूचना संख्यात्मक कोड रूप में संचरित हो।

डिजिटल संकेत: Digital Signal संकेत जिससे अंक रूप में सूचना प्रस्तुत की जा सके।

डी.वी. एस. थ्री: DBS III कम्प्यूटर प्रयुक्त प्रोग्राम प्रकार।

ड्यूवे दशमलव वर्गीकरण: Deway Decimal Classification देखिए दशमलव वर्गीकरण।

डाकूमेन्टेशन रिसर्च एण्ड ट्रेनिंग सेन्टर: Documentation Research and Training Centre यह बैंगलौर में स्थित पुस्तकालय तथा सूचना शोध का संस्थान है।

ढ

ढीली पत्र सूची प्रकार: Loose Leaf Form Catalogue सूची प्रविष्टि निश्चित आकार के मोटे पत्र पर न होकर अलग-2 पृष्ठ पर होती है। और सभी पृष्ठ फाइल फोल्डर में संयोजित रहते हैं।

त

तलोपर गमनीयता का सिद्धांत: Principle of Bottom Upward एकल यदि एक पंक्ति में लगातार उत्पन्न हो रहे हों तो उनको नीचे से ऊपर के क्रम में संयोजित करना चाहिए।

तकनीकी पत्रिका: Technical Journal पत्रिका जिसकी विषय-वस्तु तकनीकी ज्ञान के प्रचार प्रसार से जुड़ी हो।

तकनीकी पुस्तकालय: Technical Library पुस्तकालय जिसका संकलन मूलतः तकनीकी विषयों से सम्बन्धित हो।

तकनीकी प्रतिवेदन: Technical Report सामायिक तकनीकी विकास तथा वैज्ञानिक परिणामों को प्रस्तुत करने वाला प्रकाशन।

तकनीकी योग्यता: Technical Qualification तकनीकी विशष का ज्ञान।

तकनीकी सेवा: Technical Service

तकनीकी शब्द: Technical Terms

विषय विशेष के संदर्भ में प्रयुक्त शब्द।

तदर्थ समितिः Ad hoc Committee निर्धारित आवश्यकता पूर्ति अथवा सुझाव प्राप्त करने को अल्प अवधि समिति होती है। इसके सदस्य मूल समिति से अथवा बाहर से भी हो सकते हैं।

तत्काल संदर्भ सेवा: Ready Reference Service पुस्तकालय सेवा जो शीघ्रातिशीघ्र प्रदान की जाती है।

तृतीय दण्ड: Third Indentation सूची पत्र के बायें किनारे से समानान्तर काल्पनिक दूरी है जिसका प्रयोग सूचना अंकित कर नियमन के लिए किया जाता है।

तालिकाः Table लिखित सूचना प्रारूप।

तिथिः Date दिनांक/तारीख

तिथि पर्चीः Date Slip कागज की समान आकार की पर्ची जिसको पुस्तक संचरण विवरण के लिए ग्रन्थ के अन्त अथवा प्रारम्भ में प्रयोग किया जाता है।

तिथि मुद्रा/तिथि मुहरः Date Stamp मुद्रा जिसका प्रयोग पुस्तक संचरण सुनिश्चित करने के लिए किया जाता है।

तुलनात्मकताः Compatibility एक से अधिक विषयों की गुणवत्ता के आकलन की व्यवस्था है।

तैयारीः Preparation कार्य प्रारम्भ पूर्व के प्रयास।

द

दृश्य ग्रन्थ सहाय्यः Audio-visual Aids पुस्तक के अतिरिक्त सूचना संग्रह साधन जैसे टैप रिकार्ड/डिस्क फ्लोपी/फिल्मस्ट्रिप्स/दृश्य ग्रन्थ कैसिट्स इत्यादि।

दृश्य श्रव्य केन्द्रः Audio-visual centre दृश्य श्रव्य उपकरणों को प्रयोग करने का सार्वजनिक स्थान।

दशमलवः Decimal चिन्ह जिसकी स्थिति संख्या के गणितीय मूल्य को व्यक्त करती है। यह बिन्दु मात्र होता है।

दशमलव वर्गीकरणः Decimal Classification यह बहु प्रचलित वर्गीकरण प्रणाली है। जिसका आविर्भाव 1876 में मेलाविल ड्यूवे के प्रयास का परिणाम है। चार खण्ड वाला 20वाँ संशोधित संस्करण प्रकाशित हो चुका है। ज्ञान जगत् को दस भागों के निरन्तर क्रम में विभक्त कर सारणी बद्ध किया गया है।

दशमलव अंकनः Decimal Notation अंकन के दशमलव रूप में प्रयोग का प्रकार।

दशमलव अंक युक्तिः Decimal Fraction Device युक्ति जिसमें अंक दशमलव के अंश रूप में प्रयुक्त होते है। वर्गीकरण सारिणी में संख्या से पूर्व दशमलव चिन्ह का प्रयोग व्यक्त नहीं होता है।

दण्डः Indentation सूची पत्र के बायें किनारे से समानान्तर निश्चित दूरी पर व्यक्त रेखा जिनका प्रयोग सूचना पत्र पर नियंत्रण में होता है।

दरः Rate मूल्य।

दर सूचीः Rate List सूची जिसमें विभिन्न वस्तुओं का मूल्यांतर व्यक्त होता है।

दान अभिलेखः Donation Record दान प्राप्ति का अधिकारिक उल्लेख जो आवयश्कतानुसार धन तथा वस्तु के लिए अलग-2 भी हो सकता है।

द्वार-पंजीः Gate Register *देखिए* आगन्तुक पंजी।

दिन दर्शिकाः Calendar दैनिक तिथि सारिणी

द्वि-अंगीः Binary तकनीकी प्रयोग अथवा कम्प्यूटर अंक प्रणाली में जब 'एक' तथा 'शून्य' अंक का आधार रूप में प्रयोग किया जाय।

द्विअंगी संहिताः Binary Code संहिता जिसमें मात्र दो अंक 'एक' तथा 'शून्य' का प्रयोग हो।

द्विवार्षिकः Biennial प्रकाशन जिसकी आवृत्ति दो वर्ष के अन्तर से हो।

द्वितीय दण्डः Second Indentation सूची पत्र के बांयी ओर से समानान्तर निश्चित दूरी जो साधारणतः टाइप के दस अक्षर छोड़ कर होती है।

दीर्घ प्रलेखः Macro Document प्रलेख जिसमें विषय व्यापक विस्तार से विवेचित हो।

दीर्घाः Gallery स्थान जहां प्रदर्शनी आयोजित की जाती है।

दुर्लभ ग्रन्थः Rare Book ग्रन्थ एतिहासिक तथा विशेष महत्व का हो तथा मूल्य से उपलब्ध न हो।

दोष युक्त प्रतिः Defective Copy प्रति जिस के बाह्य आकार पृष्ठ, छपाई आदि में कोई त्रुटि हो।

देशीय समीपता का सिद्धांतः Principle of Spatial Contiguity पंक्ति एकल यदि निरन्तर स्थान पक्ष में उत्पन्न हो तो उनको समानान्तर सभीपता क्रम में रखना चाहिए।

देय तिथिः Due Date तिथि जो पुस्तक उधार अवधि समाप्त करती हो।

देखोः See सांकेतिक शब्द।

देयक पुस्तकः Bill Book पंजी जिसमें प्राप्त देयक विवरण अंकित होता है अथवा फाइल जिस में देयक प्रति संकलित होती है।

दैनिकः Daily प्रतिदिन प्रकाशित पत्र।

द्वैमासिकः Bi-monthly दो मास के अन्तराल से प्रकाशित पत्रिका।

ध

धर्मार्थ निधिः Endowment Fund धन जिसका प्रयोग दान रूप में होता है।

ध्यानाकर्षी शीर्षकः Catchword Title प्रभावोत्पादक अथवा कर्ण प्रिय शब्दों से बना शीर्षक और *देखिए* भ्रामक शीर्षक।

ध्वनि संचरणः Voice Mail ध्वनि की सहायता से सूचना संचरण की व्यवस्था जिसमें मशीन का प्रयोग होता है।

धर्म/गुण/लक्षणः Attribute पदार्थ/विचार/भाव के निहित गुण।

धार्मिक रचनाः Sacred Work/Sacred Book धर्म विशेष के अनुयायियों द्वारा अधिक प्रयुक्त धर्म रचना।

न

न्यायिक प्रतिवेदनः Law Report प्रतिवेदन जिसके द्वारा न्यायिक निर्णयों को सार्वजनिक किया जाता है।

नमूना पृष्ठः Sample Page चुना हुआ पृष्ठ जो कार्य योजना प्रारूप व्यक्त करे।

नव ग्रन्थः New Books पुस्तकालय द्वारा संकलित सामयिक ग्रन्थ अथवा प्रकाशक के आधुनिकतम प्रकाशन।

नवीनीकरणः Renewal उधार की अवधि का उसी ग्रन्थ के लिए विस्तार।

नया संस्करणः New Edition पूर्व प्रकाशित ग्रन्थ आवश्यक सुधार तथा आवश्यक सूचना समावेश के बाद पुनः मुद्रित हो।

नई ग्रन्थ मालाः New Series ग्रन्थमाला जिसकी प्रथम आवृति हो।

नये संग्रहः New Additions समय विशेष में पुस्तकालय अधिग्रहीत प्रलेख।

नष्ट कड़ीः Fused Link कड़ी जिसकी अन्तिम एकल संख्या किसी विचार अंश को व्यक्त नहीं करती क्योकि वह क्रमिक युक्ति, भौगोलिक युक्ति, विषय युक्ति, वर्णानुक्रम युक्ति, पक्ष युक्ति अथवा समूह युक्ति से प्राप्त की जाती है।

नाम-सूचीः Name Catalogue सूची जिसकी ग्रन्थ प्रविष्टि लेखकों/रचनाकारों के नाम के वर्णानुक्रम में व्यवस्थित होती है।

नाम संदर्भः Name Reference रचनाकार के एक से अधिक नाम प्रयोग होने की स्थिति में पूर्व नाम के संदर्भ में प्रविष्टि संयोजन होता है।

नाम/शीर्षकः Name/Heading शीर्षक जो किसी नाम/स्थान/संस्था आदि को स्पष्ट करे।

निकटस्थ ज्ञान जगतः Immediate Universe वर्गक्रम का वर्ग अपने पूर्व वर्ग से सम्बन्धित तथा समीप हो।

निकटतम वर्गीकरणः Close Classification वर्गीकरण जिसमें लघुतक वर्ग को स्वीकार किया जाय।

निकनेटः NICNET राष्ट्रीय सूचना केन्द्र, दिल्ली द्वारा विकसित कम्प्यूटर तन्त्र जिसका प्रयोग जिला केन्द्रों से सूचना संकलन में किया जा रहा है।

निर्गमः Charge संचरण ग्रन्थों का विवरण अथवा प्रयोग्ता को प्रलेख प्रदान करने की प्रक्रिया

निर्गम तरीकाः Charging System *देखिए* निर्गम प्रणाली।

निर्गम डैस्कः Charging Desk पुस्तकालय सेवा का केन्द्र जहाँ से पुस्तकालय ग्रन्थ संचरण होता है।

निर्गम प्रणालीः Charging Method तरीका जिसके प्रयोग से निर्गम सुलभ होता है।

निर्गम पर्चीः Charging Slip पर्ची जिस पर निर्गमित पुस्तक का विवरण अंकित कर स्वीकृति पत्र स्वरूप सुरक्षित रखली जाती है।

निर्गम ट्रेः Charging Tray ट्रे जिसका प्रयोग निर्गम अभिलेख संकलन के लिए होता है।

निर्देशकः Director पुस्तकालय/संस्था का सर्वोच्च सवैतनिक अधिकारी।

निर्धारित पाठ्यक्रमः Prescribed Curriculum पाठ्यक्रम जो किसी परीक्षा के लिए निश्चित होता है।

निर्गम तिथिः Date of Issue तिथि जिसको ग्रन्थ उधार दिया जाय।

निजी पुस्तकालयः Private Library निजी पुस्तकालय व्यक्ति विशेष द्वारा अथवा समूह द्वारा बिना किसी सरकारी सहायता के अपनी आवश्यकता के लिए होते है। अधिकारिक रूप से इनका प्रयोग जन साधारण के लिये अप्राप्य होता है।

निष्कासन पर्चीः Cancel Slip पर्ची जिसको संशोधन स्वीकृत के लिए प्रयोग किया जाता है।

निजी समयः Private Time समय जिसका प्रयोग व्यक्तिगत कार्यों के लिये किया जाता है।

निम्न कड़ीः Lower Link कड़ी क्रम के अन्त में प्राप्त कड़ी।

नियम/कानूनः Law/Rules सिद्धांत/निर्देश।

नियम पुस्तिकाः Manual *देखिए* हैन्ड-बुक।

नियतकालः Periodicity पत्रिका अंकों के बीच की अवधि।

नियमनः Rendering उपयोगी क्रम में रखने की कला।

नियमित अनुदानः Non-Plan Grants

निरन्तर खर्चाः Recurring Expenditure खर्चा जिसकी व्यवस्था प्रत्येक आनेवाले समय में होती है।

निरन्तर शिक्षाः Continuing Education शिक्षा जिससे विषय के सम सामायिक विकास से अवगत कराया जाता है।

निरावरणः Denudation स्थिति जिसमें विश्लेषण से विषय और एकल की बढ़ती कड़ियों के साथ निरन्तर विषय विस्तार कम तथा गुणता बढ़ती जाती है।

निरीक्षणः Checking ग्रन्थ के वाँछित आकार

गुणवत्ता की पूर्णता का अवलोकन।

निरीक्षण सूची: Check List सूची जिसका प्रयोग सत्यापन के लिए होता है।

क्रम प्रेषण: Routing पूर्व निर्धारित व्यवस्था के अन्तर्गत उपयोक्ताओं के मध्य ग्रन्थ संचरण।

निदेशिका: Directory पुस्तक जिसमें नामों से सम्बन्धित सूचना को वर्णानुक्रम में आबद्ध किया जाता है।

निवेश युक्तियाँ: Input Devices कम्प्यूटर में सूचना संचय की प्रक्रिया में प्रयुक्त मशीनी उपादान जैसे बोर्ड स्विच आदि।

निवेश तिथि: Input Date तिथि जिसको सूचना का निवेश किया जाय।

निवेश क्षेत्र: Input Area कम्प्यूटर स्मृति क्षमता भाग जो निवेश के लिए निर्धारित कर दिया जाय।

निर्बाध प्रवेश/खुला प्रवेश: Open Access पुस्तकालय जहाँ प्रयोक्ता सीधे बिना किसी बाधा के प्रलेखों तक पहुँच सके।

निष्कासन कारक: Elimination Factor/Omission Factor कुल चुने हुए ग्रन्थों में अनावश्यक ग्रन्थों का प्रतिशत।

निष्काशन पंजी: Withdrawals Register पंजी जिसमें पुस्तकालय संचय से अलग किए गए प्रलेखों का विवरण होता है।

निष्कासन: Weeding Out पुस्तकालय संकलन के प्रभावी प्रयोग के लिए अनावश्यक ग्रन्थों/ प्रलेखों को हटाने की प्रक्रिया।

निश्चय कारक शक्ति: Resolving Power ज्ञान जगत् से उत्पन्न वर्ग/ उपवर्ग को पहचान, वर्ग क्रम में रखने की क्षमता।

निश्चयकारक कारण: Resolution Factor चुने हुए प्रलेख/सूचना का सम्पूर्ण देखे गए सूचना संचय के साथ प्रतिशत।

निश्चितता की अभिधारणा: Postulate of Concreteness जब पाँच मूल-भूत श्रेणी पी. एम. ई. एस. टी को घटती निश्चितता के क्रम में संयोजित किया जाय।

निश्चित नाम समष्टि निकाय: Distinctive Name of Corporate Body व्यक्ति/स्थान के नाम से प्रारम्भ अथवा पहचानी जाने वाली संस्था।

निश्चित स्थिति: Fixed Location प्रलेखों के रखे जाने का निर्धारित स्थान।

निश्चित समय कम्प्यूटर: Real Time Computer कम्प्यूटर जो स्वचलित रूप से सूचना देता रहता है।

निहित विचार: Thought Content विषय वस्तु।

नीति: Policy दीर्घकालीन विकास से सम्बन्धित मार्गनिर्देश।

नीरस रचना: Pedestrian Work रचना जिसको किसी वर्ग में न स्वीकार किया जा सके।

नोड: Node सम्प्रेषण केन्द्र जहाँ से दूसरे केन्द्र के साथ सम्पर्क साधा जा सके।

प

पर्ची: Slip निश्चित आकार का कागज का टुकड़ा

पर्ची आकार सूची: Sheaf Form Catalogue *देखिए* खुली पृष्ठ आकार सूची।

पदार्थ: Matter मूलभूत पाँच श्रेणियों में से एक अभिधारणा है जिसकी पहचान डा. रंगनाथन ने वस्तु के रूप में की है।

पता: Address कम्प्यूटर संचित सूचना का पहचान प्रकार है।

पता पंजी: Address Register पंजी जिसका प्रयोग कम्प्यूटर व्यवस्था में सूचना संयोजन के लिए किया जाता है।

पदार्थ एकल (प्रथम चक्र): Matter Iso-

late Round (I) मूलभूत श्रेणी उर्जा से पहले के मूल श्रेणी पदार्थ की आवृत्ति।

पदानुक्रम अंकनः Hierarchical Notation अंकन जिसका प्रयोग एक ही पंक्ति/श्रेणी के दो शब्दों को क्रम प्रदान करता है।

पठन रुचि विकासः Promotion of Reading Habit पुस्तकालय प्रयोग सभ्यता विकास के लिए प्रयोक्ताओं में जागरुकता तथा पुस्तकालय सेवा में समुचित विकास का प्रयास है।

पठन कक्षः Reading Room पुस्तकालय का कक्ष जिसमें पाठक ग्रन्थों का प्रयोग करते हैं।

पठन सूचीः Reading List सूची जिससे पुस्तकालय प्रयोक्ता को उसके विषय से सम्बन्धित उपलब्ध प्रलेखों का ज्ञान होता है।

पठन सामग्रीः Reading Material देखिए पठन-सूची।

पढ़नाः Reading सूचना/ज्ञान संदोहन को प्रयास है।

पर्यायवाचीः Synonyms अनेक नाम/शब्द जब एक ही व्यक्ति/स्थान बोध को प्रयुक्त हों।

परख अवधिः Probation अवधि जिसमें परीक्षण किया जाय।

परसनल कम्प्यूटर (पी. सी.): Personal Computer कम कीमत तथा आधुनिक विकसित प्रकार के कम्प्यूटर हैं जिनका प्रयोग पुस्तकालयों में बढ़ता जा रहा है।

परामर्श मण्डलः Advisory Board नियमानुसार नियुक्त विद्वानों तथा विशेषज्ञों का समूह जो समय-2 पर पुस्तकालय सेवा सुधार के नियम सुझाता है।

परामर्श सेवाः Advisory Service देखिए पाठक सेवा।

परिगणनाः Enumeration भूत, भविष्य तथा प्रस्तावित भविष्य के विषयों को सूचीबद्ध किया जाय।

परिगणनात्मक पंक्ति एकलः Enumerated Array Isolate किसी पंक्ति के एकल जब परिगणना से उपलब्ध हो।

परिगणनात्मक युक्ति (अंकल तल): Emumeration Device (Notational Plane) युक्ति जिसमें क्रमशः अंक वर्ग अथवा एकल पक्ष में परिगणना की जाती है।

परिगणनात्मक युक्ति (विचार तल): Enumeration Device (Idea Plane) युक्ति जिसमें वर्गों, एकलों तथा पक्षों की पहचान की जाती है।

परिगणात्मक वर्गीकरणः Enumerative Classification वर्गीकरण जिसमें सम्भावित वर्गों को पहचान कर अंकन में परिवर्तित कर क्रमबद्ध कर दिया जाता है।

परिगणात्मक विशिष्ट एकलः Enumerated Special Isolate विशिष्ट एकल जिनकी पहचान कर क्रमबद्ध कर दिया गया हो।

परिगणनात्मक साधारण एकलः Enumerated Common Isolate साधारण एकल जो पहचान कर क्रमबद्ध कर दिया गया हो।

परिगणना का प्रनियमः Canon of Enumeration वर्गीकरण प्रणाली में प्रयुक्त शब्द अपने वर्ग में प्रयुक्त उपवर्गो के आधार पर हो, उनको अभिव्यक्त करे तथा सामान्य कड़ी के रूप में प्रयुक्त हो सकें।

परिपत्रः Circular Letter पत्र जिसका प्रयोग विभाग द्वारा किसी नीति/नीति परिवर्तन से अवगत कराने के लिए होता है।

परिवर्तित नामः Changed Names रचनाकार द्वारा विशेष कारणों से अलग-2 प्रयुक्त नाम जिन को स्पष्ट करने के लिए सूची कार टिप्पण का सहारा लेते हैं।

परिवर्तित शीर्षकः Transformed Title/Changed Title विश्लेषण के बाद पक्ष अभिधारणा के क्रम में सृजित शीर्षक। अथवा पूर्व प्रकाशित संस्करण प्रयुक्त शीर्षक से संशोधित अलग शीर्षक।

परिवर्णी शब्दः Acronym शब्द समूह के शब्दों के प्रथम अक्षर के योग से बना अक्षर समूह है जिससे संक्षिप्तता का निर्वाह होता है।

परिशिष्टः Appendix पूरक पाठ के रूप में ग्रन्थ के अन्त में स्पष्टीकरण के लिए दिया गया अंश।

परिशिष्ट/पूरकः Supplement खण्ड जो ग्रन्थ को पूर्णता प्रदान करता है।

परीक्षणः Testing परीक्षण क्रिया।

पहचान परक तत्वः Individualising Element शब्द जो किसी नाम के साथ जोड़ कर समानार्थी नाम की अलग पहचान व्यक्त करते हैं।

पहलूः Aspect *देखिए* पक्ष

पहुँचः Access सूचना प्राप्ति प्रक्रिया/विधि।

पहुँच केन्द्रः Access Point पूर्व निश्चित शीर्षक अथवा सूचना प्राप्त करने में प्रयुक्त शब्द/शब्द समूह।

पहुँच उपकरणः Access Tool उपकरण/प्रलेख जो पूर्व निर्धारित अथवा पहुँच केन्द्र रूप में सम्भावित शीर्षकों का संचय हो।

पहुँच समयः Access Time कम्प्यूटर संसाधित सूचना संचरण में सूचना के चुनाव तथा स्थानान्तरण के बीच लगने वाला समय।

पश्चः Back ग्रन्थ की जिल्द के दो पृष्ठों को जोड़ने वाला भाग इसका प्रयोग जिल्द साज शीर्षक तथा रचनाकार का नाम लिखने में करता है।

पश्चकारक सामान्य एकल विचारः Posteriorising Common Isolate Idea सामान्य एकल विचार जिसके प्रयोग से उत्पन्न वर्ग मुख्य वर्ग का अनुगामी हो जाता है।

पश्च किनाराः Back Margin यह ग्रन्थ के बांई ओर छोड़ा गया हाशिया है जिसका प्रयोग पृष्ठ सिलाई में किया जाता है।

पश्चमुखी तीरः Backward Arrow यह तीर चिन्ह है जिसका प्रयोग द्वि बिन्दु वर्गीकरण प्रणाली में हुआ है।

पश्च स्थानः Back Space जब टंकण युक्ति को उसके स्थान से पीछे ले जाकर प्रयोग किया जाय। यह प्रयोग कम्प्यूटर में व्यापक रूप से होता है।

पक्षः Phase/Facet मिश्रित वर्ग, मिश्रित एकल तथा मिश्रित पंक्ति एकल का हिस्सा होता है अथवा अभिलक्षण आधार पर प्राप्त विभाग है जिसको वर्गीकरण में प्रयोग किया जाता है।

पक्ष प्रथमः Phase I वर्गीकरण में पक्ष को जब पहली बार पहचाना जाय

पक्ष द्वितीयः Phase II वर्गीकरण में पक्ष जब प्रथम पक्ष के बाद पहचाना जाय।

पक्ष दूरस्थ बिन्दुः Facet Telescoping Point एकल परिगणना की दूरस्थ स्थिति जहाँ पक्ष परिवर्तन होता है।

पक्ष युक्तिः Phase Device युक्ति जिससे पक्ष संयोजन हो।

पक्ष युक्ति (अंकन तल): Phase Device (Notational Plane) युक्ति जिसमें पक्ष सम्बन्ध संकेत चिन्ह तथा अंक की सहायता से व्यक्त किया जाय।

पक्ष युक्ति (विचार तल): Phase Device (Idea Plane) युक्ति जिसमें

पक्ष सम्बन्ध तथा उसके प्रयोग पर विचार किया जाय।

पक्ष विश्लेषण: Facet Analysis विषय को उद्देश्य के अनुसार उसके पक्षो में विभक्त करने की प्रक्रिया है।

पक्ष सम्बन्ध: Phase Relation एक पक्ष दूसरे पक्ष के निकट हो सम्बन्ध व्यक्त करे।

पक्ष-सूत्र: Facet Formula अभिधारणा आधारित सूत्र जिससे विषय को उसके विकास क्रम तथा उपयोगी क्रम में सारणीबद्ध किया जाय।

पक्ष संश्लेषण: Facet Synthesis पक्षों के योग से वर्ग निर्माण की प्रक्रिया।

पत्र: Leaf/Card *देखिए* सूची पत्र।

पत्र अनुक्रमाणिका: Card Index अनुक्रमाणिका जिसमें पत्र प्रयुक्त हो।

पत्र आकार सूची: Card Form Catalogue *देखिए* पत्र सूची।

पत्रक: Leaflet लघु पुस्तिका।

पत्र निर्गम प्रणाली: Card Issue System निर्गम प्रणाली जिसमें पत्रों का प्रयोग है। जिनमें से एक पत्र प्रयोक्ता की पहचान तथा अन्य प्रलेख का प्रतिनिधित्व करता है। प्रलेख के परिचालन की अवस्था में दोनों पत्र आदान-प्रदान अनुभाग में रोक लिए जाते है।

पत्र-दराज: Card Drawer धातु/लकड़ी की छोटी पेटी जिसमें सूची पत्र क्रमशः रखे जाते हैं।

पत्र ट्रे: Card Tray ट्रे जिसमें पत्र क्रमशः संयोजित कर पत्र मंजूषा में रखे जाते हैं। अतः पत्र पेटिका का एकभाग है।

पत्र-पेटिका: Card Catalogue लकड़ी/स्टील की बनी सूची पत्र संग्राहक दराज इकाई है।

पत्र-सूची: Card Catalogue समान आकार के मानक पत्रों पर निश्चित नीति से बनी सूची।

पत्र-सूची-पेटिका: Card Catalogue Cabinet लकड़ी/स्टील की बनी सूची पत्र संयोजक अनेक दराजों के योग से बनी निश्चित आकार पेटी।

पत्रिका: Periodical निश्चित समयान्तर से निरन्तर प्रकाशित रचना है जो किसी सामान्य/विशेष उद्देश्य से जूड़ी होती है। रचनाकार प्रत्येक खण्ड में अलग-2 हो सकते हैं। पहले खण्ड की रचना संख्या अथवा रचनाकार से सामान्यतः सम्बन्ध नहीं होता तथा संकलित सूचना प्राथमिक एवम् समसामयिक आवश्यकता होती है।

पत्रिका अंक: Issue पत्रिका के निर्धारित खण्ड का एक भाग।

पत्रिका नियंत्रण: Serial Control

पत्रिका पूरक: Supplement to a Periodical पत्रिका अंक किसी विशेष अवसर अथवा कारण से अंक संख्या से अलग प्रकाशित हो।

पत्रिका प्रदर्शक रैक: Perodical Display Rack रैक जिस पर पत्रिकाओं को सार्वजनिक किया जाता है।

पत्रिका लेख: Periodical Article लेख जो किसी पत्रिका में प्रकाशित हुआ हो।

पत्रिका पेटी: Periodical Box बक्सा जिसमें अलग अंको को संकलित किया जाता है।

पत्रिका भण्डार: Periodical Stock स्थान जहाँ पर पत्रिका खण्डों को सुरक्षित क्रम में रखा जाता है।

पत्रिका स्टेन्ड: Periodical Stand विशेष उपकरण जिस पर पत्रिका प्रयोक्ता की सूचना तथा प्रयोग सुविधा को रख दी जाती है।

पत्रिका सूची: Serial Catalogue सूची

जिसमें क्रमिक प्रकाशनों की प्रविष्टि होती है।

प्रकार: Type गुण आधारित प्रकार।

प्रकाशक: Publisher व्यक्ति/संस्था जो प्रलेख प्रकाशन कार्य करते हैं।

प्रकाशक सूची: Publisher's Catalogue प्रकाशक प्रकाशनों की सूची जिसका प्रयोग व्यवसायिक प्रोत्साहन के लिए किया जाता है।

प्रकाशन: Publication रचना जो मुद्रित रूप में उपलब्ध हो।

प्रकाशन आदि विवरण: Imprint सूचीकरण में प्रकाशक का नाम, स्थान तथा वर्ष के विवरण को प्रकाशन आदि विवरण जाना जाता है।

प्रकाशन सूचीकरण: Cataloguing in Source/Pre-natal प्रकाशन पूर्व की केन्द्रीय सूचीकरण व्यवस्था है तथा मुद्रित प्रविष्टि ग्रन्थ के साथ उपलब्ध करा दी जाती है।

प्रकाशन तिथि: Date of Publication पुस्तक के प्रकाशित होने की तिथि। सामान्यतः प्रकाशन वर्ष अंकित होता है।

प्रकाशन विभाग: Publication Division पुस्तक प्रकाशन की सरकारी संस्था है हिन्दी अंग्रेजी तथा अन्य भारतीय भाषाओं की 6800 पुस्तक 1991 तक प्रकाशित कर चुकी है। देश की सभ्यता, संस्कृति तथा आदर्श पुरुषों की जीवनी विशेष रूप से प्रकाशित की गई है।

प्रकाशित मूलः Publication Price मूल्य जो प्रकाशन पर अंकित हो।

प्रकाशनावधि: Periodicity अवधि जिस में कोई प्रकाशन प्रकाशित होता है।

प्रशिक्षण: Training कार्य सम्पादन प्रकार जानने की क्रिया।

प्राक्कथन: Preface आमुख/भूमिका/प्रारम्भिक विवरण जिसमें रचना का उद्देश्य, प्राथमिकताएं तथा विधि आदि का उल्लेख होता है।

प्राकृतिक अभिलक्षण: Natural Characteristic वस्तुओं के वंशानुक्रम प्राप्त अभिलक्षण जिनसे उन्हें पहचाना जाता है।

प्राकृतिक सम्पदा: Natural Material वस्तु जो सीधे प्रकृति से प्राप्त हुई हो तथा अपने मूल रूप में हो।

प्रत्यावर्तन का सिद्धांत: Principle of Inversion सिद्धांत के अनुसार मुख्य वर्ग के पक्ष, पक्ष सूत्र के अनुसार प्रत्येक चक्र में ह्रासमान क्रम में व्यक्त होंगे।

प्रत्येक पुस्तक का पाठक: Every Book Has It's Reader डा. रंगनाथन द्वारा प्रतिपादित पुस्तकालय विज्ञान का तीसरा नियम है जिसके अनुसार प्रलेख व्यवस्था इस प्रकार की हो कि प्रत्येक पुस्तक की उपयोगिता सुनिश्चित की जा सके।

प्रत्येक पाठक की पुस्तक: Every Reader has his/her Book डा. रंगनाथन प्रतिपादित पुस्तकालय विज्ञान का दूसरा नियम जिसके अनुसार पुस्तक चयन में अथवा पुस्तकालय सेवा में प्रत्येक प्रयोक्ता की रुचि को स्थान अवश्य मिलना चाहिए।

प्रति: Copy प्रलेख की एक जिल्द।

प्रतिनिधि पुस्तक: Representative Book विषय विशेष के मूल विचारों से सम्बन्धित पुस्तक।

प्रति नियमन: Copy Filing प्रतियों को क्रमशः संयोजित करना।

प्रतिलिपि: Copy पूर्व लिखित प्रलेख की नकल।

प्रतिवेदन: Report किसी संस्था के समसामयिक कार्यकलापों के बारे में प्रकाशित प्राथमिक सूचना संचय।

प्रतिलिपि कारक: Photocopier प्रतिलिपिकरण मशीन।

प्रतिलिपिकरण सेवाः Reprography Service अभिलेख अथवा उसके किसी भाग की चित्र प्रतिलिपि मशीन की सहायता से उपलब्ध कराई जाय।

प्रतिलिपिकरणः Reprography मूल ग्रन्थ की नकल प्राप्त करना।

प्रतिबन्धित प्रकाशनः Restricted Document/Banned Book/Suspended Book/Discontinued Book प्रकाशन जिसका प्रसार किन्ही विशेष कारणों से रोक दिया गया हो। अथवा प्रकाशनोपरान्त उपलब्ध न हो सकती हो। इसका कारण पुस्तक की विवादित विषय वस्तु भी हो सकती है।

प्रतिस्थापन्नः Replacement ग्रन्थ की स्थानापन्न प्रति। इस व्यवस्था की आवश्यकता ग्रन्थ के अधिक प्रयोग अथवा अप्राप्य होने की स्थिति में होती है।

प्रतीक/चिन्हः Symbol वह आकार जिसकी सहायता से किसी भाव/विचार को एक से अधिक बार के प्रयोग में सुगमता से व्यक्त किया जा सके।

प्रतीक/करैक्टरः Character चिन्ह/संकेत/अक्षर/अंक जो सूचना का प्रतिनिधित्व करता है।

प्रतीकात्मक मैटा-भाषाः Symbolic Meta Language इस प्रकार की भाषा को निश्चित प्रतीक विकसित करते हैं।

प्रतीक्षा सूचीः Waiting List साधारणतः बहुचर्चित एवम् अधिक उपयोगी प्रेलख के अधिकाधिक संचरण के लिए प्रयोक्ताओं की आवश्यकता क्रम में सूची बनाई जाती है।

पृथक्करण/अलगकरणः Abstraction वर्गीकरण में समूह/वर्ग संयोजन क्रिया।

पृथक्करणः Individualization अनेक तत्त्वों को छटनी प्रक्रिया में अलग-2 करना।

प्रथम उर्ध्वस्थः First Vertical सूची पत्र की प्रथम समानान्तर रेखा जिसका प्रयोग शीर्षक पंक्ति के रूप में होता है। इस पर आहवान संख्या अथवा पहुँच शब्द लिखा जाता है।

प्रथम कड़ीः First Link शृंखला की निम्नतम स्तर कड़ी।

प्रथम दण्डः First Indentation सूची पत्र के बांई ओर से निश्चित दूरी लगभग आठ अक्षर पर प्रविष्टि सूचना नियमन के लिए प्रयुक्त रेखा।

प्रथम नामः First Name एक से अधिक नाम प्रयोग की स्थिति में रचनाकार पहचान नाम।

प्रथम प्रूफः First Proof जब किसी विषय को ग्रन्थ आकार देने के लिए प्रथमबार त्रुटि निरीक्षण किया जाता है।

प्रथम संस्करणः First Edition प्रलेख का संस्करण जिसकी प्रतियाँ साथ प्रकाशित हुई है तथा इससे पूर्व यह प्रकाशन नहीं हुआ है।

प्रदर्शक आधारः Display आधार/उपादान जहाँ पुस्तक प्रदर्शन को रखी जाती हैं।

प्रदर्शकः Display/Demonstration सूचना का दृश्यावलोकन।

प्रदर्शक बक्सः Display Case देखिए पुस्तक प्रदर्शक बक्स/प्रदर्शनी।

प्रदर्शक पट्टः Display Board पट्ट जिसका प्रयोग पुस्तकालय द्वारा प्राप्त नई अथवा विशेष विषय से जुड़ी सूचना/ ग्रन्थ प्रदर्शन के लिए किया जाता है।

प्रदर्शनीः Exhibition देखिए पुस्तक प्रदर्शनी।

प्रनियमः Canon डा. रंगनाथन द्वारा प्रतिपादित वर्गीकरण सहयोगी सूत्र हैं।

प्रणाली विश्लेषणः System Analysis.

प्रबन्धः Management निर्धारित उद्देश्य

प्राप्त करने की नीति, व्यवस्था तथा अनुसाशन से सम्बन्धित निर्णय प्राप्त करने की निरन्तर प्रक्रिया हैं सम्पूर्ण कार्य की सफलता का आघार हैं।

प्रबन्ध सूचना प्रणाली: Management Information System प्रबन्ध सूचना प्रणाली के प्रभावी प्रयोग की व्यवस्था।

प्रबर्धित वर्ग: Amplified Class विषय के निश्चित वर्ग विन्यास के समान छद्मनाम के योग से उत्पन्न वर्ग विन्यास।

प्रविष्टि नामकरण: Naming of Entry प्रथम पंक्ति पर अंकित संख्या अथवा शब्दों के आघार पर प्रविष्टि पहचान।

प्रवेश अभिलेख: Admission Record *देखिए* पंजीयन अभिलेख।

प्रवेश पर्ची: Admission Slip *देखिए* प्रवेश पत्र।

प्रमाणीकरण: Certification प्रमाण कार्य करने की क्रिया।

प्रवेश पत्र: Admission Card पुस्तकालय सुविधा प्राप्त करने के लिए दिया गया अधिकार/पहचान पत्र होता है इसको साघारणतः विभाग का प्रशासन विभाग प्रदान करता है।

प्रभावी पक्ष: Influencing Phase पक्ष सम्बन्धों में जो पक्ष अन्य पक्ष को प्रभावित करता है।

प्रभारी: Incharge *देखिए* पुस्तकाध्यक्ष।

प्रभावी कड़ी: Effective Link देखिए वांछित कड़ी।

प्रमाणिक प्रतिलिपि: Authenticated Copy रचना जिसका उत्तरदायित्व स्वीकृत किया जा चुका है।

प्रयोक्ता: User व्यक्ति जो पुस्तकालय संकलन प्रयोग करता है।

प्रयोक्ता सेवा: User Service सेवा जिसके द्वारा प्रयोक्ता को पुस्तकालय उपयोग के बारे में आवश्यक जानकारी दी जाए।

प्रयोक्ता रूपरेखा: User Profile प्रयोक्ता की रुचि उससे सम्बन्धित अन्य आवश्यक सूचना की अनुक्रमाणिका।

प्रलेखक: Documentalist अधिकारी जो प्रलेखन कार्य करता है।

प्रलेखन: Documentation सूचना संकलन, व्यवस्थापन जिससे शोधार्थी शीघ्राति-शीघ्र प्रयोग कर सके। उसके कार्य में सहयोग हो तथा सम्बन्धित विषय में व्यापक संदर्भ प्राप्त हो सके।

प्रलेखन कार्य: Documentation Work कार्य जिसके अन्तर्गत प्रलेखन-सूची आदि तैयार की जाती है।

प्रलेखन केन्द्र: Documentation Centre केन्द्र जहाँ सूचना एकत्रितकर आवश्यकतानुसार उपयोगी क्रम में संयोजित कर उपलब्ध करायी जाती है। सूचना सम्प्रेषण के लिए अनुक्रमाणिका/सारांश पत्रिका का प्रकाशन करते है।

प्रलेखन विज्ञान: Documentation Science प्रलेखन निरन्तर सूचना संकलन कर आवश्यकतानुसार वर्गीकरण कर विश्रिष्टि उपयोक्ता को उपलब्ध कराने का विज्ञान है। इसका उद्देश्य अल्प अवधि में समसामायिक सूचना को उपयोगी तक शीघ्रता से पहुँचाना है।

प्रलेखन सेवा: Documentation Service प्रलेखन सेवा, सूचना संकलन वर्गीकरण तथा सम्प्रेषण की समग्र प्रक्रिया है जिसका प्रयोग विशेष प्रयोक्ता करता हैं।

प्रलेखन सूची: Documentation List किसी विशेष प्रयोजन से पुस्तकों/लेखों की विषयवार सूची। साघारणतः वर्तमान में किसी विषय पर विचार तथा प्रतिक्रिया से अवगत कराना होता है।

प्रलेख विवरणिका: Documentation

Profile यह विवरणिका साधारणतः कम्प्यूटर पर ग्रन्थात्मक सूचना प्रदर्शन का आधार होती है।

प्रलेख प्रदाय सेवाः Document Delivery Service पुस्तकालय सेवा सहयोग से अन्य पुस्तकालयों के अभिलेख अथवा उनके आवश्यक अंश प्राप्त कर प्रयोक्ता को उपलब्ध कराये जाते हैं।

प्रलेख पूर्तिः Document Supply *देखिए* प्रलेख प्रदाय सेवा।

प्रविष्टिः Entry सूची में अंकित सूचना की इकाई अथवा पहचान है।

प्रविष्टि तत्वः Entry Element सूचना/सूचना समूह जिनको स्थान निर्धारण अथवा सकेतों के आधार पर अलग-2 पहचाना जा सके।

पृष्ठादि विवरण तथा प्रकाशनादि अनुभागः Collation and Imprint Section प्रविष्टि अनुभाग जिसमें आकार, खण्ड संख्या पृष्ठ, चित्र, मान चित्र, आदि की सूचना होती है।

प्रसार कार्यः Extension Work सूचना सेवा का व्यापक प्रसार।

प्रसार सेवाः Extension Service पुस्तकालय परिसर से बाहर सेवा विस्तार।

प्रारूपः Draft.

प्रविष्टि शब्दः Entry Word मुख्य शीर्षक/उपशीर्षक का आरम्भिक शब्द जिसके प्रयोग से प्रविष्टि को वर्णानुक्रम प्रदान किया जाता है।

प्रश्न चिन्हः Question Mark अपूर्णता द्योतक-चिन्ह।

प्रश्नावलीः Questionnaire प्रश्नों की सूची।

प्रश्नोत्तरमयः Catechism प्रश्नोंत्तर के रूप में कार्य।

प्रशिक्षितः Trained व्यक्ति विशेष जिसने प्रशिक्षण प्राप्त कर लिया है।

प्रशिक्षणार्थीः Trainee व्यक्ति विशेष जो प्रशिक्षण लेता है।

पृष्ठ संख्या रहित ग्रन्थः Unpaged Book ग्रन्थ जिसके पृष्ठों को क्रम संख्या न प्रदान की गई हो।

पृष्ठः Page ग्रन्थ प्रयुक्त पत्र का एक ओर का भाग।

पृष्ठांकनः Pagination क्रमिक पृष्ठ अंकित करने की प्रणाली।

पृष्ठादि विवरणः Collation प्रलेख विवरण जिसमें भौतिक आकार-खण्ड पृष्ठ संख्या, चित्र, चार्ट, आकार सम्बन्धी सूचना होती है।

प्राथमिक अभिलेखः Primary Document विषय पर मुख्य तथा प्रामाणिक सूचना संचय होता है।

प्राथमिक प्रकाशनः Primary Periodical *देखिए* प्राथमिक पत्रिका।

प्राथमिक पत्रिकाः Primary Journal पत्रिका जिसकी रचना प्रथम बार प्रकाशित हो अथवा शोध परिणाम व्यक्त करती हो।

प्राथमिक स्कूल पुस्तकालयः Primary School Library प्राथमिक स्कूल के बच्चों में पुस्तक प्रयोग की उपयोगिता बढ़ाने के लिए बच्चों की रुचि के संकलन प्रधानतः उपलब्ध होते है।

प्राप्ति ट्रेः Receipt Tray ट्रे जिसमें पुस्तकालय ग्रन्थ प्राप्ति-पत्र संकलित किए जाते हैं।

प्रामाणिकः Authentic जिसको अधिकारिक रूप से स्वीकृति प्राप्त हो।

प्राथमिक शृंखलाः Primary Chain वर्गीकरण से उत्पन्न शृंखला जो सीधे ज्ञान जगत से जुड़ी होती है।

प्राथमिक स्रोतः Primary Source रचना- कार द्वारा कथन के प्रमाण में पहले

से स्वीकृत तथ्यों का उल्लेख व्यक्त करने वाले ग्रन्थ।

प्रारंभिकः Starter चिन्ह जिसका प्रयोग विषय युक्ति की पहचान के लिए अंकों के पूर्व सदैव किया जाता है। जो अंको को एक इकाई रूप में प्रस्तुत कराता है।

प्रारम्भिक ग्रन्थ-सूचीः Retrospective Bibliography ग्रन्थ-सूची जिसमें नई रचनाओं के साथ पूर्व प्रकाशित रचनाएं भी रहती हैं।

प्रारम्भिक एकल विचारः Seminal Insolate Idea एकल जिसको एक ही एकल संख्या द्वारा वर्ग संख्या के साथ जोड़ा जाता है चाहे कितने ही अलग-2 शब्दों में व्यक्त हुआ हो।

प्रासंगिकता का प्रनियमः Canon of Context वर्गीकरण प्रणाली प्रयुक्त शब्द की पहचान श्रृंखला क्रम में प्रयुक्त अन्य शब्दों के अनुसंगिक हो।

प्रिय/समार्थित भाषाः Favoured Language भाषा जिसमें अधिकांशत पुस्तकालय संकलन हो।

पीठः Spine *देखिए* पश्च।

प्रोढ़ शिक्षाः Adult Education अधिक आयु के स्त्री-पुरुषों की शिक्षा व्यवस्था।

प्रेसीजः Precis परिवर्णी शब्द जिसका प्रयोग अनुक्रमणिका प्रकार के लिए होता है।

प्रैस चिन्हः Press Mark चिन्ह जिसके द्वारा ग्रन्थों में स्थिति बोध कराया जाया है।

पंक्ति क्रमः Ranking ज्ञान जगत से उत्पन्न विभाग, उपविभागों को श्रेणीबद्ध रखना।

पंक्ति अन्तर्वेधन केन्द्रः Array Telescoping Point अन्तर्वोधित पंक्ति एकल जिसका कम से कम एक उप एकल होता है।

पंक्ति एकल विचारः Array Isolate Idea वर्गीकरण वैचारिक इकाई जिसको परिगणित कर पंक्ति क्रम में रखा जाता है।

पंक्ति में समायोजन का प्रनियमः Canon of Hospitality in Array वर्ग निर्माण की प्रक्रिया में अन्त तक नई वर्ग संख्या को उपयुक्त स्थान पर बिना किसी बाधा स्वीकृत किया जाय।

पंक्ति में समायोजनः Hospitality in Array *देखिए* पंक्ति में समायोजन का प्रनियम।

पंक्ति क्रमः Order of an Array ज्ञान जगत के अनेक अभिलक्षणों के आधार पर वर्ग पंक्ति समूह बनाना।

पंजी/रजिस्टरः Register संग्रह/अंकित विवरण।

पंजीकरणः Registration पुस्तकालय सदस्यता प्रदान करना।

पंजीकरण पत्र/प्रपत्रः Registration Card /Form पुस्तकालय सदस्यता पत्र।

पंजी निर्गम प्रणालीः Register Issue System निर्गम का प्राचीनतम प्रकार है। जिसमें पंजी के पृष्ठ प्रयोक्ता को निर्धारित कर दिए जाते हैं तथा निर्गम की स्थिति में ग्रन्थ से सम्बन्धित सूचना निर्धारित पृष्ठ पर अंकित करने के बाद प्रयोक्ता से प्राप्ति हस्ताक्षर करा लिये जाते हैं।

पंजी आकार सूचीः Register Form Catalogue यह सूची प्रकार है जिसमें पंजी में सूची प्रविष्टि वर्णक्रम में अंकित की जाती है। अलग-2 विषयों के लिए अलग-2 पंजी का भी प्रयोग किया जा सकता है।

पंजीयन पत्रः Registration Card पत्र जिसमें सदस्य संख्या तथा सदस्य का नाम होता हैं। यह पुस्तकालय प्रयोग के लिए प्रयोक्ता पहचान एवम् अधिकार पत्र होता है।

पार्चमेन्टः Parchment संसाधित चमड़ा जिसको लिखने के लिए प्रयोग किया जाता

है।

पाठक/प्रयोक्ता: Reader/User/ Clientele व्यक्ति जो पुस्तकालय प्रयोग करता है।

पाठक परामर्श दात्री सेवा: Reader's Advisory Service सेवा जिसके द्वारा पाठकों को पुस्तकालय संकलन के प्रभावी प्रयोग की जानकारी दी जाती है।

पाठक का समय बचाओं: Save the Time of the Reader डा. रंगनाथन द्वारा प्रतिपादित पुस्तकालय विज्ञान का चौथा नियम है जिसका उद्देश्य पुस्तकालय सेवा, कार्यक्षमता विकास तथा पुस्तकालय के प्रति पाठको में झुकाव पैदा करना है।

पाठक पत्र: Reader's Ticket देखिए पुस्तकालय टिकिट/पुस्तकालय पत्र।

पाठ्यपुस्तक पुस्तकालय: Text Book Library इस प्रकार के पुस्तकालय विद्यालय/ महाविद्यालय स्तर पर हैं जिनसे विशेष वर्ग के विद्यार्थियों की सहायतार्थ सम्पूर्ण सत्र के लिए पाठ्य पुस्तकें उपलब्ध कराई जाती हैं।

पाठक-मुद्रक: Reader-Printer स्वचालित मशीन जिससे पाठक रचना का वांछित अंश प्रतिलिपि रूप में उपलब्ध कर सकता है/ देख सकता है।

पिछला अंक: Back Issue/Back Number देखिए पिछली फाइल/पिछली संख्या।

पिछला शीर्षक: Back Title शीर्षक जो कि पुस्तक के पीछे आवरण को जोड़ने वाली पीठ पर अंकित होता है।

पिछली फाइल: Back File पत्रिका के पिछले अंक अथवा फाइल का पूर्वा पर सम्बन्ध रखने वाली सूचना।

पी एम ई एस टी: PMEST डा. रंगनाथन के पाँच मूल श्रेणि अभिधारणा शब्दों पर आधारित परिवर्णी शब्द हैं जिसमें व्यक्तित्व, पदार्थ, उर्जा, स्थान तथा समय को क्रमशः रखा गया है।

पुनः खरीद पुस्तक: Second-hand book पुस्तक प्रयोग के बाद पुनः बेची हो/खरीदी जाय।

पुनः प्राप्तिः Retrieval सूचना प्राप्त करने की प्रक्रिया।

पुनः निर्गमः Re-issue देखिए नवीनीकरण।

पुनर्बन्धन: Rebinding पुनः बनाई गई जिल्द।

पुनः बुलाना: Recall अधिकाधिक प्रयोग के लिए पुस्तकालय ग्रन्थ प्रयोक्ता से प्राप्त कर पुनः सार्वजनिक करने की प्रक्रिया।

पुनर्मुद्रण: Reprint रचना को बिना किसी परिवर्तन/शंसोधन के फिर से मुद्रित किया जाय।

पुस्तक: Book पुस्तक/ग्रन्थ/प्रलेख/अभिलेख लिखा अथवा छपा हुआ सूचना संग्रह है जो विचार का प्रतिपादन/विस्तार होता है। आकार वैभिन्य तथा अनेक खण्ड, उपखण्ड हो सकते है।

पुस्तक पत्र: Book Card पत्र पर पुस्तक से सम्बन्धित आवश्यक चुनी हुई सूचना अंकित होती है। जो पुस्तक के साथ ही रहता है। पुस्तक निर्गम की स्थिति में पुस्तक का प्रतिनिधित्व करता है।

पुस्तक आवरण: Book Jacket आवरण पुस्तक को सुरक्षा तथा पुस्तक और रचनाकार के बारे में संक्षिप्त विवरण देता है।

पुस्तक उपयोग के लिए है: Books are for Use डा. रंगनाथन द्वारा प्रतिपादित पुस्तकालय विज्ञान का प्रथम नियम है जिसके अनुसार पुस्तकें भविष्य के लिए सुरक्षित रखने की अपेक्षा वर्तमान के लिए अधिक आवश्यक है अतः उनके उपयोग को ध्यान में रखकर ही पुस्तकालय संचय, संयोजन, संचरण की व्यवस्था होनी चाहिए।

पुस्तक क्रय केन्द्रः Book Stall स्थान जहाँ पुस्तक व्यापार हो।

पुस्तक क्रयादेश सूचीः Book Order List चुनी हुई पुस्तकों की सूची जिससे पुस्तकें खरीदी जायें।

पुस्तक का आकारः Bulk of a Book पुस्तक का स्वरूप जिसका निर्धारण उसकी चौड़ाई, लम्बाई तथा मौटाई से होता है।

पुस्तक क्रम व्यवस्थाः Shelving पुस्तकों को वर्गीकरण प्रणाली के अनुसार उचित क्रम प्रदान करना।

पुस्तक-कोशः Book Fund धन राशि जिससे पुस्तकें खरीदी जाती हैं।

पुस्तक के अतिरिक्त समानः Non-book Material सूचना सम्प्रेषण तथा संचय के आधुनिक इलैक्ट्रोनिक साज समान जिनका प्रयोग सूचना सम्प्रेषण के लिये मशीन की सहायता से होता हैं।

पुस्तक घाटाः Loss of Books पुस्तक सेवा प्रक्रिया में पुस्तक अप्राप्य हो जाए।

पुस्तक चयनः Book Selection प्रक्रिया जिससे पुस्तकालय के उद्देश्य अनुसार पुस्तक चयन किया जाए।

पुस्तक चयन पत्रः Book Selection Card प्रत्येक पुस्तक के लिए एक पत्र संक्षिप्त सूचना अंकन से बनाया जाता है। जो पुस्तक का प्रतिनिधित्व करता है तथा चयन निर्णय के लिये उपयोग किया जाता है।

पुस्तक ट्रेः Book Tray ट्रे जो पुस्तक रखने में प्रयुक्त होती है।

पुस्तक पश्च आवरणः Back Cover ग्रन्थ के अन्तिम पृष्ठ का आवरण जिस पर कभी-2 लेखक के बारे में संक्षिप्त विवरण रहता है।

पुस्तक प्रदर्शकः Book Stand उपादान जो पुस्तक प्रदर्शित करने में प्रयुक्त होता है।

पुस्तक प्रदर्शनीः Book Exhibition उपयोगिता स्पष्ट करने/ध्यानाकर्षण के लिए पुस्तकें सार्वजनिक की जायें।

पुस्तक मेलाः Book Fair अधिकाधिक ग्राहक आकर्षित करने का विक्रेताओं का प्रयास तथा पुस्तक प्रेमीयों को उनकी रुचि की पुस्तकों से एक साथ मिलाने की योजना का परिणाम है। मेला आयोजन शहर, प्रान्त, देश अथवा अन्तर्राष्ट्रीय स्तर पर होते रहते हैं।

पुस्तक पर्चीः Book Slip पर्ची जिस पर ग्रन्थात्मक सूचना आवश्यकतानुसार अंकित की जाती है।

पुस्तक पॉकेट/पुस्तक जेबः Book Pocket पुस्तक पत्र संरक्षण के लिए पुस्तक की जिल्द के अन्दर की ओर कागज की बनी होती है।

पुस्तक बाजारः Book Market स्थान जहाँ पर पुस्तक क्रय विक्रय की सुविधा उपलब्ध हो।

पुस्तक बैंकः Book Bank देखिए पाठ्य पुस्तक पुस्तकालय।

पुस्तक भण्डारः Stacks/Book Stock स्थान जहाँ पुस्तकें संग्रहीत की जाएं।

पुस्तक भण्डार कक्षः Stock Room देखिए पुस्तक भण्डार।

पुस्तक व्यवसायः Book Trade पुस्तक उत्पादन, वितरण तथा खरीदने बेचने का कार्य।

पुस्तक वार्ताः Book Talk पुस्तकों से सम्बन्धित बातचीत।

पुस्तक वाहकः Book Lifter व्यक्ति जो पुस्तकों को एक स्थान से दूसरे स्थान पर पहुँचाता है।

पुस्तक वाहनः Book Trolly पहिये लगी दो या तीन रैक होती हैं जिन पर रखकर

पुस्तकें स्थानान्तरित की जाती हैं।

पुस्तक विक्रेताः Book Seller व्यक्ति जो पुस्तक व्यापार करता है।

पुस्तक समीक्षाः Book Review पुस्तक की विषय वस्तु का मूल्यांकन करने की क्रिया।

पुस्तक सूचीः Book Catalogue सूची जिसमें पुस्तक सम्बन्धी सूचना होती है।

पुस्तक संख्याः Book Number संख्या जिसको अनेक अंक/चिन्ह और दोनों ही के योग से पुस्तक को अन्य पुस्तकों के मध्य पहचान देने के लिए प्रयोग किया जाता है।

पुस्तक संख्या का प्रनियमः Canon of Book Number एक ही वर्ग के ग्रन्थ की अलग-2 पहचान के लिए वर्गीकरण में पुस्तक संख्या का योग होता है।

पुस्तक सग्रहः Book Collection *देखिए* पुस्तक भण्डार।

पुस्तक संग्रह केन्द्रः Book Deposit Centre स्थान जहाँ पुस्तकों का संयच किया जाए।

पुस्तक संयोजकः Book Supporter एल अथवा टी के आकार का स्टील का टुकडा पुस्तकों को इच्छित स्थिति में रखने के लिये प्रयोग में लाया जाता है।

पुस्तक संसाघन केन्द्रः Book Processing Centre स्थान जहाँ पर पुस्तकों का वर्गीकरण/सूचीकरण आदि होता है।

पुस्तकालयः Library परम्परात्मक रूप में हमारी संस्कृति की धरोहर है। वही आधुनिक अर्थ में सम्पूर्ण भानवता विकास के सूचना सम्प्रेषण केन्द्र है।

पुस्तकाध्यक्ष/ पुस्तकालयाध्यक्षः Librarian व्यक्ति जिसका उत्तरदायित्व पुस्तकालय व्यवस्था तथा सूचना सेवा प्रदान करना है।

पुस्तकालयाध्यक्षताः Librarianship पुस्तकालय सेवाओं का सम्पादन।

पुस्तकालय अधिकारीः Library Authority पुस्तकालय संचालन के अधिकार पालन का उत्तरदायित्व है *और देखिए* पुस्तकालयाध्यक्ष।

पुस्तकालय आय-व्ययः Library Accounts विवरण जिससे पुस्तकालय की आय-व्यय का उल्लेख हो।

पुस्तकालय अधिनियमः Library Act अधिनियम जिससे पुस्तकालय विकास सुनिश्चित हो।

पुस्तकालय कार्यकलापः Library Activities *देखिए* पुस्तकालय सेवायें।

पुस्तकालय अभिलेखः Library Document पुस्तकालय सेवा प्रदान करने के लिए अनेक अभिलेख जैसे अवाप्ति पंजी, निर्गम पंजी तथा धन प्राप्ति पुस्तक आदि-2 प्रयोग होते हैं। और देखिए अभिलेख/प्रलेख/ग्रन्थ।

पुस्तकालय अर्थ व्यवस्थाः Library Economy आय व्यय का विवरण।

पुस्तकालय उपकरः Library Cess नियमानुसार पुस्तकालय सेवा के लिए प्रशासन द्वारा प्राप्त किया गया धन।

पुस्तकालय उपकरणः Library Equipment *देखिए* उपकरण।

पुस्तकालय एक विकसित संस्था हैः Library is a growing organism पुस्तकालय विज्ञान का पाँचवां नियम है जिसके अनुसार पुस्तकालय अवयव पुस्तक, कर्मचारी, पाठक तथा सेवा प्रकार सभी निरन्तर विकसित तथा वृद्धिशील है।

पुस्तकालय कर्मचारीः Library Staff/ Library Worker कर्मचारी जिनका सम्बन्ध पुस्तकालय सेवा से होता है।

पुस्तकालय कार्यः Library function सूचना संचय, संसाघन एवम् सम्प्रेषण सम्बन्धी

कार्य।

पुस्तकालय कोशः Library Fund धन जिसका प्रयोग पुस्तकालय सेवा प्रसार के लिए हो।

पुस्तकालय छूटः Library Discount छूट जो पुस्तक खरीद पर दी जाती है।

पुस्तकालय जिल्दसाजीः Library Binding *देखिए* जिल्द-साजी।

पुस्तकालय टिकिट/पुस्तकालय पत्रः Library Ticket पुस्तकालय द्वारा दिया गया अधिकार पत्र जिससे ग्रन्थ उधार प्राप्त किये जा सकते हैं *और देखिए* पाठक पत्र।

पुस्तकालय तन्त्रः Library Network जब एक से अधिक पुस्तकालय/सूचना केन्द्रों को तकनीकी व्यवस्था में जोड़कर उनका कार्य क्षेत्र/संसाधन प्रयोग बढ़ा दिया जाय तो तन्त्र बन जाता है।

पुस्तकालय नियमः Library Rules पुस्तकालय सेवा व्यवस्था के प्रभावी प्रयोग के लिए निर्देश।

पुस्तकालय नियोजनः Library Planning भविष्य की कार्य प्रणाली का प्रारूप।

पुस्तकालय नीतिः Library Policy नीति जिसको पुस्तकालय संचालन के लिए निर्धारित किया जाए।

पुस्तकालय लेखन प्रकारः Library Hand एक विशेष स्पष्ट लेखन प्रकार जिसको साधारणतः सूची पत्र अंकित करने में प्रयोग किया जाता है।

पुस्तकालय प्रशासनः Library Administration व्यवस्था प्रक्रिया जिससे पुस्तकालय संसाधनों का प्रभावी प्रयोग किया जाता है।

पुस्तकालय प्रशिक्षुः Apprentice in Library पुस्तकालय सेवा उत्तरदायित्व वहन करने से पहले प्रयोगात्मक/तकनीकी कार्य का ज्ञान प्राप्त करना।

पुस्तकालय व्ययः Library Expenditure व्यय जिससे सूचना सेवा प्रदान जाती है।

पुस्तकालय बजटः Library Budget *देखिए* बजट।

पुस्तकालय भवन तथा साजसामानः Library Building and Furniture.

पुस्तकालय वर्गीकरणः Library Classification पुस्तकालय संकलन का विषयानुसार प्रस्तुतीकरण/वर्गीकरण।

पुस्तकालय विकासः Library Extension प्रयास जिससे पुस्तकालय उपयोगिता का विकास हो।

पुस्तकालय वित्तः Library Finance *देखिए* पुस्तकालय कोश।

पुस्तकालय एवम् सूचना विज्ञान स्नातकः Bachelor in Library and Information Science (BLISc) पुस्तकालय तथा सूचना विज्ञान की स्नातक उपाधि।

पुस्तकालय विवरणिकाः Library Brochure विवरणिका जिसमें पुस्तकालय के वर्तमान क्रिया-कलापों का उल्लेख हो।

पुस्तकालय विज्ञानः Library Science *देखिए* पुस्तकालय एवम् सूचना विज्ञान।

पुस्तकालय विज्ञान का स्नातकः Bachelor in Library Science (B.Lib.) पुस्तकालय विज्ञान में स्नातक उपाधि *और देखिए* पुस्तकालय एवम् सूचना विज्ञान।

पुस्तकालय विज्ञान के नियमः Laws of Library Science *देखिए* पुस्तकालय विज्ञान के पाँच नियम।

पुस्तकालय विज्ञान के पाँच नियमः Five Laws of Library Science डा. रंगनाथन ने पुस्तकालय विज्ञान के सम्यक विकास के लिए निम्न पाँच नियम सुझाये

हैं।

(1) पुस्तकें उपयोग के लिए हैं।
(2) प्रत्येक प्रयोक्ता को पुस्तक मिलें।
(3) प्रत्येक पुस्तक को प्रयोक्ता मिलें।
(4) प्रयोक्ता का समय बचाओ।
(5) पुस्तकालय विकासशील संस्था है।

पुस्तकालय विज्ञानी शिक्षा: Education for Librarianship *देखिए* पुस्तकालय विज्ञान शिक्षा।

पुस्तकालय सलाहाकार समिति: Library Advisory Committee पुस्तकालय के निश्चित उद्देश्य प्राप्त करने को नीति निर्धारण कर सेवा सुधार के सुझाव देती है। इसकी सदस्य संख्या संस्थागत नियमों के अनुसार होती है।

पुस्तकालय विशेष का संकलन: Library Holdings *देखिए* पुस्तकालय संकलन/संकलन।

पुस्तकालय शुल्क: Library Fees सेवा व्यवस्था प्रयोग के बदले लिया गया आंशिक धन।

पुस्तकालय स्कूल: Library School संस्था जहाँ पुस्तकालय विज्ञान की पढ़ाई होती है।

पुस्तकालय स्वचालन: Library Automation पुस्तकालय सेवा व्यवस्था में स्वचालित मशीन जैसे कम्प्यूटर का प्रयोग।

पुस्तकालय स्थिति: Library Location पुस्तकालय स्थान जहाँ वह स्थित है।

पुस्तकालय समय: Library Hours पुस्तकालय सेवा अवधि।

पुस्तकालय समिति: Library Committee *देखिए* सलाहाकार समिति।

सलाहाकार समिति: Advisory Committee *देखिए* पुस्तकालय सलाहकार समिति

पुस्तकालय सहयोग: Library Co-operation व्यवस्था जिससे एक से अधिक पुस्तकालय अपने संसाधन/तकनीकी ज्ञान का प्रयोग मिलकर एक दूसरे के लिए करते है।

पुस्तकालय-सूची: Library Catalogue किसी पुस्तकालय के संकलन का विवरण प्रस्तुत करती है। इसका आकार पंजी/पत्र रूप में हो सकता है इसमें पुस्तकालय में उपलब्ध ग्रन्थों की सूचना निर्धारित प्रारूप में रहती है।

पुस्तकालय सूची के कार्य: Functions of the Catalogue प्रमुख रूप से किसी विषय, लेखक तथा पुस्तक संस्करण के बारे में जाना जा सकता है तथा संकलित पुस्तक की उपलब्धता का ज्ञान होता है।

पुस्तकालय सेवा: Library Service सेवा जिससे सूचना संकलन तथा सम्प्रेषण सुचारु किया जाता है।

पुस्तकालय संकलन: Library Holdings *देखिए* पुस्तकालय संग्रह।

पुस्तकालय संस्करण: Library Edition संस्करण जिसका उत्पादन पुस्तकालय प्रयोग तथा दीर्घकालीन रख रखाव को ध्यान में रख कर किया गया हो। साधारणत: इसकी जिल्द मोटे मजबूत आवरण की होती है।

पुस्तकालय संगठन: Library Organisation पुस्तकालय के निर्धारित लक्ष प्राप्त करने की व्यवस्था।

पुस्तकालय संग्रह: Library Collection *देखिए* पुस्तकालय सामग्री/पुस्तकालय संसाधन/पुस्तकालय संकलन/पुस्तकालय संग्रह/संग्रह।

पुस्तकालय संसाधन: Library Resources प्रमुख रूप से वित्त, संकलन तथा मानव शक्ति होते हैं।

पुस्तकालय संघ: Library Associations पुस्तकालय कर्मचारियों के सामूहिक

प्रयास विकास के लिए व्यवसायिक अनुभव का आदान-प्रदान करते हैं। इस प्रकार के अनेक संघ राष्ट्रीय तथा प्रादेशिक स्तर पर कार्यरत है।

पुस्तकालय संघों का अन्तर्राष्ट्रीय फैडरेशन (इफ्ला): International Federation of Library Associations पुस्तकालय संघों का अन्तर्राष्ट्रीय संघ है जो कि विश्व स्तर पर पुस्तकालय एवम् सूचना विज्ञान के विकास के कार्यक्रम चलाता है।

पुस्तिका: Manual/Hand Book विषय के समझने के लिए संक्षिप्त विशेष पुस्तक।

पूर्तिकर प्रति: Back up Copy प्रति जो कि कम्प्यूटर प्रयोग की स्थिति में सुरक्षा रूप में सामान्य प्रति के अतिरिक्त होती है।

पूर्तिकर: Back up कम्प्यूटर व्यवस्था में सुरक्षा तथा तकनीकी अव्यवस्था से बचने के लिए दुहरी सूचना संकलन प्रणाली।

पूर्ति-पत्र: Continued Card पत्र जो सूची पत्र प्रविष्टि को पूर्णता प्रदान करता है।

पूर्व उपविभाजन: Anterior Sub-division विषय का उपवर्ग जो वर्गीकरण क्रम में मुख्य विषय पूर्व रखा जाए।

पूर्ण किया: Update मूल सूचना संकलन में वर्तमान सूचना का समावेश।

पूर्णता का प्रनियम: Canon of Exhaustiveness ज्ञान जगत से उत्पन्न वर्ग तथा उनसे उत्पन्न वर्ग पंक्ति पूर्ण होनी चाहिए।

पूर्ण प्रविष्टि: Closed Entry प्रविष्टि जिसमें निर्धारित ग्रन्थ से सम्बन्धित सूचना व्यवस्थितक्रम में अंकित हो और सूचना सभाहित करने का प्रावधान न हो।

पूर्ण बिन्दु: Full Point वाक्य के अन्त में सम्पूर्णता व्यक्त करने वाला विराम चिन्ह।

पूर्ण शीर्षक: Full Title *देखिए* मुख्य शीर्षक।

पूर्ण शृंखला: Complete Chain शृंखला जिसकी प्रथम कड़ी ज्ञान जगत से तो अन्तिम कड़ी उत्पन्न वर्ग से जुड़ी हो।

पूरक पत्र: Continuation Card/ Continued Card मुख्य पत्र का विस्तार पत्र है जो प्रविष्टि को पूर्णता प्रदान करता है। *और देखिए* पूर्ति पत्र।

पूरक पक्ष: Supplement Facet प्रलेख संख्या का भाग जो कि संख्या का पूरक हो।

पूरक संख्या: Supplement Number ग्रन्थ/प्रलेख संख्या का भाग जिसके द्वारा पूरक की पहचान खण्ड तथा अन्य पूरकों के मध्य निश्चित होती है।

पूर्वकारक अंक: Anteriorising Digit अंक जिसके मुख्य वर्ग के अन्त में प्रयोग करने से उत्पन्न वर्ग मुख्य वर्ग का अनुगामी होता है।

पूर्वकारक सामान्य एकल: Anteriorising Common Isolate पूर्व कारक सामान्य एकल मुख्य वर्ग से सीधे जुड़ते हैं बीच में किसी चिन्ह का प्रयोग नहीं होता। इस प्रयोग से सृजित वर्ग में मुख्य विषय को समझने में सहयोगी ग्रन्थ रखे जाते हैं।

पूर्वकारक सामान्य एकल विचार: Anteriorising Common Isolate Idea *देखिए* पूर्वकारक सामान्य एकल।

पूर्व दत्त मूल्य प्रकाशन: Prepaid Publication प्रकाशन जिसको प्राप्त करने से पूर्व मूल्य आग्रिम चुका दिया जाता है।

पूर्व संयोजक अनुक्रमणिका प्रणाली: Post Coordinate Indexing System अनुक्रमणिका जिसमें प्रविष्टि सामान्यक्रम में रहती है जिसके सम्भावित योग से प्रयोक्ता विषय से परिचित होता है।

पूर्वाग्रह सम्बन्धः Bias Relation पक्ष सम्बन्ध को जानने के लिए प्रथम पक्ष प्रयास के आधार पर ही सम्बन्ध को जाना जाए।

पेटेण्ट/संरक्षक अधिकारः Patent प्रकाशन जिसमें अप्रकाशित प्रमाणित सरकारी शोध परिणाम जो अन्यत्र इस रूप में उपलब्ध नहीं का समावेश होता है।

पेपीरसः Papyrus वृक्ष विशेष के तने का पत्र जिसका प्राचीन काल में प्रयोग कागज के रूप में होता रहा है।

फ

फाइलः File व्यवस्थित सूचना संग्रह जिसको एक इकाई मान लिया जाए।

फाइल करने की मंजूषाः Filing Cabinet स्टील/लकड़ी की विशेष प्रकार की अलमारी जिसमें फाइल क्रमशः रखी जाती है।

फारमेट/आकारः Format सूचना अथवा सूचना प्रकार का आकार।

फिल्म पुस्तकालयः Film Library पुस्तकालय जिसका संकलन फिल्मों पर आधारित होता है। सूचना आधुनिक तकनीकी सहयोग से व्यवस्थित/सम्प्रेषित की जाती है।

फुलस्कैपः Foolscap मानक आकार का कागज।

फोरट्रानः FORTRAN कम्प्यूटर प्रयुक्त प्रोगाम भाषा प्रकार।

ब

बजट आवण्टन रजिस्टर/पंजीः Budget Allocation Register पंजी जिसमें वित्त सम्बन्धी विवरण अंकित किया जाता है।

बाल पुस्तकालयः Children's Library पुस्तकालय जिसका संकलन बच्चों की आवश्यकतानुसार होता है।

बढ़ती जटिलता का सिद्धांतः Principle of Increasing Complexity यदि एक दुरुहता अलग-अलग स्तर की हो तो यह ठीक होगा कि बढ़ती दुरुहता के क्रम में वर्गों को सारिणी में रखा जाए।

बहु खण्डीय पुस्तकः Multi-volumed Book पुस्तक जिसकी सम्पूर्णता अनेक खण्डों के योग से होती है। व्यापक विषय को अनेक खण्डों में अभिव्यक्ति मिलती है।

बढ़ती मात्रा का सिद्धांतः Principle of Increasing Quantity वर्गीकरण का आधार परिमाण हो तो एकल का क्रम परिमाण से प्रयुक्त अभिलक्षणों के अनुसार होना चाहिए।

बजट/आय व्ययः Budget भविष्य की प्रस्तावित योजना पूर्ति के लिए आय-व्यय का विवरण।

बम्बई पुस्तकालय संघः Bombay Library Association इस संघ की स्थापना 1944 में पुस्तकालय सेवा तथा व्यवसाय बम्बई शहर में विकसित करने को हुई थी।

वर्ष संख्याः Year Number प्रलेख के प्रकाशन वर्ष की अनुवाद सूचक संख्या।

वर्ष पक्षः Year Facet ग्रन्थ संख्या का अंश जिससे प्रकाशन वर्ष संख्या व्यक्त होती है।

बृहत प्रलेखः Macro Document देखिए बृहत विचार।

बृहत विचारः Macro Thought व्यापक विचार/ विषय।

बाइटः Bite सूचना की इकाई है।

वांछित क्रम का प्रनियमः Canon of Favoured Sequence वर्ग क्रम स्वाभाविकता के साथ, वर्गीकरण प्रणाली के अनुसार प्रोक्ता की सुविधानुसार वर्गक्रम रखना चाहिए।

वाधित अलमारीः Closed Shelves *देखिए* बाधित प्रवेश।

बाधित प्रवेशः Closed Access प्रयोक्ता को चुनाव के लिए पुस्तक सम्पर्क की स्वतन्त्रता नहीं होती है।

बाह्य परिधीयः Peritheral विषय के अन्तिम छोर की ओर तथा बाहरी परिवेश में हो।

बाहिक क्षमताः Channel Capacity समय विशेष में द्विधारी अंक अथवा इसी प्रकार के समान चिन्हों को इकाई रूप में निश्चित समयावधि में स्थानान्तरित करने की शक्ति।

बाहिक/पथः Channel मानव, मशीन अथवा विद्युत प्रभुक्त युक्ति जिसमें संकेतों को एक स्थान से दूसरे स्थान पर स्थानान्तरित किया जाता है।

बिटः Bit कम्प्यूटर भाषा प्रयुक्त शब्द इकाई।

विषय संदर्भः Subject Reference एक विषय से दूसरे सम्बन्धित विषय को संकेत।

बिस्को समय संख्याः Bisco Time Number समयानुक्रम में ग्रन्थों को व्यवस्थित करने के लिए डब्लू एस विस्को ने अक्षरों के स्थान पर संक्षेपित दिनाँक का पुस्तक संख्या में प्रयोग किया है।

ब्रिटिश पुस्तकालयः British Library यह ब्रिटेन का राष्ट्रीय पुस्तकालय है इसका कार्य केन्द्र में रहकर देश के व्यवसाय, शिक्षा तथा ज्ञान का प्रसार करना है।

ब्रिटिश नेशनल बिबलोग्राफी/ब्रिटिश राष्ट्रीय ग्रन्थ सूचीः British National Bibliography ग्रेट ब्रिटेन में प्रकाशित अँग्रेजी माध्यम की पुस्तकों की सूची है प्रविष्टियाँ अन्तर्राष्ट्रीय मानक पत्रों पर उपलब्ध है।

ब्रूनेट वर्गीकरणः Brunet Classification चेकेस चार्ल्य ब्रुनेट प्रतिपादित वर्गीकरण प्रणाली का प्रादुर्भाव प्रथम 1809 में हुआ था।

बेसिकः BASIC कम्प्यूटर प्रोग्राम में प्रयुक्त भाषा है।

बेसिक भाषाः BASIC Language *देखिए* बेसिक

बेचनेवालाः Vendor व्यक्ति जो बेचने का काम करता है।

बेकन वर्गीकरणः Bacon Classification शैक्षणिक विकास क्रम में 1605 में फ्रान्सिस बेकन की वर्गीकरण प्रणाली की रचना हुई।

भ

भाग/अंश/खण्डः Part/Section

भारतीय नामः Indian Name नाम जिससे भारतीयता का बोध हो।

भारतीय प्रकाशनः Indian Publication प्रकाशन जिनका उत्पादन भारतीय प्रकाशकों ने किया है।

भारतीय पुस्तकालय संघः Indian Library Association (ILA) इस राष्ट्रीय संस्था की स्थापना 1933 में कलकत्ता पुस्तकालय सम्मेलन के समय हुई थी इसके संचालक मण्डल का चुनाव दो वर्ष के लिए 'पत्र मत' द्वारा होता है। संघ के सूचना सम्प्रेषण के लिए पत्र तथा अपना प्रकाशन है। यह प्रतिवर्ष राष्ट्रीय सम्मेलन आयोजन कर विषय से सम्बन्धित सूचना विन्मय की व्यवस्था करता है तथा इसके सदस्य सम्पूर्ण भारतवर्ष में हैं।

भारतीय राष्ट्रीय वैज्ञानिक प्रलेखन केन्द्रः Indian National Scientific Documentation Centre (INSDOC) इस केन्द्र की स्थापना देश के वैज्ञानिकों की सूचना आवश्यकता को ध्यान में रख कर की गई थी। यह केन्द्र

आवश्यकतानुसार सूचना/लेख प्रतिलिपि/अनुवाद उपलब्ध कराता है।

भारोबीय संख्या: Indo-Arabic Numbers संख्या जिसको अरब प्रणाली से प्राप्त कर भारतीयता में अपना लिया गया है।

भाव चित्र: Ideograph/Pictograph एक विशेष चित्रांकन/चित्रांकन प्रकार जो अंकन को आकृति प्रदान करता है अथवा भाव तथा विचार का मूर्त रूप होता है।

भ्रामक शीर्षक: Fanciful Title/Misleading Title शीर्षक जिससे वर्णित विषय स्पष्ट नहीं होता।

भाषा: Language कम्प्यूटर की भाषा में संकेत/नियम समूह है जो सूचना संचय तथा सम्प्रेषण में सहयोगी है।

भाषा उप विभाजन: Language Subdivision भाषा पर आधारित विषय उपखण्ड।

भाषा पक्ष: Language Facet ग्रन्थ संख्या का अंश जिससे ग्रन्थ की भाषा को अभिव्यक्ति मिलती है।

भाषा वर्गीकरण: Language Classification जब वर्गीकरण का आधार भाषा को स्वीकृत किया जाय।

भाषा संख्या: Language Number क्रम बोधक संख्या जो प्रलेख की भाषा बोध का अनुवाद होती है।

भित्ति चित्र सिद्धांत: Wall-Picture-Principle जब दो पक्ष 'क' और 'ख' किसी विषय में इस प्रकार हो कि 'ख' के बिना क को न समझा जा सके तो 'क' 'ख'पक्ष से पहले आता है।

भूमिका: Introduction ग्रन्थ का आरम्भिक लेख जिसमें ग्रन्थ का उद्देश्य, कार्य बोध तथा विस्तार का संक्षिप्त विवरण होता है।

भौगोलिक क्षेत्र: Geographical Area क्षेत्र जो सीमायें व्यक्त करता है।

भौगोलिक युक्ति: Geographical Device संख्या जो स्थान बोध के लिए किसी वर्ग के साथ जुड़ती है।

भंगक्रम: Broken Order वर्गीकरण प्रणाली क्रम के साथ आवश्यकतातुसार क्रम परिवर्तन के साथ ग्रन्थ व्यवस्थित किए जाँय।

भण्डार: Stock/Repository संकनलनों को सुरक्षित रखने का स्थान।

भण्डारण/संग्रहण: Storage प्रक्रिया जिससे सूचना/ग्रन्थ एकत्रित किए जाते हैं।

भण्डार मार्ग दर्शक: Stock Guide मार्ग दर्शक जो प्रयोक्ता को ग्रन्थ के स्थान की ओर इंगित करता है।

भंडारण पुस्तक: Stock Book देखिए अवाप्ति पंजी/संग्रह पंजी।

भण्डार जाँच: Stock Verification/Stock Checking सत्यापन प्रक्रिया जिससे पुस्तकालय पंजी में पंजीकृत ग्रन्थों की भौतिक स्थिति का आकलन करना होता है।

म

मदर कन्ट्री: Mother Country पुस्तकालय जिस देश का है।

मजबूत जिल्द: Hard Bound मजबूती के लिए मोटे कागज/कपड़ा की सहायता से बनी जिल्द।

मध्यवर्गीय सेवा: Intermediate Service मध्य स्तर का प्रयास जिसका उद्देश्य सीधे सेवा प्रदान करता है।

मण्डल: Zone भू भाग का क्षेत्र अथवा वर्गीकरण प्रणाली पंक्ति समूह जिसका निर्माण एक ही युक्ति से होता है।

मण्डलीय एकल: Zonal Isolate भौगोलिक गुणों का उप विभाग जो उसमें अन्तर्निहित

है।

मशीनी शब्दः Machine Word सूचना की इकाई जिसकी मानक अंक संख्या का कम्प्यूटर में अनेक बार प्रयोग होता है।

मशीन द्वारा पठनीय अंक आधारः Machine Readable Database मशीन द्वारा प्रयुक्त माध्यम पर उपलब्ध सूचना संकलन।

मशीन द्वारा पठनीय सूचीः Machine Readable Catalogue सूची जिसका प्रयोग कम्प्यूटर आदि मशीन के द्वारा ही किया जा सकता हो।

मशीनी भाषाः Machine Language सांकेतिक भाषा जिसका प्रयोग मशीन की युक्ति से होता है।

मशीनी खोजः Machine for Search प्रयास जिसमें मशीन/कम्प्यूटर के प्रयोग से सूचना का चुनाव तथा सम्प्रेषण होता है।

माइक्रोफार्मः Microform तकनीकी प्रणाली से अभिलेख को परिवर्तित कर मशीन के प्रयोग योग्य बना दिया जाता है। यह इलैक्ट्रोन आधारित व्यवस्था है जिसमें बड़े-2 ग्रन्थ छोटे आकार की फिल्म में बदल दिये जाते हैं। जिनको अकेले आँखों की सहायता से नहीं प्रयोग किया जा सकता।

माइक्रोफोर्म पठन कक्षः Microform Reading Room विशेष कक्ष जहाँ आधुनिक उपकरण प्रयोग कर सूचना प्राप्त की जाती है।

माइक्रोफिशः Microfiche समतल मानक फिल्म जिस पर सूचना चित्रांकित की जाती है।

मार्कः MARK कम्प्यूटर पठनीय सूची परियोजना का परिवर्णीनाम।

माध्यमः Media सूचना सम्प्रेषण के साधन।

माध्यम कार्यक्रमः Media Programme कार्यक्रम जिनका प्रसारण माध्यम प्रकार उपयोग के लिए होता है।

मान्यताः Recognition उपलब्ध निर्देशों के अनुसार स्वीकृति।

माध्यम केन्द्रः Media Centre केन्द्र जहाँ से माध्यम गति विधि नियन्त्रित होती है।

माध्यमिक स्कूल पुस्तकालयः Secondary School Library इस प्रकार के पुस्तकालय के संकलन तथा सेवा सम्बन्धित विद्यार्थियों के शिक्षण कार्यक्रम में सहयोग के साथ व्यक्तित्व विकास में सहयोगी होते हैं।

मानक/मानदण्डः Standard प्रकाशन जिसमें गुणों के स्वीकृत स्तर से सम्बन्धित मानक प्रकाशित होते हैं।

मानक आकारः Standard Format ग्रन्थात्मक सूचना का पूर्व निर्धारित नियमानुसार आकार।

मानक आकार पत्रः Standard Size Card कोई भी पत्र जिसका आकार स्वीकृत नियमों के अनुसार हो।

मानक उप विभाजनः Standard Subdivision वर्गीकरण प्रणाली में ग्रन्थ के स्वरूप अभिव्यक्ति के निए निश्चित उप विभाग प्रयोग करती है। जिनका आधार अलग-2 गुण होते हैं।

मानक प्रतिः Standard Copy पूर्व निर्धारित उच्च मानकों के आधार पर बनी प्रति।

मानक शब्दों का शीर्षकः Title in Standard Terms शीर्षक के प्रमुख शब्दों को वर्गीकरण प्रयुक्त शब्दावली से प्रतिस्थापित कर सहयोगी चिन्हों के साथ व्यक्त किया जाए।

मानचित्रः Map 'भू' भाग का कागज पर चित्रण है।

मान चित्रावलीः Atlases मान चित्रों/चित्रों का संकलन होती है।

मासिक प्रगति प्रतिवेदनः Monthly Progress Report माह के कार्य कलाप का विवरण अथवा कार्य विशेष की माह के अन्तर्गत प्रगति सूचना।

मास्टर पत्रः Master Card पत्र जिस पर सर्वाधिक सूचना होती है तथा जिसके योग से अन्य पत्र बनाये जाते हैं।

मात्राः Quantity परिमाण।

मासिक पत्रिकाः Monthly Magazine पत्रिका जिसका प्रकाशन माह के अन्तर से होता है।

मिश्रित अंकनः Mixed Notation वर्गीकरण की अंकन प्रणाली जिसमें एक से अधिक प्रकार के अंकन का प्रयोग हो।

मिश्रित अंकन का प्रनियमः Canon of Mixed Notation प्रनियम के अनुसार वर्गीकरण प्रणाली प्रयुक्त अंकन मिश्रित प्रकार का होना चाहिए।

मिश्रित एकल क्रमः Order of Complex Isolate प्रयुक्त एकल की संख्या क्रम व्यवस्था।

मिथ्या झुकावः False Drop चुने हुए विषय से असम्बद्ध संदर्भ।

मिश्रित-पंक्ति एकलः Complex Array Isolate पंक्ति एकल जिसका सृजन पंक्ति में उपलब्ध दो अलग-2 एकल योग से होता है।

मिश्रित पंक्ति एकल क्रमः Order of Complex Array Isolate पंक्ति एकल संख्या जिससे इसका निर्माण होता है।

मिश्रित विषयः Complex Subject मूल विषय के साथ जुड़े हुए अन्य अनेक पक्षों से बना विषय अथवा विषय जिसमें एक से अधिक गुणों का समावेश हो।

मिश्रित वर्गः Complex Class वर्ग जिसके संयोजन में दो और उससे अधिक मूल अथवा यौगिक विषय होते हैं।

मिश्रित वर्ग क्रमः Order of a Complex Class मिश्रित वर्ग के योग में प्रयुक्त मूल/यौगिक संख्या क्रम।

मुक्त करनाः Discharge प्रयोक्ता को ग्रन्थ उधार से मुक्त करना तथा आवती पत्र आदि आवश्यक अभिलेख बनाने की प्रक्रिया है।

मुफ्त प्रवेश प्रणालीः Free Access System प्रयोग प्रणाली अथवा पुस्तक सेवा जो प्रयोक्ता को पुस्तकालय संचय के समीप तक चुनाव के लिए स्वतन्त्रता प्राप्त कराती है।

मुख पत्रः House Organ *देखिए* ग्रह पत्रिका।

मुख पत्रः Organ संस्था का प्रकाशन जो साम्प्रतिक सूचना सम्प्रेषित करता है।

मुख्य आधारः Mainframe कम्प्यूटर का मुख्य भाग जो केन्द्रीय संसाधन इकाई के रूप में कार्य करता है तथा जिस पर एक से अधिक प्रसार उपकरण एक साथ प्रयोग हो सकते हैं।

मुख्य आधार कम्प्यूटरः Mainfram Computer कम्प्यूटर अनेक टर्मिनल्स उपयोग से एक साथ अनेक कार्य कर सकता है। व्यक्तिगत कम्प्यूटर की अपेक्षा अधिक प्रयोक्ताओं को एक साथ प्रयोग सुविधा प्रदान करता है *और देखिए* मुख्य आधार।

मुख्य केन्द्र/मुख्यालयः Headquarters संस्थान का नीति निर्धारक/प्रशासनिक कार्यालय।

मुख्य पत्रः Main Card सूची पत्र जिस पर मुख्य प्रविष्टि अंकित हो जिसकी सहायता से अन्य प्रविष्टि बनाई जा सकती है। मुख्य पत्र होता है।

मुख्य पुस्तकालयः Main Library *देखिए*

केन्द्रीय पुस्तकालय

मुख्य सूचीः Main Catalogue केन्द्रीय सूची होती है। पुस्तकालय के सभी, ग्रन्थों की सूचना होती है।

मुख्य शब्दः Keyword रचना के भाव तथा विचारों को व्यक्त करने वाले चुने हुए शब्द।

मुख्य प्रविष्टिः Main Entry प्रविष्टि जिसमें नियमानुसार सर्वाधिक सूचना होती है तथा अतिरिक्त प्रविष्टि बनाने में सहयोगी होती है।

मुख्य वर्गः Main Class ज्ञान जगत से वर्गीकरण प्रणाली द्वारा उत्पन्न प्रथम वर्ग पंक्ति है *और देखिए* मूल वर्ग।

मुख्य विषयः Main Subject रचना में विवेचित विषयों में प्रधान विषय।

मुख्य शीर्षकः Main Title एकाधिक शीर्षकों में प्रथम शीर्षक अथवा जिसके साथ कोई उप शीर्षक अथवा सह शीर्षक हो।

मुख्य शीर्षक पृष्ठः Main Title Page पृष्ठ जिस पर मुख्य शीर्षक अंकित हो।

मुख्य सूची प्रविष्टिः Main Catalogue Entry *देखिए* मुख्य प्रविष्टि।

मुद्रकः Printer प्रकाशक/छपाई मशीन जिससे छपी प्रति प्राप्त की जाती है।

मुद्रित सूचीः Printed Catalogue सूची को मुद्रित कराया जाय *और देखिए* पुस्तक आकार सूची।

मुद्रणः Printing छपाई कार्य।

मुद्रण एवम् प्रकाशनः Printing and Publication.

मूल्यांकनः Evaluation पद्धति जिसके द्वारा विभिन्न विषय के श्रेष्ठ ग्रन्थों का आकलन कर सुधार के लिए जानकारी प्राप्त की जाती है।

मूल्यांकन खरीद पक्षः Evaluation Acquisition Facet पुस्तक का गुण है जिसके सुनिश्चित होने पर खरीदने का कार्य प्रारम्भ हो।

मूल्यांकन खरीद संख्याः Evaluation Acquisition Number संख्या जिसका आधार किसी विषय पर उपलब्ध रचनाओं से चुनी हुई रचना जिनको पुस्तकालय के लिए खरीदा जाना है को दी जाती है।

मूल्यांकन पक्षः Evaluation Facet *देखिए* मूल्यांकन खरीद पक्ष।

मूल्यांकन संख्याः Evaluation Number *देखिए* मूल्यांकन खरीद पक्ष।

मूल प्रलेखः Host Document प्रलेख को जब अन्य रचना के लिए प्रयुक्त ग्रन्थ के रूप में देखा जाए।

मूल्य लागत लाभः Cost Benefit लागत मूल तथा सेवा उपलब्धि के बीच सम्बन्ध।

मूल/आधार संख्याः Base Number वर्गीकरण प्रणाली में प्रयुक्त अंकन है जिसके संयोजन से आवश्यक वर्ग संख्या बनाई जा सकती है।

मूल अंकः Substantive Digit अंक अपने क्रमिक मूल्य के साथ विशेष विचार को व्यक्त करता है।

मूल प्रविष्टिः Basic Entry *देखिए* मुख्य प्रविष्टि।

मूल पुस्तकः Basic Book विषय के विकास का प्रथम प्रामाणिक प्रकाशन/मूल विषय वस्तु पर आधारित ग्रन्थ।

मूलभूत श्रेणी की अभिधारणाः Postulate of Fundamental Catagories डा. रंगनाथन के अनुसार व्यक्तित्व, पदार्थ, शक्ति, स्थान तथा समय केवल पाँच ही मूलभूत श्रेणी किसी विषय की अभिधारणा हो सकती है।

मूलभूत श्रेणीः Fundamental Category रंगनाथन की विषय के सम्बन्ध में

प्रतिपादित अभिधारणा है देखिए मूलभूत श्रेणी की अभिधारणा।

मेलविल ड्यूवेः Melvil Dewey आधुनिक पुस्तकालय विज्ञान के जनक तथा सर्वाधिक प्रयुक्त वर्गीकरण प्रणाली डी. डी. सी के बनाने वाले अमेरिकी पुस्तकालय विज्ञानी।

मैरिल पुस्तक संख्याः Marril Book Number डब्लू एस मैरिल की पुस्तक संख्या संयोजन प्रणाली जिसमें पुस्तक वर्णक्रम अथवा घटते दिनांक क्रम में रखी जाती है।

मैगाबाइटः Megabyte कम्प्यूटर की स्मरण शक्ति मापक संख्या।

मैडलर्सः Medlars चिकित्सा साहित्य विश्लेषण तथा पुनः प्राप्ति प्रक्रिया का परिवर्णी शब्द है। चिकित्सा विज्ञान के इस व्यापक सूचना संचय को राष्ट्रीय चिकित्सा विज्ञान पुस्तकालय अमेरिका द्वारा विकसित किया गया है।

मैडीलाइनः Mediline कम्प्यूटर आधारित अन्तर्राष्ट्रीय सेवा जिससे चिकित्सा साहित्य में खोज परक सूचना सम्प्रेषण होता है।

मोनोग्राफः Monograph किसी एक विषय पर विद्वतापूर्ण रचना।

मोड्मः Modem दूर संचार तथा कम्प्यूटर के बीच सम्बन्ध स्थापित करने वाली युक्ति।

मोड्यूलः Module किसी प्रणाली की अलग-2 इकाई जिनके योग से प्रणाली की पहचान होती है।

मौखिक स्तर के प्रनियमः Canon of Verbal Plane स्मृति पटल पर कार्य करने के लिए कुछ विशेषताओं का पहचान प्रकार है।

मौलिक रचनाएँः Original Works रचनाएँ जिनके विचार रचनाकार के हैं।

मौलिक संस्करणः Original Edition संस्करण जिसकी प्रथम आवृति है और देखिए मौलिक रचनाएँ।

माँग पत्रः Requisition Card/Requisition slip पत्र जिसमें प्रयोक्ता अपना प्रयोजन अंकित करता है।

य

यात्री मार्ग दर्शकः Travel Guide यात्रियों की सुविधा के लिए मुख्य स्थान ठहरने की व्यवस्था तथा यातायात की सूचना देने वाली लघु पुस्तिका।

युक्तिः Device कार्य सम्पादन प्रकार।

युवाओं का पुस्तकालयः Adolescent Library पुस्तकालय जिसमें युवकों के प्रयोग का संचय हो।

यूनीमार्कः UNIMARK सूची प्रकार है।

यूनीवर्सल डेसीमल वर्गीकरणः Universal Decimal Classification 1905 में पॉल आरलैट तथा डी लाँ फाउन्टेन द्वारा निर्मित विश्लेषित संश्लेषित वर्गीकरण प्रणाली है। जिसमें सीमित रूप में वर्ग सारणी उपलब्ध रहती है।

यूनीसिस्टः UNISIST यूनेस्को द्वारा 1971 में विकासित सूचना प्रणाली है।

यूनैस्कोः UNESCO यह अन्तर्राष्ट्रीय संस्था 1946 से कार्यरत है पुस्तकालय तथा प्रलेखन विकास/विस्तार के कार्यक्रम चला रही है सेमिनार के साथ-2 सलाहकार रूप में भी कार्य करती है।

योजनाः Plan/Planning/Scheme उद्देश्यों को कार्यरूप देने की प्रक्रिया है अथवा किसी संस्था व्यवस्था के नीति परक कार्यक्रम जिनसे वर्तमान और भविष्य के कार्यक्रम निश्चित किए जायें।

योजना अनुदानः Plan Grant प्रयोजन विशेष के लिए निर्धारित अनुदान।

योजना व्ययः Plan Expenditure व्यय जब योजना आवण्टित धन से हो।

योजना व्ययः Non-Recurring Expenditure राष्ट्रीय अथवा संस्था कोश

का अंश जो लगातार उपलब्ध नहीं होता है।

योजनाबद्ध एकल विचार (व्यवस्थित): Systematic Isolate Idea एकल विचार जिसकी संख्या का निर्धारण सिद्धांत पर आधारित हो।

यौगिक नाम: Compound Name जब एक से अधिक नाम/नाम अंश को किसी संयोजक चिन्ह से जोड़ दिया जाय।

यौगिक वर्ग का क्रम: Order of a Compound Class वर्ग में एकल पक्ष की संख्या स्थिति।

र

रख रखाव: Maintenance व्यवस्था जिससे कार्य प्रणाली की क्षमता को बनाये रखा जाता है।

रचना: Article/Work एक/एक से अधिक रचनाकारों की रचना जिसको किसी पत्रिका में प्रकाशित किया जाना हो।

रसायन शास्त्र तथा रसायनिक प्राद्योगिकी का राष्ट्रीय सूचना केन्द्र: National Information Centre for Chemistry and Chemical Technology (NICHEM) निसात के अर्न्तगत विकसित सूचना केन्द्र 1986 से पूना में कार्य कर रहा है। कम्प्यूटर प्रयोग कर रसायन शास्त्र तथा रसायन प्रोद्योगिकी की सूचना का संकलन तथा सम्प्रेषण किया जाता है।

रक्षा विज्ञान सूचना एवम् प्रलेखन केन्द्र: Defence Science Information and Documentation Centre (DESIDOC) यह सूचना केन्द्र भारतीय शोध एवम् विकास संस्थान का अंग है। संस्थान के वैज्ञानिकों की सूचना आवश्यकता के लिए अनेक अन्य संस्थानों से सूचना उपलब्ध कराता है सूचना सम्प्रेषण के लिए संस्थान पत्र तथा पत्रिका प्रकाशित करता है।

राइडर का अन्तर्राष्ट्रीय वर्गीकरण: Rider's International Classification फ्रैमैन्ट राइडर द्वारा विकसित वर्गीकरण प्रणाली है जिसका प्रथम प्रादुर्भाव 1961 में हुआ था।

राज्य केन्द्रीय पुस्तकालय: State Central Library राज्य द्वारा प्रकाशित/राज्य से सम्बन्धित विषयों पर संकलित पुस्तकों का केन्द्र होता है।

राजा राम मोहन राय फाउन्डेन पुस्तकालय: Raja Ram Mohun Roy Library Foundation राष्ट्रीय स्तर पर सार्वजनिक पुस्तकालयों के विकास तथा क्रियान्वन की संस्था है। जिसका मुख्य आफिस कलकता में है।

राष्ट्रीय ग्रन्थ सूची: National Bibliography किसी राष्ट्र द्वारा प्रकाशित/राष्ट्र के बारे में प्रकाशित ग्रन्थों की सूची होती जाती है।

राष्ट्रीय कलाभवन: National Gallery कलाभवन जिसमें राष्ट्र की सर्वोच्च कला कृतियों का प्रदर्शन किया जाता है।

राष्ट्रीय पुस्तकालय: National Library देश में प्रकाशित प्रत्येक पुस्तक को 1944 के कानून के अर्न्तगत प्राप्त कर राष्ट्रीय संग्रह रूप में रखता है तथा संग्रहीत सूचना सम्प्रेषण सेवा संचालित करता है। संकलन प्रक्रिया में यूनाइटैड नेशन्स का विशेष संचय है। निरन्तर संचय प्रकिया से उपलब्ध ग्रन्थों के आधार पर देश की ऐतिहासिक, सामाजिक, वैज्ञानिक तथा तकनीकी विकास प्रक्रिया का अनुमान लगाया जा सकता है।

राष्ट्रीय पुस्तकालय न्यास: National Book Trust स्वायत्तशासी संस्था राष्ट्रीय पुस्तक न्यास की स्थापना 1957 में पुस्तकों के प्रति जागरूकता पैदा करने के लिए हुई

जब से ही संस्था पुस्तक प्रकाशन, वितरण के साथ पुस्तक मेले आयोजन करने का कार्य सुचारु रूप से कर रही है।

राष्ट्रीय समाज विज्ञान प्रलेखन केन्द्रः National Social Science Documentation Centre यह केन्द्र 1985 से भारतीय समाज विज्ञान शोध परिषद के अधीन कार्यरत है अनेक कार्य प्रणाली जैसे शोध प्रबन्ध संकलन, विषय ग्रन्थ सूची आदि के द्वारा शोध के प्रचार प्रसार का काम करता है।

राष्ट्रीय सूचना केन्द्रः National Informatic Centre राष्ट्र की राजघानी नई देहली में स्थिति है। कम्प्यूटर प्रयोग की सहायता से जिलास्तर से सूचना प्राप्त कर भारतीय निति निर्धारण व्यवस्था में सहयोग करता हैं।

राष्ट्रीय सूचना प्रणालीः National Information System प्रणाली जिससे राष्ट्रीय सूचना केन्द्र/पुस्तकालय की व्यवस्था की जाती है।

राष्ट्रीय शैक्षणिक शोध केन्द्रः National Educational Research Centre शैक्षणिक तथा शोध सम्बन्धी आवश्यकता के अन्तर्गत भारतीय विचार धारा से सम्बन्धित रचनाओं को प्रोत्साहित करने के लिए इस प्रकार के केन्द्र कार्य कर रहे है।

रिक्त अंकः Empty Digit अंक का प्रयोग वर्गीकरण में विशेष वर्ग अथवा अर्थ अभिव्यक्ति के लिये न होकर उसके सामान्य मूल्य में हो।

रिक्त एवम् रिक्त कारक अंकः Empty and Emptying Digit अंक अपने सामान्य मूल्य के साथ किसी अन्य विशेष अर्थ/मूल्य के लिये न प्रयुक्त होते हुए पूर्ववर्ती अंक को विशेष अर्थ/मूल्य से वंचित करता है।

रिक्त कारक अंकः Emptying Digit अंक जो क्रमिक मूल्य के साथ पूर्ववर्ती अंक को मूल अर्थ से वंचित कर देता है।

रिक्त कारक सार गर्भित अंकः Emptying Substantive Digit देखिए रिक्त कारक अंक।

रीड ऑनली मैमोरीः Read only Memory (ROM) कम्प्यूटर में उपलब्ध स्मृति जिसका प्रयोग प्रोग्राम के उपयोग के लिए किया जाता है।

रीडरः Reader पाठक अथवा कम्प्यूटर प्रयोग में इच्छित सूचना प्राप्ति के निर्देश पर कार्य करने वाली युक्ति।

रूप पक्षः Form Facet पुस्तक के आकार को व्यक्त करने वाला पक्ष जिसको अभिव्यक्ति पुस्तक संख्या में मिलती है।

रूपान्तरणः Adaptation किसी रचना का रूपान्तरण करणवश पुनः लिखा जाना है जिसको विचार तथा अभिव्यक्ति की गुणवत्ता के आघार पर अलग रचना नहीं स्वीकार किया जाता। रूपान्तरण वास्तविक अथवा मूल भाषा और किसी भी अन्य भाषा में हो सकता है स्वतन्त्र अनुवाद प्रकार है।

रूपवर्गः Form Classes वर्ग जिनका आधार प्रलेखों का आकार होता है।

रूप विभाजनः Form Division वर्गीकरण का भाग जिससे वर्ग के विशेष प्रकार को पहचाना जाता है।

रूप संख्याः Form Number संख्या जिसकी सहायता से वर्ग में ग्रन्थ के प्रकार का क्रम निर्धारित होता है।

रेखा अंशः Dash (—) चिन्ह का प्रयोग संयोजन व्यक्त करने को होता है।

रेखा चित्रः Diagram, Outline रेखात्मक अभिव्यक्ति

रैकः Rack पुस्तक रखने का उपादान।

रैन्डम ऐक्सिस मैमोरीः Random Ac-

cess Memory कम्प्यूटर की मुख्य स्मृति।

ल

लचीला अंकनः Flexible Notation अंकन जिसमें अनेक अंक विषय के नये क्षेत्र व्यक्त करने के लिए प्रयोग किये जा सकते है इस व्यवस्था में पूर्वनिर्धारित वर्गीकरण व्यवस्था के बदला नहीं जाता है।

लचीलापनः Flexibility अंकन की क्षमता अथवा वह गुण है जिससे नये विषयों को अंकन में व्यक्त किया जाता है।

लघु पुस्तिकाः Pamphlet or Booklet आवश्यक सूचना की आकस्मिक पूर्ति के उद्देश्य से प्रकाशित कम पृष्ठ वाली छोटी पुस्तक अथचा कागज की जिल्द में कम पृष्ठ की पुस्तक।

लघु प्रलेखः Micro Document रचना जिसमें विषय का विस्तार कम होता है।

लघु संस्करणः Pocket Edition छोटे आकार की पुस्तक।

लटकता हुआ दण्डः Hanging Indentation सूची पत्र के बांयी ओर अदृश्य कल्पित रेखा जिसका प्रयोग सूचना संयोजन में होता है।

लाइब्रेरी ऑफ कॉंग्रेसः Library of Congress (LC) अमेरीका का राष्ट्रीय पुस्तकालय है कापी राइट के अर्न्तगत ग्रन्थ संग्रह से संसार का सबसे बड़ा सूचना केन्द्र बन गया हैं। व्यापक सेवा व्यवस्था में छः हजार योग्य तकनीकी कार्यकर्त्ता लगे हुए हैं।

लाइब्रेरी ऑफ कॉंग्रेस वर्गीकरणः Library of Congress Classification लाइब्रेरी ऑफ कॉंग्रेस अमेरिका द्वारा 1904 में प्रकाशित वर्गीकरण प्रणाली है।

लिपिः Script किसी भाषा की अभिव्यक्ति का लिखित प्रकार है।

लिपि विज्ञानः Paleography प्राचीन ग्रन्थों में प्रयुक्त लिपि के अध्ययन से सम्बन्धित विज्ञान।

लुप्त एकलः Missing Isolate एकल की अनुपस्थिति से शृंखला में अन्तर हो जाता है।

लुप्त कड़ीः Missing Link शृंखला में अन्तर के बाद कड़ी जो लुप्त एकल की ओर संकेत करे।

लेखकः Author विचारों/भावों को आत्मसात कर समसामायिक सत्य के अनुरूप व्यक्त करने वाला व्यक्ति/व्यक्ति समूह।

लेखक अनुभागः Author Section प्रविष्टि का अनुभाग जिसमें ग्रन्थ के रचनाकार का उल्लेख हो।

लेखक कथन का पूरकः Supplement to Author Statement लेखक की जन्मतिथि/प्रयुक्त अन्य नाम सम्बन्धी सूचना आदि।

लेखक प्रतिः Author's Copy रचना कार को प्रकाशक से प्राप्त निःशुल्क प्रति।

लेखक संशोधनः Author's Proof ग्रन्थ की टंकित/मुद्रित प्रथम प्रति जिसका संशोधन रचनाकार को करना हो।

लेखक पत्रः Author Card सूची प्रविष्टि पत्र जिसकी प्रथम सूचना लेखक होता है।

लेखक प्रविष्टिः Author Entry यह प्रविष्टि अतिरिक्त प्रविष्टि होती है। इसकी प्रथम सूचना रचनाकार होता है। प्रविष्टि संयोजन से एक लेखक की रचनाओं को एक स्थान पर देखा जा सकता है।

लेखक विश्लेषिकः Author Analytical अतिरिक्त सूची प्रविष्टि है जो लेखक का नाम स्पष्ट करती है तथा मूख्य ग्रन्थ का उल्लेख रखती है। जहाँ ग्रन्थ संलग्न है।

लेखक-सूचीः Author Catalogue सूची जिसमे लेखक प्रविष्टियों को वर्णामुक्रम में रखा जाए।

लेखक संदेश: Author Statement लेखक से सम्बन्धित सूचना।

लेखक संख्या: Author Number संख्या जो वर्गीकरण में लेखक को व्यक्त करती है।

लेखाकरण: Accounting नियमित आय-व्यय का विवरण।

लेख चित्र: Illustrations *देखिए* चित्र।

लेखा-परीक्षक: Auditor अधिकारी जो नियमों के अन्तर्गत आय-व्यय की वैधता का निरीक्षण करता है।

लेखा परीक्षण: Auditing/Audit आय व्यय की नियमों के अन्तर्गत निरीक्षण प्रक्रिया।

लेबल: Label कागज/कपड़े का छोटा निश्चित आकार जिसका प्रयोग पुस्तक के ऊपर आह्वान संख्या अंकित करने के लिए होता है।

लोकप्रिय पुस्तक: Popular Book पुस्तक जिसका अधिक प्रयोग हो।

व

व्यक्तित्व: Personality अन्य वस्तु/व्यक्तियों के बीच पहचान।

व्यक्तित्व एकल: Personality Isolate विषय विश्लेषण से मूलभूत श्रेणी प्राप्त करने की प्रक्रिया में समय, स्थान, पदार्थ, उर्जा प्राप्त करने के बाद शेष व्यक्तित्त्व श्रेणी जानी जाती है।

व्यक्तित्व तथा पदार्थ चक्र की अभिधारण: Postulate of Rounds for Personality and Matter व्यक्तित्त्व तथा पदार्थ के लिए यह भी सम्भव है वह दुबारा शक्ति की प्रथम अथवा द्वितीय आवृत्ति के बाद व्यक्त हो तो यह उनका आवृत्ति चक्र होगा।

व्यक्ति परक लेखक: Personal Author व्यक्ति जो रचना के लिए स्वयं उत्तरदायी हो।

व्यवधान: Noise कम्प्यूटर में व्यक्त अंवाछित संकेत जिनकी उपस्थिति वांछित संकेत सम्प्रेषण तन्त्र में बाधक होती है।

व्यवधानकारक: Noise Factor चुने हुये ग्रन्थों में अवांछित प्रलेखों का प्रतिशत।

व्यवस्था: Organisation आवश्यकतानुसार संसाघन संयोजन।

व्यवस्था विन्यास: Arrangement आवश्यकतानुसार वर्गों का क्रम संयोजन।

व्यवसाय: Profession.

व्यवसायिक: Professional व्यक्ति जिसको तकनीकी ज्ञान हो।

व्यवसायिक सहायक: Professional Assistant व्यक्ति जो तकनीकी कार्य में सहायता करता है।

व्यापक वर्गीकरण: Broad Classification विषय का कुछ मूल उपवर्गों में वर्गीकरण।

व्यापार पत्रिका: Trade Journal पत्रिका जिसका कार्य व्यापारिक आवश्यकता पूर्ति हो।

व्यापार साहित्य: Trade Literature प्रलेख जिनमें व्यापार से सम्बन्धित सूचना एवम् उत्पादों के बारे में विवरण रहते हैं।

व्यापारिक छूट: Trade Discount पुस्तक क्रय विक्रय के समय अंकित मूल्य में दी गई छूट जो पुस्तक विक्रेताओं को उपलब्ध होती है।

व्यापारिक पुस्तक सूची: Trade Catalogue पुस्तक व्यवसायियों द्वारा प्रकाशित पुस्तक सूची।

वर्ग: Class विषय का भाग जिसका आघार समान गुण धर्मिता होती है।

वर्ग अनुक्रमाणिका प्रविष्टि: Class Index Entry वर्गीकरण सूची प्रणाली की प्रविष्टि है जिसमें वर्ग के लिए वर्ग संख्या अंकित होती है।

वर्ग क्रम: Order of a Class अभिलक्षणों का वरीयता क्रम जिसके आधार पर वर्ग निर्माण किया जाता है।

वर्ग अनुक्रमाणिका: Index to Classification वर्ग संख्या क्रम अथवा स्वाभाविक विषय भाषा शब्दों में व्यक्त कोश।

वर्ग आयाम: Dimensions of Class अनेक पक्ष मिश्रित अथवा यौगिक पक्ष मिल कर वर्ग आयाम को निश्चित करते हैं।

वर्ग विधि: Scheme of Classes वर्गीकरण प्रणाली।

वर्ग संख्या: Class Number प्रलेख का अंको में अनुवाद। वर्गीकरण प्रणाली में वर्ग को व्यक्त करने वाली संख्या। प्रलेख का अन्य प्रलेखों के मध्य स्थान नियत करती है।

वर्गीकरण: Classification विशेषता अथवा उपयोगिता क्रम में वस्तुओं का संयोजन करने की प्रक्रिया।

वर्गीकरण करना: Classifying क्रिया जिससे गुण अथवा अवगुणों के आधार पर वस्तुओं को अलग-2 किया जाता है।

वर्गीकरण सारिणी: Schedules of Classification सारिणी जिसमें ज्ञान जगत से उत्पन्न वर्गों को प्राकृतिक भाषा में रखा जाता है।

वर्गीकरण नियम: Rules of Classification वर्गीकरण प्रणाली की प्रामाणिकता सुनिश्चित करने वाले निर्देश जिनका प्रयोग वर्गीकरण करने वाले की आवश्यकता होती है।

वर्गीकरण सिद्धान्त: Principles of Classification *देखिए* वर्गीकरण के नियम।

वर्गीकरण-पद्धति: Classification Scheme पद्धति जिसके द्वारा अनेकानेक विषयों को विषयानुसार उपयोगी क्रम के वर्गों में रखा जाता है तथा स्वीकृत शब्दावली के साथ अंकन प्रदान किया जाता है।

वर्गीकरण चरण: Steps in Classification डा. रंगनाथन ने वर्गीकरण प्रणाली में वर्गसंख्या निर्धारण के आठ निम्न चरण व्यक्त्त किए हैं : व्यक्त शीर्षक विस्तार; सार शीर्षक; विश्लेषित शीर्षक परिवर्तित शीर्षक; मानक/स्वीकृत शब्द पहचान; पक्ष संख्या स्थानापन्न; वर्ग संख्या और वर्ग संख्या विश्लेषण सत्यापन।

वर्गीकरण विद: Classificationist व्यक्ति जो वर्गीकरण पद्धति बनाता है।

वर्गीकृत-क्रम: Classified Arrangement क्रम व्यवस्था जिस का आधार विषय का वर्ग आधार पर विभक्तीकरण हो।

वर्गीकरणात्मक-भाषा: Classificatory Language वर्गीकरण में प्रयुक्त अंकन के अंकों पर आधारित क्रत्रिम भाषा।

वर्गीकृत सूची: Classified Catalogue इस में सूची दो भागों में होती है। अतिरिक्त विषय प्रविष्टियों को विषय क्रम में रखा जाता है। वर्गीकरण का आधार आवश्यकतानुसार निश्चित किया जाता है।

वर्गीकृत सूची संहिता: Classified Catalogue Code सूची संहिता प्रकार है जिसमें वर्गीकृत सूची प्रविष्टि बनाने के नियम है।

वर्गीकरण संहिता: Classification Code नियमावली जिसकी सहायता से वर्गीकरण पद्धति का प्रयोग किया जाता है।

वर्धमान मूर्तता का सिद्धान्त: Principle of Increasing Concreteness जब दो वर्गों में एक अधिक निश्चित हो तो दूसरा निश्चित का अनुसरण करता है।

वर्णानुक्रम सरिणी का सिद्धान्त: Principle of Alphabetical Sequence यदि एकल प्रयुक्त नाम अन्तर्राष्ट्रीय स्तर पर स्वीकृत तथा आधुनिक हैं तो उनको वर्णानुक्रम में वर्गीकरण के नियमानुसार रखना चाहिए।

वर्णानुक्रमिक: Alphabetical.

वर्णानुक्रमिक युक्ति: Alphabetical Device इस युक्ति में वर्ण के प्रयोग से एक ही लेखक की रचनाओं/मशीन आदि के अनेक प्रकारों को पहचान प्रदान की जाती है।

वर्णानुक्रमिक वर्ग फाइल प्रणाली: Alphabetical Classed Filing System विषय पर उपलब्ध सूचना को वर्ग उपवर्गों में विभक्त कर वर्णानुक्रम में संयोजित किया जाता है।

वर्णानुक्रमिक व्यंवस्था: Alphabetical Arrangement व्यवस्था का आधार वर्णानुक्रम हो।

वर्णानुक्रमिक संहिता: Alphabetical Code इस संहिता का प्रयोग कम्प्यूटर में सूचना संग्रह के लिए भी होता है जिसमें सूचना शब्द/अक्षर प्रयोग से प्राप्त की जा सकती है।

वर्णानुक्रमिक वर्ग सूची: Alphabetical-Classed Catalogue सूची प्रकार है जिसमें प्रविष्टि विषय के स्थान पर मुख्य-2 शीर्षक शब्द के आधार पर वर्णनात्मक क्रम में रखी जाती है। यह अनुक्रमाणिका से भिन्न होती है।

वर्णानुक्रमिक-सूची: Alphabetical Catalogue इस सूची प्रकार में सभी अतिरिक्त प्रविष्टि पत्र वर्णानुक्रम में आवद्ध रहते है।

वर्णानुक्रमाणिका: Alphabetical Index सूची जिसको वर्णो के क्रम के आधार पर बनाया जाता है।

वर्णानुक्रमण: Alphabetisation प्रक्रिया जिससे वर्णो को क्रमवद्ध किया जाता है।

वर्णनात्मक युक्ति: Alphabetical Device युक्ति जिसमें वर्ग पहचान के लिए वर्ण/अक्षर का वर्ग निर्माण में प्रयोग होता है।

वर्णनात्मक संहिता: Alphabetic Code *देखिए* वर्णानुक्रमिक संहिता।

वर्तमान कृषि शोध सूचना संस्थान: Current Agricultural Research Information System (CARIS) प्रणाली जिससे वर्तमान की कृषि शोध संबंधी सूचनाएँ एकत्रित की जाती है।

वंशानुक्रम: Hierarchy वर्गीकरण प्रणाली में शब्द जब अपने पूर्व तथा पश्च प्रयुक्त शब्दों के साथ सम्बन्ध निर्वाह में प्रयुक्त हो।

वस्तु: Item वस्तु जिसको गुणों के आधार पर पहचाना जा सके।

वंशानुक्रम: Filiatory Sequence ज्ञान जगत से उत्पन्न वर्गो का क्रमिक संयोजन अथवा समीपी वर्गो के क्रम में संयोजक।

वाक्यांश: Phrase स्वीकृत वाक्य भाग जिसको प्रभावोत्पादकता के कारण यथावत प्रयोग किया जाता है।

वाम उत्तर सिद्धान्त: Principle of Left to Right यदि पंक्ति में उत्पन्न एकल को समानान्तर पंक्ति में रखना हो तो उनका क्रम बायें से दाये होना चाहिए।

वास्तुकला: Architecture कला जिससे पुस्तकालय भवन/साज सामान को इच्छित आकार/सौन्दर्य प्रदान किया जाता है।

वास्तविक नाम: Real Name नाम करण जो पहचान प्रदान करता है अथवा दूसरे नाम यदि है तो उनको भी पहचान प्रदान करता है।

वास्तविक मूल्यः Net Price व्यवसायिक छूट आदि निकाल कर शेष देय मूल्य।

वार्षिकीः Annual क्रमिक प्रकाशित वार्षिक खण्ड, बहुखण्डी पुस्तक का पूरक होता है तथा वर्ष भर की गति विधि का विवरण प्रस्तुत करता है।

बांछित क्रमः Preferred Order क्रम जिसमें वर्गीकरण के वर्ग रखे जाते हैं।

बांछित कड़ीः Sought Link कड़ी जो व्यर्थ या अनावश्यक न हो।

वार्षिक प्रतिवेदनः Annual Report प्रकाशन जो कि विभाग की गतिविधियों का वार्षिक विवरण होता है अथवा विशेष विषयों पर प्राणमिक सूचना रखता है।

विकास क्रम में उत्तरता का सिद्धान्तः Principle of Later in Evolution यदि कोई एकल पंक्ति में अलग-2 समय में उत्पन्न हो तो उसका क्रम विकास के उत्तरता के क्रम में होना चाहिए।

विकेन्द्रीकरणः Decentralisation जब सेवा अनेक केन्द्रों पर संचालित की जाय।

विक्रेता सूचीः Book Seller's Catalogue सूची जिसको पुस्तक विक्रेता अपने उपयोग के लिए अथवा उसके पास उपलब्ध संचय को सार्वजनिक करने के लिए बनाता है।

विच्छिन्न पंक्तिः Discontinued Array वर्ग पंक्ति जो लगातार नये वर्गों को नहीं स्वीकारती।

विच्छेदनः Dissection विषय का उसमें उपलब्ध अभिलक्षणों के आधार पर वर्गों में विभक्ती करण है।

विचारः Thought ज्ञान के अंश।

विचार तलः Verbal Plane वर्गीकरण प्रक्रिया का स्तर जब शब्दों से अंकन के बारे में विचार होता है।

विचार धरातल के वर्गीकरण प्रनियमः Canon's of Classification (Idea Plane) इस प्रकार के प्रनियमों को चार समूहों में रख गया है:- 1. गुण के प्रनियम; 2. पंक्ति के प्रनियम; 3. शृंखला के प्रनियम और 4. क्रमिक सारिणी के प्रनियम।

वितरक वाहनः Delivery Van वाहन जिसके द्वारा पुस्तकालय की पठन सामग्री एक स्थान से दूसरे स्थान पर पहुँचाई जाती है।

वित्तः Finance धन सम्बन्धी कार्य।

वित्त अभिलेखः Financial Record अभिलेख जिसमें वित्त सम्बन्धी प्रामाणिक विवरण रहता है।

वित्त-अनुमानः Financial Estimate आगामी समय की आवश्यकताओं के लिए वित्त सम्बन्धी अनुमान।

वित्त प्रशासनः Financial Management प्रशासन जो वित्त सम्बन्धी व्यवस्था की देख-रेख करता है।

वित्त विवरणः Financial Statement प्रस्तावित धन सम्बन्धी विवरण।

वित्तीय साधनः Financial Resources धन प्राप्त करने के साधन।

विद्वित समाजः Learned Society समाज जिसके सदस्य विद्वान/शिक्षित हों।

विदेशी प्रकाशनः Foreign Publication अपने देश के अतिरिक्त अथवा अन्य देशों के प्रकाशन।

विदेशी सूचना केन्द्रः Foreign Information Centre देश से सम्बन्धित सभ्यता, संस्कृति, इतिहास तथा विज्ञान से संम्बन्धित सूचना को विदेशों को उपलब्ध कराते हैं।

विधि/कानून पुस्तकालयः Law Library इस प्रकार के पुस्तकालयों के संकलन विधि से सम्बन्धित होते हैं।

विघेय-क्रियाकर्त्ता-उपकरण सिद्धान्तः Act and-Action-Actor-Tool Principle.

विन्यास पंक्तिः Array समकक्ष वर्गों का समूह।

विनिमयः Exchange व्यवस्था जिसके अर्न्तगत बिना मूल्य चुकाए प्रकाशन के बदले में विभागीय प्रकाशनों का आदान-प्रदान होता है।

विपरीत अनुवाद सत्यापनः Verification of Reverse Translation वर्ग संख्या का उसके पक्षों में विश्लेषण करने के उपरान्त उनका नाम-करण तथा अंकन का शीर्षक के संदर्भ में अनुवाद कर, अर्थ अभिव्यक्ति निश्चित करने की क्रिया है।

विभागः Department सम्पूर्ण निकाय का एक भाग जो विशेष कार्य करता है।

विभागीय प्रकाशनः Departmental Publication प्रकाशन जिनके द्वारा विभागीय गतिविधि/प्रगति को स्पष्ट किया जाता है।

विभागीय पुस्तकालयः Departmental Library पुस्तकालय जिनके संकलन सम्बद्ध विभागों की आवश्यकता पूर्ति के साघन होते है।

विभागीय संचयः Departmental Collection विभाग की आवश्यकता पूर्ति करने वाला संचय अथवा विभाग द्वारा उत्पन्न संचय।

विभागीय सूचीः Departmental Catalogue सूची जिसकी प्रविष्टि विभाग विशेष के संचय को व्यक्त करती है।

विभेदीकरण का प्रनियमः Canon of Differentiation वर्गीकरण के आधार में प्रयुक्त अभिलक्षण इकाई को अलग-2 कर कम से कम दो वर्गों को जन्म देने वाले होने चाहिए।

विभाजन गुणः Division Characteristic गुण जिनको वर्गीकरण का आधार बनाया जाय।

विभाजनः Division वर्गीकरण में वांछित गुणों के आधार पर वर्ग प्राप्त करने की क्रिया।

विभाजित विशेष एकलः Devised Special Isolate गणनात्मक युक्ति प्राप्त विशेष एकल।

विरल एकत्रणः Loose Assembly विषयों का संयोजन अधिक समीपता के साथ न हो।

विलम्बित पुस्तकः Over-due Book उधार की अवधि समाप्त होने पर भी प्रयोक्ता के पास रखी पुस्तक।

विलम्ब सूचनाः Over-due Notice उधार ग्रन्थ को प्राप्त करने को दिया गया स्मरण पत्र।

विलम्बित शुल्कः Overdue Charges निश्चित अवधि के उपरान्त नियमानुसार शेष अवधि के लिए लिया गया शुल्क। इस शुल्क की मात्रा विभाग निर्धारित करता है।

विलम्बीः Defaulter व्यक्ति जो पुस्तकालय ग्रन्थों को देय तिथि तक नहीं लौटा पाता।

विवरणः Statement नियमित सूचना प्राप्त करने के लिए दिया गया निर्देश जिसकी सहायता से सूचना प्राप्त की जा सकती है।

विवरणकारः Descriptor विषय को अभिव्यक्त करता है।

विवरणात्मक सूची करणः Descriptive Cataloguing सूची जिसमें सूचना का समायोजन व्यापक रूप से होता हैं।

विवराणिकाः Prospectus शैक्षणिक संस्था द्वारा प्रस्ताविक शैक्षाणिक कार्यक्रम तथा प्रार्थना पत्र के प्रारूप सम्बन्धी सूचना प्रदान करती हैं।

विवरणात्मक तत्त्वः Descriptive Element विषय के स्पष्टीकरण के लिए

व्यक्ति के नाम के साथ जोड़े जाने वाले शब्द जिससे उसके कार्य का पता चलता है।

विवरणिका: Brochure विषय की साधारण जानकारी से सम्बन्धित अंकित सूचना सम्बन्धी कुछ पृष्ठ मात्र जो एक साथ जुड़े हो सकते हैं।

विश्लेषिक अनुक्रमणिका: Analytical Index विषय शीर्षकों के अन्तर्गत वर्णानुक्रमणिका होती है।

विश्लेषिक टिप्पण: Analytical Note टिप्पण विश्लेषिक प्रविष्टि का वह भाग है जिसमें मूल रचना के बारे में उल्लेख रहता है।

विश्लेषिक प्रविष्टि: Analytical Entry यह इतर प्रविष्टि रचना का संदर्भ व्यक्त करती है। तथा विषय के पूर्वापर सम्बन्ध को अभिव्यक्त करती है।

विश्लेषिक संश्लेषित वर्गीकरण: Analytico Synthetic Classification वर्गीकरण जिसमें पहले वर्ग प्राप्त करने के लिए विश्लेषण होता है तथा प्रणाली के नियमानुसार संश्लेषित कर वर्ग निर्धारित किया जाता है।

विश्लेषित शीर्षक: Analysed Title शीर्षक के मुख्य शब्दों को पहचान कर मूलभूतश्रेणी की अभिधारण क्रम में रख दिया जाता है।

विश्वविद्यालय पुस्तकालय समिति: University Library Committee यह समिति वि. वि. पुस्तकालयाध्य के लिए सलाहकर के रूप में कार्य करती है। इराके सदस्य प्रशासक, शिक्षक तथा पुस्तकालय व्यवसायी होते हैं।

विशेष एकल: Special Isolate एकल जो सामान्य नहीं हैं इनका प्रयोग विशेष परिस्थिति में होता है।

विशिष्टता का प्रनियम: Canon of Exclusiveness वर्गीकरण में पंक्तिवर्ग आपस में विशिष्ट होने चाहिए।

विश्व कोश: Thesaurus चुने हुए शब्द समानार्थी सम्बन्धों के साथ वर्णाक्रम में संयोजित होते है।

विश्वकोश: Encyclopaedia किसी विषय अथवा सम्पूर्ण ज्ञान जगत का संक्षिप्त प्रमाणिक परिचय वर्गानुक्रम में संयोजित होता है।

विश्वविद्यालय अनुदान आयोग–अनुदान: U.G.C. Grants केन्द्रीय स्वायत्तशासी संस्था विश्व-विद्यालय अनुदान आयोग द्वारा शिक्षा कार्यक्रम के अन्तर्गत आवण्टित अनुदान।

विश्वविद्यालय पुस्तकालय: University Library विश्वविद्यालय के पाठ्यक्रम तथा युवाओं में राष्ट्रीय विकास के प्रति चेतना उत्पन्न करने वाले संकलन तथा सूचना सम्प्रेषण सेवा प्रदान कर पुस्तकालय शिक्षा संस्था से जुड़े होते हैं।

विशेषताएँ: Specifications *देखिए* मानक।

विशेष प्रविष्टि: Specific Entry प्रविष्टि जिसमें विशेष प्रलेख का उल्लेख होता है।

विशेष पुस्तकालय तथा सूचना केन्द्रों का भारतीय संघ: Indian Association of Special Libraries and Information Centres (IASLIC) इस पंजीकृत संस्था का मुख्य कार्यालय कलकत्ता में है। यह पुस्तकालय सेवा विकास के कार्य में संलग्न है।

विशेष-सूचना: Specific Information सूचना जो विशेष उद्देश्य के लिये हो।

विशिष्ट युक्ति: Classic Device.

विशेष संस्करण: Special Edition ग्रन्थ का सामायिक उद्देश्य अथवा विशेष आवश्यकता पर आधारित संस्करण।

विशेष एकल विचार: Special Isolate Idea एकल विचार जिसके विशेष गुणों के कारण विशेष अंकन द्वारा व्यक्त किया जाता है।

विशेष अंक: Special Issue *देखिए* विशेष संख्या।

विशेष बड़ी जिल्द: Deluxe Binding कलात्मक बड़े आकार वाली जिल्द।

विशेष पुस्तकालय: Special Library चुने हुए विषय से सम्बन्धित संकलन ही कुछ चुने हुए प्रयोक्ताओं के लिए रखे जाते हैं। सर्व साधारण के प्रयोग के ग्रन्थ इनकी आवश्यकता नहीं होते।

विशेष परामर्श: Expert Advise.

विशेष सूची: Special List सूची जो विशेष उद्देश्य पूर्ति के लिए हो।

विशेष संग्रह: Special Collection विशेष उद्देश्य से एकत्रित संग्रह।

विस्तार पत्र: Extension Card *देखिए* निरन्तर पत्र।

विस्तृत संस्करण: Enlarged Edition *देखिए* संशोधित संस्करण।

विषय: Subject विचार/विषय वस्तु जो विवेच्य है। अथवा प्रलेख का आन्तरिक रूप जो कथा-वस्तु से बनता है।

विषय ग्रन्थ सूची: Subject Bibliography ग्रन्थ-सूची जिसमें किसी विषय पर ही पूर्व तथा वर्तमान में प्रकाशित ग्रन्थ प्रविष्टि होती हैं।

विषय वर्गीकरण: Subject Classification जेम्स डफ ब्राउन द्वारा 1906 में प्रथम बार इसकी रचना की गई।

विषय-विश्लेषिक: Subject Analytical अतिरिक्त प्रविष्टि जिसको विषय व्यक्त करने के लिए बनाया जाता है।

विषय-प्रदेश: Subject Region विषय के समान गुणों के कारण भौगोलिक भिन्नताओं के रहते हुए भी जब भौगोलिक भाग इकाई मान लिया जाता है।

विषय प्रविष्टि: Subject Entry विषय को प्रविष्टि की प्रथम पंक्ति में लिखा जाता हैं।

विषय व्यवस्था: Subject Arrangement विषय के आधार पर ग्रन्थ संयोजन हो।

विषय युक्ति: Subject Device वर्गीकरण में जब वर्ग संख्या को एकल रूप में प्रयोग कर मुख्य विषय के साथ जोड़ा जाए।

विषय सारिणी: Table of Contents प्रलेख में वर्णित अध्यायों के पृष्ठ संदर्भ के साथ सूची जो ग्रन्थ के प्रारम्भ में होती है।

विषय-सूची: Subject Catalogue विषय से सम्बन्धित प्रविष्टियों की वर्णानुक्रम में सूची होती है।

विषय शीर्षक: Subject Heading शब्द/शब्द समूह जिससे प्रलेख का विषय स्पष्ट होता है। समानता निर्वाह के लिए मानक विषय शीर्षक सूची बनाई जाती हैं।

विषय-संदर्भ: Subject Reference एक विषय से दूसरे विषय को संकेत।

विषय विशेषज्ञ: Subject Specialist व्यक्ति जिसको विषय का गहन अध्ययन हो।

विसम पृष्ठांकन: Irregular Paging पृष्ठ संख्या जो क्रमशः न हो।

विज्ञापन पत्र: Poster तात्कालिक सूचना संवाहक।

विज्ञान तथा तकनीकी राष्ट्रीय सूचना प्रणाली: National Information System for Science and Technology (NISSAT) विज्ञान तथा तकनीकी क्षेत्र में अनावश्यक अपव्यय को रोककर सूचना प्रयोग में सुधार लाने के लिए 'निसात' की स्थापना की गई थी।

वीडियो टेपः Video Tape चुम्बकीय गुण युक्त टेप जिसका प्रयोग सूचना एकत्र कर दृश्य-श्रव्य उपकरण पर प्रयोग करना है।

वीडियो डिस्कः Video Disc मशीन (कम्प्यूटर) प्रयुक्त उपकरण है। जिसमें धातू के विशेष प्रकार के पत्रों पर सूचना अंकित कर समाहित कर दिया जाता है।

बेतरतीव-प्रवेशः Random Access सूचना प्राप्ति के लिए सारिणी में प्रवेश विधि।

वैकल्पिक शीर्षकः Alternative Title वैकल्पिक शीर्षक मूल शीर्षक के साथ और अथवा समानार्थक शब्द प्रयोग से जुड़ा होता है अथवा शीर्षक एक से अधिक भाषाओं में होता है। इसका कारण शीर्षक को व्यापक अभिव्यक्ति देना होता है।

वैचारिक धरातलः Idea Plane विषय का वैचारिक स्मृति से उद्भव होता है। इसके बाद शब्द/अंकन युक्त किया जाता है।

वैदिक वर्गीकरणः Vedic Classification वर्गीकरण प्रणाली जिसका प्रयोग वेद, उपनिषद, पुरान, भगवद् गीता तथा तन्त्रों के लिए होता है।

वैयक्तिक सेवाः Personal Service सीधे व्यक्ति से व्यक्ति सम्पर्क द्वारा दी गई सेवा।

वैयक्तिक सेवकः Personal Staff कर्मचारी जो व्यक्ति की सहायता के लिये लगाया गया हो।

वैज्ञानिक प्रशासनः Scientific Management *देखिए* आधुनिक प्रशासन।

वैज्ञानिक शब्दावलीः Scientific Terms शब्द जिनका प्रयोग वैज्ञानिक विषयों में होता है।

श

शक्ति चक्र की अभिधारणाः Postulate of Rounds for Energy किसी भी एक विषय में ही शक्ति एक से अधिकबार भी उत्पन्न हो सकती है।

शब्दः Term शब्द/शब्द समूह जिससे किसी भाषा में भाव और विचारों को प्रामाणिक अभिव्यक्ति मिलती है तथा वर्गीकरण में वर्ग की अभिव्यक्ति का माध्यम होता है।

शब्द कोशः Glossary/Dictionary चयनित शब्द अपने आशय के साथ वर्णानुक्रम में संयोजित रहते है।

शब्द कोश-सूचीः Dictionary Catalogue सूची भाग जिसकी प्रविष्टियों अक्षर क्रम में व्यवस्थित होती हैं।

शब्द प्रविष्टिः Word Entry प्रविष्टि की प्रथम सूचना पंक्ति शब्द से प्रारम्भ होती है *और देखिए* प्रविष्टि शब्द।

शब्द पुस्तकः Word Book *देखिए* शब्द कोश।

शब्द-समूहः Word Group शब्द एक से अधिक विषय की अभिव्यक्ति के लिए प्रयुक्त होते हैं।

शब्द संसाधनः Word Processing कम्प्यूटर प्रयुक्त प्रौग्राम।

शब्दानु क्रमाणिकाः Word-by-word Filing प्रविष्टियों का शब्दों के प्रथम अक्षर/वर्ण क्रम में व्यवस्थित करना।

शब्दावलीः Terminology विषय की अभिव्यक्ति में प्रयुक्त शब्द समूह।

शाखा पुस्तकालयः Branch Library पुस्तकालय विस्तार सेवा।

शाब्दिक धरातलः Verbal Plane धरातल जिस पर विचार को शब्द रूप में परिगणित किया जाता है जहाँ शब्द/शब्द समूह वाक्य तथा कथन अंश प्राकृतिक भाषा रूप में होते है।

शाब्दिक स्मृति सहाय्य का प्रनियमः Canon of Verbal Mnemonics वर्ण का स्मृति सहाय्य युक्ति के रूप में उसी

अवस्था में प्रयोग करना चाहिए जब अन्य युक्ति से वर्गीकरण स्पष्ट न हो पाता हो।

शासकीयः Official Organ *देखिए* शासकीय प्रकाशन

शासकीय प्रकाशनः Official Publication सरकार/शासकीय संस्था द्वारा प्रकाशित प्रकाशन।

शिक्षाः Qualification/Education माध्यम जिससें व्यक्ति अपने आप परिवेश/समाज को जान कर उसके अंग के रूप में व्यवहार करता है।

शिक्षा का माध्यमः Medium of Education

शिक्षितः Literate व्यक्ति तो समझ, पढ़ तथा अभिव्यक्त कर सकता है।

शीफः Sheaf कागज का अंश।

शीघ्र चुनाव कारकः Rapid Selector मशीनी युक्ति जिससे फिल्म/दृश्य पटल पर देख कर सूचना चुनी जाती है।

शीर्षकः Heading/Title प्रलेख के विषय को स्पष्ट करने वाला शब्द/शब्द समूह जो रचना का प्रतिनिधित्व करता है।

शीर्ष पंक्तिः Head Line पंक्ति जिसके वाक्य अधिक स्पष्ट अक्षरों में तथा विषय की ओर ध्यान आर्कषित करने के लिए लिखें जाते हैं।

शीर्षक टिप्पण परिवर्तितः Change of Title Note टिप्पण जिसमें रचना के लिए प्रयुक्त अन्य शीर्षक का उल्लेख होता है जो पूर्व संस्करण में व्यक्त हो चुका है।

शीर्षक अनुभागः Title Section सूची पत्र का सूचीकरण निर्देशो द्वारा प्रयुक्त भाग जिसमें शीर्षक सम्बन्धी सूचना का उल्लेख होता है।

शीर्षक आवरणः Title Cover ग्रन्थ आवरण पृष्ठ जिसपर शीर्षक अंकित हो।

शीर्षक प्रविष्टिः Title Entry शीर्षक अधिक ग्राह्य होने की स्थिति में अतिरिक्त प्रविष्टि बनाई जाती है। जिसमें प्रथम सूचना शीर्षक से प्रारम्भ होती है।

शीर्षक पृष्ठः Title Page प्रलेख का साधारणतः प्रारम्भिक पृष्ठ जिस पर शीर्षक सम्बन्धी सूचना अंकित हो।

शीर्षक पृष्ठ प्रसारः Over Flow of Title Page शीर्षक संबंधी सूचना शीर्षक पृष्ठ से आगे वाले पृष्ठ पर अंकित हो।

शीर्षक विवरणः Title Statement विवरण जहाँ शीर्षक का उल्लेख हो।

शीर्षक विश्लेषकः Title Analytical शीर्षक अतिरिक्त प्रविष्टि है।

शीर्षक पत्रः Title Card सूची पत्र जो शीर्षक अतिरिक्त प्रविष्टि होता है।

शीर्षक सूचीः Title Catalogue सूची जिसमें शीर्षक प्रविष्टियों को वर्णानुक्रम में रखा जाता है।

शुद्ध अंकन का प्रनियमः Canon of Pure Notation वर्गीकरण में प्रयुक्त अंकन शुद्ध होना चाहिए।

शुद्ध अंकनः Pure Notation वर्गीकरण प्रणाली एक ही प्रकार के अंकन को वर्ग व्यवस्था में प्रयोग करे।

शुल्कः Subscription पत्रिका प्राप्ति के लिए दिया गया मूल्य।

शेषः Sequel रचना एक से अन्य रचना तक अग्रसरित होती हो।

शेष प्रलेखः Remainder विदेश में प्रकाशित न बिकपाने की स्थिति में शेष प्रलेख जिनको मूल्य कम होने के कारण भारतीय पुस्तक व्यवसाथियों द्वारा भारत के बाजार में बेचा जाता है। साधारणतः इनकी कागज की जिल्द होती है तथा मूल्य अंकित नहीं होता है। पुस्तक व्यवसाय से जुड़े लोगों के धन उपार्जन का मुख्य साधन है।

शोध प्रबन्धः Thesis/Doctoral the-

sis/Dissertation शोधकर्त्ता द्वारा किसी विषय पर किया गया प्रामाणिक गहन अध्ययन।

शोधः Research निश्चित विषय पर गहन वैज्ञानिक अध्ययन।

शोध पुस्तकालयः Research Library इस प्रकार के पुस्तकालय शोध से सम्बन्धित सूचनाओं के संचय के साथ-2 पाठक को सूचना सम्प्रेषण सेवा प्रदान करते हैं।

शोध मोनोग्राफः Research, Monograph शोध परिणाम पर आधारित प्रतिवेदन है।

शैल्फः Shelf लकड़ी अथवा स्टील की अलमारी जिसमें पुस्तकें रखी जाती है।

शैल्फ चिन्हः Shelf Mark चिन्ह/संख्या जिससे शैल्फ की स्थिति अथवा उसमें चयनित ग्रन्थों के बारे में ज्ञान होता है।

शैल्फ मार्ग दर्शकः Shelf Guide शैल्फ पर रखे ग्रन्थों के वर्ग का संकेतक।

शैल्फ सूचीः Shelf List सूची जिसमें प्रत्येक प्रलेख खण्ड का एक सूची पत्र उसी क्रम में रखा जाता है जिसमें पुस्तकालय में ग्रन्थ रखे गये है। मुख्य-पत्र संयोजित किया जाता है।

शैल्फ संख्याः Shelf Number संख्या जो किसी शैल्फ की स्थिति निश्चित करती है।

शैल्फ संसोधनः Shelf Rectification प्रयास जिसके द्वारा प्रलेखों को शैल्फ पर वर्गीकरण व्यवस्थानुसार रखा जाए।

शैक्षणिकः Academic शिक्षा से जुड़ा हुआ।

शैक्षणिक पुस्तकालयः Academic Library शिक्षा संस्थानों से जुड़े पुस्तकालय जिनके द्वारा शिक्षा के निश्चित मानदण्ड प्राप्त करने के लिए सूचना संकलन किया जाता है। इनके शिक्षा संस्थाओं के भेद के अनुसार अनेक भेद जैसे विश्वविद्यालय पुस्तकालय/कालेज पुस्तकालय/संकाय पुस्तकालय/स्कूल पुस्तकालय किए जा सकते हैं।

स्कूल पुस्तकालयः School Library यह स्कूल शिक्षा के आदर्श प्राप्त करने का माध्यम होते हैं। अध्यापक/विद्यार्थियों की अध्ययन आवश्यकता पूर्ति के साधन होते हैं।

स्कूल संस्करणः School Edition संस्करण विशेष रूप से विद्यार्थियों की आवश्यकतानुसार कम मूल्य पर बना हो।

स्तम्भः Coloumn पृष्ठ का विभाजन

स्तरः Round वर्गीकरण में पक्ष अथवा एकल की एक से अधिक बार आवृत्ति।

स्तर की अभिधारणः Postulate of Level पक्ष एक ही अथवा अनेक स्तरों पर एक से अधिक बार उत्पन्न होता है।

स्तरणः Lamination पतले पारदर्शी आवरण जिससे पृष्ठ को सुरक्षा दी जाती है अथवा वर्गीकरण में एक से अधिक वर्गो का मिश्रण।

स्थानः Space दो अंकित चिन्ह/अक्षरों के बीच की दूरी अथवा वर्गीकरण में शब्द से भौगोलिक सीमांकन से अभिप्राय है।

स्थान एकलः Space Isolate पृथ्वीतल का अनेक भाग/उपविभाग/द्वीप/देश/राज्य/जिला/तहसील आदि के रूप में पहचान कर वर्गीकरण किया जाता है।

स्थानान्तरणः Transfer कार्यक्षमता परिवर्तन के साथ कार्य का स्थान परिवर्तित हो जाता है।

स्थान तथा समय पक्ष की अभिधारणाः Postulate of Space and Time Facet साधारणतः स्थान तथा समय पक्ष सारणी के अन्त में होने चाहिए।

स्थानीय पहुँचः Local Access स्थानीय सूचना संकलन अथवा अनेक कम्प्यूटर सूचना

संग्रहों तक पहुँचना।

स्थानीय क्षेत्र तन्त्रः Local Area Network क्षेत्र विशेष के कम्प्यूटरों को एक दूसरे से जोड़ कर बनाया गया तन्त्र।

स्थायित्व का प्रनियमः Canon of Permanence वर्गीकरण के उद्देश्य में जब तक परिवर्तन नहीं होता तब तक वर्गीकरण के आधार स्वरूप स्वीकृत अभिलक्षण अपरिवर्तित रहने चाहिए।

स्थायी आदेशः Standing Order प्रत्येक नव प्रकाशित/पुनः प्रकाशित ग्रन्थ प्राप्त करने की स्थायी खरीद व्यवस्था।

स्मरण पत्रः Reminder पुस्तकालय प्रयोक्ता को पुस्तक लौटाने के लिए दिया गया पत्र।

स्मरण शक्तिः Memory सूचना संग्रह करने की कम्प्यूटर क्षमता जहाँ से पुनः आवश्यकता पड़ने पर सूचना प्राप्त की जा सकती है *और देखिए* संग्रह।

स्मरण-शक्ति क्षमताः Memory Capacity कम्प्यूटर में प्रयुक्त स्मरण शक्ति क्षमता अलग-2 होती है जिसके आधार पर इसका नाम करण किया जाता है।

स्मरण सूचनाः Reminder Notice *देखिए* स्मरण पत्र

स्मारक ग्रन्थः Souvenir Volume विशेष प्रयोजन व्यक्त करने वाला खण्ड।

स्मृति सहायकः Mnemonics कोई भी शब्द/चिन्ह/परिवर्णी शब्द/अंकन पूर्ण वर्गीकरण में अनेक बार उत्पन्न भाव के लिए एक से अधिक बार प्रयोग होता है।

स्मृति सहायक युक्तिः Mnemonic Device युक्ति जिससे वर्गीकरण प्रयुक्त अंको की स्मृति में सहयोग मिलता है।

स्वकृत क्रियाः Manual Operation मानव शक्ति संचालित क्रिया।

स्वतः अनुक्रमणः Auto Index तकनीकी सहायता से अनुक्रमण करना।

स्वतः संक्षेपणः Auto Abstract तकनीकी सहायता से रचनाओं के मुख्य शब्द संयोजन से संक्षेपण प्रस्तुत करना।

स्वत्वाधिकार पुस्तकालयः Copyright Library पुस्तकालय जिसके संचय को कानूनी अधिकार के अन्तर्गत देश में प्रकाशित प्रत्येक प्रलेख की प्रति प्राप्त होती है।

स्वाचालित अभिलेखः Automatic Record मशीन द्वारा नियमित सूचना संग्रह।

स्वचालित निर्गम प्रणालीः Automated Circulation System कम्प्यूटर प्रयुक्त निर्गम प्रणाली।

स्ववर्गीग्रन्थः Classic ग्रन्थ जिसकी अधिक प्रसिद्धि से वर्ग के रूप में पहचान बन चुकी हो।

स्ववर्गी ग्रन्थ प्रनियमः Canon of Classics वर्ग विशेष से सम्बन्धित सभी संस्करण अनुवाद/समीक्षा/इसी प्रकार के अन्य प्रयास साथ-2 होने चाहिए।

स्ववर्गी लेखकः Classical Author लेखक जिनकी रचना पहचान के कारण सभी कालों में पढ़ी जाती है।

स्वत्वाधिकारः Copyright लेखक/प्रकाशक/संस्था को रचना सम्बन्धी कानूनी अधिकार।

स्वामित्व चिन्हः Ownership Mark रबर की मुहर/छपी हुई कागज की पर्ची होती है। जिस पर पुस्तकालय का नाम होता है। जिसको प्रत्येक ग्रन्थ पर लगा दिया जाता है।

स्वायत्तशासी निकायः Autonomous Body निकाय जिसकी स्वतन्त्र कार्य प्रणाली होती है।

स्वास्थ्य विज्ञान पुस्तकालयः Health Science Library स्वास्थ्य विज्ञान के शैक्षणिक कार्यक्रम से जुड़े संकलन वाला

पुस्तकालय।

स्वीकृत पाठ्यक्रमः Recommended Curricula स्वीकृत विषय वस्तु जिसके आधार पर परीक्षा निशिचत होती है।

स्वीकृत क्षमताः Hospitality अंकन का गुण जिससे नये वर्गों को वर्गीकरण में अंकन प्राप्त हाता है।

स्थिति से दूर का सिद्धांतः Principle of Away from Position पंक्ति एकल यदि बिन्दु से प्रारम्भ करने हो तो बिन्दु से दुरस्थ पंक्ति का क्रम होना चाहिए।

स्विचबोर्डः Switch Board बिजली प्रयोग करने का उपकरण।

स्पैन्सर वर्गीकरणः Spenser Classification हरबर्ट स्पैन्सर द्वारा वैज्ञानिक विषयों के वर्गीकरण में उपयोगी 1864 में प्रदत्त प्रणाली।

स्रोतः Source प्रारम्भिक केन्द्र।

स्रोत प्रलेखः Source Document मूल प्रलेख।

स्रोत केन्द्रः Resource Centre केन्द्र जहाँ सूचना संकलन संसाधन तथा सम्प्रेषण होता है।

स्रोत सामग्रीः Resource Material देखिए मुख्य स्रोत

सत्ताः Entity कोई भी व्यक्त रूप।

सत्यापनः Verification वस्तु स्थिति तथा संकलनों की स्थिति जानने का तरीका है।

सदृश एकल विचारः Quasi Isolate Idea पंक्ति अभिलक्षण जब एकल रूप में जाना जाय।

सदृश अंकः Quasi Digit अंक समूह को इकाई रूप में समझा जाय।

सदृश वर्गः Quasi Class रचना को जब वर्गीकरण प्रणाली में वर्ग रूप मान लिया जाय तथा शीर्षक सारिणी में सूचीबद्ध हो।

सदस्यः Member पुस्तकालय प्रयोग की सुविधा प्राप्त व्यक्ति।

सदस्यताः Membership अधिकार जिससे पुस्तकालय सेवा ली जा सके।

सदस्यता सूचीः Membership list सूची जिसमें पुस्तकालय प्रयोग करने वालों के नाम होते हैं।

सदस्यता अभिलेखः Membership Record पंजी जिसमें पुस्तकालय सदस्यों/प्रयोक्ताओं का विवरण रहता है।

सम्पूर्ण मूल्यः Absolute Value विषय के निकटस्थ।

सम्मेलनः Conference निश्चित विषय पर बातचीत करने को एकत्रित विशेषज्ञों का अवसर।

समकक्ष वर्गः Co-ordinate Classes एक ही पंक्ति के वर्ग।

समकक्ष वर्ग प्रनियतः Canon of Co-ordinate Classes वर्गों के बीच कोई भी एफनिटी वर्ग न आकर अधिक एफनिटी वर्ग आना चाहिए।

समर्थित देशः Favoured Country देश जिससे सम्बन्धित सर्वाधिक सूचना संचयित हो तथा पुस्तकालय की व्यवस्था कर रहा हो।

समर्थित प्रणालीः Favoured System चयनित प्रणाली है जिसका चुनाव प्रयोग आधिक्य के आधार पर किया जाता है।

समार्थित मुख्य संख्याः Favoured Focus Number अंक/संख्या जो समर्थित वर्ग को व्यक्त करे।

सम ध्वनीय भिन्नार्थक शब्दः Homonym शब्द स्थान परिवर्तन से अर्थ परिवर्तन कर लें।

समजीवी स्मृति सहाय्य प्रनियमः Canon of Seminal Mnemonics सम्पूर्ण वर्गीकरण प्रणाली में समान विचारों को

व्यक्त करने के लिए एक ही प्रकार के अंकन का वर्ग अभिव्यक्ति में प्रयोग हो चाहे वह किसी भी पंक्ति, कितने ही शब्द अथवा संदर्भो में क्यो न व्यक्त हुआ हो।

समपृष्ठः Even Page पृष्ठ जिसकी संख्या सम हो।

समपद स्मृति सहाय्य प्रनियमः Canon of Scheduled Mnemonics किसी भी वर्गीकरण प्रणाली में सामान्य सारणी समूह होने चाहिए जिनको अलग-2 पंक्ति क्रम में अनेक वर्गों में उत्पन्न होने पर सारिणी की व्यवस्था के अनुसार मुख्य विषय से जोड़ा जा सकता है।

समरूपता का प्रनियमः Canon of Consistency वर्गीकरण के आधार में प्रयुक्त अभिलक्षणों का प्रयोग सारिणी क्रम में होना चाहिए जब तक कि वर्गीकरण के उद्देश्य में परिवर्तन नहीं होता।

समरूपी तारतम्यता का प्रनियमः Canon of Consistent Sequence यदि समान वर्ग आवृति विभिन्न पंक्तियों में हो तो उनकी सारिणी सभी पंक्तियों में समान होनी चाहिए जब तक कि उद्देश्य नहीं बदलता है।

समय सारिणीः Time Table तालिका जिसमें विभिन्न समयों का उल्लेख हो।

समष्टि लेखकः Corporate Author रचना में सन्निहित विचारों के लिए एक व्यक्ति के स्थान पर संस्था जिम्मेदार होती है।

समष्टि निकायः Corporate Body व्यक्ति समूह जो किसी सामान्य कार्य के लिए मिलकर कार्य करता है।

समष्टि प्रविष्टिः Corporate Entry.

समरुपता का प्रनियमः Canon of Uniformity वर्ग में प्रयुक्त अंक संख्या वर्ग के नियमित क्रम को व्यक्त करे।

समाचारः News साम्प्रतिक सूचना।

समाचार कतरनः News Clipping समाचार पत्रों में प्रकाशित साम्प्रतिक घटनाओं से सम्बन्ध सूचना का काटकर निकाला हुआ भाग।

समाचार पत्रः Newsletter किसी संस्था की समसामायिक गति विधियों का निश्चित अन्तर से विवरण प्रस्तुत करने वाला प्रकाशन

समाचार पत्रः Newspaper अधुनातन सूचनाओं को प्रसारित करने वाला पत्र।

समाचार पत्र प्रदर्शकः Newspaper Stand स्टेन्ड जिस पर समाचार पत्र पढ़ने को रखे जाते हैं।

समानान्तर वर्गः Collateral Classes एक ही क्रम के वर्ग जो एक पंक्ति में उत्पन्न न हुए हों।

समानान्तर शीर्षकः Parallel Title शीर्षक जिसके समानान्तर अन्य भाषाओं में शीर्षक साथ हो।

समानान्तर पंक्तियाँः Collateral Arrays सामान्य ज्ञान जगत् से उत्पन्न एक ही क्रम की पंक्तियाँ।

समानधर्मिता का प्रनियमः Canon of Concomitance वर्गीकरण के आधार में प्रयुक्त अभिलक्षणों में सहधार्मिता नहीं होनी चाहिए जिससे कि समान वर्ग पंक्ति निर्माण की स्थिति को रोका जा सके।

समान शीर्षकः Uniform Title बहुखण्डी ग्रन्थ का मानक शीर्षक जिसका प्रयोग सभी खण्डों पर किया जाता है।

समाप्त प्रकाशनः Out of Print Publication प्रकाशित ग्रन्थ की प्रति बाजार में उपलब्ध न हो तथा प्रकाशन बन्द कर दिया गया हो।

समायोज्य वर्गीकरणः Adjustable Classification जेम्स डफ ब्राउन की वर्गीकरण प्रणाली जिसको छोटे अंग्रेजी

पुस्तकालयों के लिए संख्या/अक्षरों के योग से बनाया गया था।

समायोजन युक्तिः Interpolated Device युक्ति जिससे दो वर्गों के मध्य नये वर्ग को अंकन प्रदान किया जाय।

समाहित संख्याः Interpolated Number संख्या जिसमें रिक्त कारक अंक आगामी अंक से पहले रहता है।

समाहानः Interpolation दो स्थितियों के मध्य अन्य स्थिति। एकल को स्थान प्रदान करना।

समीक्षाः Review समालोचनात्मक रचना

समीक्षा पत्रिकाः Review Periodical पत्रिका जिसमें प्रकाशित समीक्षाओं को पुनः प्रकाशित किया जाता है।

समुच्चयः Assemblage विषय युक्ति प्रयोग से नये वर्ग निर्माण न कर पाने की स्थिति में वर्ग सम्पर्क से वर्ग बनाने की प्रक्रिया है।

समूहः Group वर्गीकरण में ज्ञान जगत के अभिलक्षणों के आधार पर वर्ग समूह उत्पन्न किए जाते हैं।

समूह अंकन युक्तिः Group Notation Device अंकन समूह को इकाई रूप में प्रयुक्त किया जाय।

सरकिटः Circuit विद्युत प्रवाह जाल।

सरकारी पुस्तकालयः Government Library पुस्तकालय जिसका कार्य क्षेत्र सरकारी आवश्यकता पूर्ति तथा व्यवस्था खर्च सरकार वहन करती है। यह अनेक प्रकार के जैसे राष्ट्रीय, विभागीय तथा सूचना केन्द्र हो सकते है।

सरकारी प्रलेखः Government Document प्रलेख जिसका सृजन सरकारी विभाग अथवा सरकारी प्रयास से होता है।

सरकारी प्रकाशकः Government Publication *देखिए* सरकारी प्रलेख।

सरल आधारः Simple Base वर्गीकरण आधार जिसमें एक ही प्रकार के अंकों का प्रयोग हुआ हो।

सरल पुस्तकः Simple Book सम्बन्धित विषय की साधारण व्याख्या करती हो तथा सयुंक्त पुस्तक न हो।

सरल शीर्षकः Simple Heading शीर्षक जिसमें एक शब्द खण्ड हो।

सलाहकार पत्रः Guide Card पत्र सूची में अक्षर क्रम के निर्देशक होते हैं।

सलाहाकार पुस्तकः Guide Book विषय विशेष के बारे में साधारण ज्ञान देने वाली पुस्तक।

सलाहाकार समितिः Advisory Committee समिति पुस्तकालय सेवा नीति निर्धारित करती है साधारणतः पुस्तकाध्यक्ष समिति का सदस्य सचिव होता है। इस प्रकार की समिति का गठन राष्ट्रीय स्तर पर पुस्तकालय सेवाओं के आकलन के लिए सरकार द्वारा समय-2 पर किया जाता है।

सर्वेक्षणः Survey प्रामाणिक सूचना एकत्रित करने की प्रक्रिया।

सर्वाधिकार सुरक्षितः All Rights Reserved प्रतिलिपि प्राप्त करने सम्बधी अधिकार-सूचना जो ग्रन्थ के प्रारम्भ में अंकित होती है।

सस्ता संस्करणः Cheap Edition अल्प मूल्य संस्करण।

सहकारी सूचीकरणः Co-operative Cataloguing सूचीकरण में मितव्यता के लिए एक से अधिक पुस्तकालयों द्वारा मिलकर एक केन्द्र पर सूचीकरण किया जाता है। तथा बाद में आवश्यकतानुसार सूची पत्रों की संख्या स्वयम् प्राप्त कर ली जाती है। व्यय समान रूप से वहन किया जाता है।

सहकारी संकलनः Co-operative Acquisition/Co-operative

storage सूचना संकलन का सामूहिक प्रकार।

सहचारी पुस्तक: Associated Book पूर्व रचना के बारे में अन्य प्रलेख।

सह वितरण शीलता: Co-extensiveness वर्ग संख्या प्रधान रूप से वर्णित अभिलक्षणों का प्रतिनिधित्व करती है।

सहयोग: Sharing पुस्तकालय संसाधन/संचय/ सेवाओं को एक से अधिक पुस्तकालयों द्वारा प्रयोग किया जाता है।

सहयोगी कर्मचारी: Supporting Staff कर्मचारीगण जो व्यवसायिक/प्रशासनिक अधिकारियों की सहायता में नियुक्त होते हैं।

सहयोगी क्रम: Helpful Order वर्गीकरण प्रणाली क्रम जिससे वाँछित सूचना प्रयोक्ता को सुलभ होती है।

सहयोगी सारणी क्रम का प्रनियम: Canon of Helpful Sequence वर्गों का पंक्ति क्रम उद्देश्य का सहयोगी होना चाहिए।

सहयोगी लेखक: Collaborator व्यक्ति जो रचनाकार के कार्य में सहयोगी होता है यह सहयोग सम्पूर्ण ग्रन्थ रचना अथवा अंशमात्र के लिए हो सकता है।

सहयोगी टिप्पण: Add to Note वर्गीकरण प्रणाली के प्रयोग को व्यापक बनाने के लिए इस प्रकार के टिप्पण का प्रयोग किया जाता है जिसका संदेश होता है कि वर्ग विशेष के आधार पर दूसरे वर्ग के भाग, उपविभाग किए जा सकते हैं तथा उक्त अनुसार वर्ग संयोजन किया जाना चाहिए।

सहयोगी सारिणीक्रम: Helpful Sequence सारिणी क्रम जब उद्देश्य सहयोगी होता है।

सहायक: Assistant व्यक्ति/कर्मचारी जो अधिकारी के आदेशानुसार कार्य करता है।

सहायक-पत्रिका: Secondary Journal/Secondary Periodical पत्रिका जिसकी विषय वस्तु में प्रकाशित लेख/आलोचना/सारांश आदि होते हैं।

सहायक-प्रलेख: Secondary Document प्रलेख जिसको मूल प्रलेखों के उपयोग के लिए बनाया जाय।

सहायता प्राप्त पुस्तकालय: Aided Library पुस्तकालय जो अर्थ अथवा अन्य सहायता प्राप्त करने की शर्त पूरी करता है और नियमित व्यवस्था प्राप्त करने के लिए संस्था/सरकार/व्यक्ति का सहयोग प्राप्त प्राप्त करता है।

सक्षम अधिकारी: Competent Authority व्यक्ति/संस्था जिसको अधिकार प्राप्त होते हैं।

साधारण संयुक्त पुस्तक: Ordinary Composite Book एक से अधिक स्वतन्त्र रचनाओं को एक ही जिल्द में रख दिया जाय। इसका एक सामान्य शीर्षक भी हो सकता है।

साधारण उप-विभाग: Common Subdivision देखिए रूप-विभाग।

साज-समान: Furniture पुस्तकालय सेवा सम्बन्धी साज समान।

साझा-सूचीकरण: Shared Cataloguing एक से अधिक पुस्तकालय मिल कर सूचीकरण करते हैं।

सामान्य प्रविष्टि: General Entry प्रविष्टि जिसका निर्माण सामान्य नीति के अन्तर्गत होता है।

सामान्य वर्ग: Generalia Class वर्गीकरण प्रणाली का प्रथम वर्ग होता है। जिसके सरिणीबद्ध वर्ग एक विषय से सम्बन्धित न होकर आंशिक रूप से एक से अधिक विषयों से जुड़े होते है और किसी एक वर्ग की पहचान नहीं हो सकते।

साप्ताहिक: Weekly पत्रिका जिसका प्रकाशन

पन्द्रह दिन के अन्तर से होता है।

सम्मान जनक संग्रहः Comprehensive Collection देखिए संग्रह।

सापेक्ष अनुक्रमाणिकाः Relative Index वर्गीकरण में प्रयुक्त मानक शब्दों का कोश होती है जिसके प्रयोग से वर्गीकरण में अंकन पहचाना जाता है।

सापेक्षता का प्रनियमः Canon of Relativity वर्ग संख्या में प्रयुक्त अंको की संख्या वर्गो के अनुपातिक क्रम मे होनी चाहिए जिनको यह व्यक्त करती है।

सापेक्ष स्थानः Relative Location प्रलेखों का उनके आपसी सम्बन्ध क्रम में संयोजन।

साफ्टवेयरः Software कम्प्यूटर प्रोग्राम जिसके योग से कम्प्यूटर का प्रयोग होता है।

साम्प्रतिक निर्देशिकाः Current Directory (CD) कम्प्यूटर में अंकित सूचना की तालिका।

साम्प्रतिक विषय तालिकाः Current Contents विषय विशेष पर वर्तमान अवधि में उत्पन्न रचनाओं का संक्षेप में सम्प्रेषण प्रकार।

साम्प्रतिक समीक्षाः Current Review देखिए समीक्षा।

साम्प्रतिकता का प्रनियमः Canon of Currency वर्गीकरण प्रणाली में प्रयुक्त शब्द आधुनिकतम होने चाहिए। तथा इन शब्दों का प्रयोग विषय विज्ञानियों द्वारा सुनिश्चित होने पर ही वर्गीकरण प्रणाली में स्वीकृत हो।

साम्प्रतिक सूचनाः Current Information देखिए सूचना।

साम्प्रतिक-सूचीः Current List सूची जिससे पुस्तकालय द्वारा वर्तमान में प्राप्त संचय का ज्ञान होता है।

साम्प्रतिक सूचना सेवाः Current Awareness Service पुस्तकालय में उपलब्ध सूचनाओं के विषयों के प्रयोक्ताओं को इस बारे में सूचित करना।

साम्प्रतिक संख्याः Current Number पत्रिका का नवीनतम अंक

सामान्य एकलः Common Isolate एकल जिसको सामान्य गुण के काण अनेक वर्गों के साथ जोड़ा जा सकता है।

सामान्य एकल विचारः Common Isolate Idea एकल विचार जिसको निश्चित अंकन द्वारा किसी वर्ग के साथ जोड़ा जा सकता है वर्ग परिवर्तन की स्थिति में सामान्य एकल प्रयुक्त अंकन नहीं बदलता है।

सामान्य प्रकाशनः Ordinary Publication प्रकाशन जिसका विशेष उद्देश्य न हो।

सामान्य पक्षः Common Facet वर्ग/वर्ग प्रणाली में कही भी उत्पन्न हो सकता है। इसमें प्रयुक्त गुण सामान्य प्रकार के होते है। जो किसी भी वर्ग के अनुगामी हो सकते है।

सामान्य पत्रः Ordinary Letter साधारणतः कार्य को प्रयुक्त पत्र।

सामान्य पुस्तकः General Book पुस्तक जिससे विषय का सामान्य परिचय प्राप्त होता है।

सामान्य पुस्तकालयः General Library पुस्तकालय जिनका संकलन/प्रयोक्ता किसी निश्चित उद्देश्य के आधार पर निश्चित नहीं किए जातें।

सामान्य पाठकः General Reader पाठक जिसका कोई विशेष अध्ययन क्षेत्र नहीं होता।

सामान्य विषयः General Subject विषय जिससे सामान्य ज्ञान प्राप्त होता है।

सामान्य सम्बन्धः General Relation

दो पक्षों के बीच पूर्वाग्रह रहित सम्बन्ध।

सामान्य सम्बन्ध पक्ष: General Relation Phase एक ही प्रकार के एकल के बीच का सम्बन्ध होता है।

सामूहिक शीर्षक: Collective Title शीर्षक जिसके अन्तर्गत अनेक रचनाकारों की रचनाएं प्रकाशित होती हैं।

सामूहिक/समूह: Aggregate बिना किसी व्यवस्था में कोई भी संग्रह।

सार: Extract रचना का मूल अंश/संक्षिप्त कथावस्तु।

सारकरण: Abstracting सार करने की क्रिया।

सारकरण सेवा: Abstraction Service संस्था/व्यक्ति जो सार उपलब्ध कराने का प्रबन्ध करता है।

सारकरण पत्रिका: Abstracting Periodical विषय विशेष पर छपी रचनाओं की मूल सूचनाओं को सार रूप में प्रस्तुत करती है।

सार पत्रिका: Abstract Bulletin *देखिए* सारकरण पत्रिका।

सार शीर्षक: Kernel Title मुख्य शब्दों में व्यक्त शीर्षक।

सारांश: Summary विषय की मुख्य बातों को प्रस्तुत किया जाय।

सारिणी/तालिका: Schedule वर्गीकरण से प्राप्त उपवर्गों का उनके वर्गानुक्रम में सूचीबद्ध स्वरूप।

सारिणी संयोग विन्यास: Arrangement by a Combination एक से अधिक वर्गीकरण प्रणालियों के सहयोग से किया गया वर्गीकरण विन्यास।

सार्वजनिक अभिलेख: Public Record अभिलेख जो कि सार्वजनिक है अथवा सभी को सुलभ है।

सावधिक पत्रिका: Periodical Bulletin *देखिए* पत्रिका।

सार्वजनिक पुस्तकालय: Public Library पुस्तकालय जिसकी सेवाएँ बिना किसी बाधा के सम्पूर्ण समाज को उपलब्ध हों तथा पूर्ण अथवा आंशिक रखरखाव सार्वजनिक रूप से एकत्रित साधनों से हो।

सार्वजनिक पुस्तकालय अधिनियम: Public Library Act नियम जिससे सार्वजनिक पुस्तकालय स्थापना तथा विकास हो।

सार्वजनिक पुस्तकालय कानून: Public Library Law *देखिए* सार्वजनिक पुस्तकालय आधिनियम।

सार्वजनिक पुस्तकालय घोषणा पत्र: Public Library Manifesto इस आशय का अभिलेख यूनेस्को द्वारा 1949 में प्रथम प्रकाशित हुआ था।

सार्वजनिक पुस्तकालय प्रणाली: Public Library System

साहित्य सहायक: Literature Guide विषय पर उपलब्ध सदर्भ ग्रन्थ।

सिद्धान्त: Principles *देखिए* नियम।

साहित्यिक आवृत्ति: Literary warrant विषय पर प्रकाशित रचनायें।

साहित्यिक कृति: Literary Work साहित्य की अनेक विघा कविता/कहानी/नाटक/उनन्यास आदि-2 जिनमें सत्य सुग्राह्य बनाया जाता है।

साहित्यिक खोज: Literature Search विषय से सम्बन्धित सूचना का संचय।

साहित्यिक मौंग का सिद्धान्त: Principle of Literary warrant पंक्ति एकल क्रम उपलब्ध साहित्य के ह्रासमान क्रम में होना चाहिए।

साहित्यिक शीर्षक: Literary Title शीर्षक जिसका शब्द चयन साहित्यिक अभिरूचि के अनुसार होता है। पुस्तकालय वर्गीकरण साहित्यिक शीर्षक को वर्णक्रम में सूचीबद्ध

करता है।

सीधा उप-विभाजनः Direct Sub-division.

सीधी छपाईः Direct Printing मशीनी व्यवस्था अथवा कम्प्यूटर प्रयोग में कम्प्यूटर से सीधे प्रिन्ट प्राप्त करने की क्रिया।

सीधा प्रवेशः Direct Entry प्रवेश बाधा रहित हो।

सीधा सम्पर्कः On Line Operation एक कम्प्यूटर संकलन से दूसरे कम्प्यूटर संकलन तक पहुँचने की व्यवस्था।

सीधा पहुँच सेवाः On Line Search Service *देखिए* सीधा सम्पर्क।

सीधा पहुँचः On Line Access *देखिए* सीधा सम्पर्क।

सी. डी. रोमः C D ROM इलैक्ट्रॉनिक माध्यम पर सूचना संग्रह का प्रकार।

सी डी एस/आई एस आई एसः CDS/ISIS यूनेस्को द्वारा विकसित कम्प्यूटर द्वारा सूचना संसाधन की व्यवस्था (प्रोग्राम) है। यह विशेष रूप से प्रलेखों के सूचना प्रयोग को ध्यान कर बनाया गया है।

सुझाव पुस्तकः Suggestion Book पंजी जिसमें सुझाव एकत्रित किए जाते हैं।

सुलेखनः Caligraphy सुन्दर लिखने की कला।

सुनियोजित समृद्ध अंकः Systematic Rich Digit अंक जो क्रमिक मूल्य के साथ विशेष विचार सुनियोजित स्मृति सिद्धान्त के अन्तर्गत व्यक्त करता है।

सुनिश्चिता का प्रनियमः Canon of Ascertainability वर्गीकरण के लिए प्रयुक्त गुण निश्चित होना चाहिए।

सुव्यवस्थित स्मृति सहाय्य प्रनियमः Canon of Systematic Mnemonic वर्गीकरण प्रणाली में प्रयुक्त सारिणी एक ही क्रम पर आधारित समृति सहाय्य हो।

सुस्पष्टता का प्रनियमः Canon of Distinctiveness प्रनियम का उद्देश्य पुस्तकालय आह्वान संख्या के अवयवों की पहचान स्पष्ट करना है अतः वर्ग संख्या/पुस्तक संख्या/खण्ड संख्या को पृथकता के साथ लिखा जाना चाहिए।

सूचनाः Information/Data कोई ज्ञान अंश विकास प्रक्रिया में परवर्ती ज्ञान समीपता पाकर नवीनता ग्रहण करता है तो वह भी ज्ञान/सूचना बन जाता है। 'डाटा' शब्द कमप्यूटर प्रणाली में सूचना की इकाई का द्योतक है। अथवा मानव जिज्ञासा जनित ज्ञान भंण्डार का नाम है जिसको सर्वकालिक परिभाषा में बांधना सम्भव नहीं है।

सूचना की आधिकता/सूचना विस्फोटः Explosion of Information सूचना का तीव्रातितीव्र निरन्तर विस्तार।

सूचना अधिकारीः Information Officer व्यक्ति जो सूचना संचय, व्यवस्था तथा उपलब्ध कराने के कार्य से जुड़ा हो।

सूचना संग्रहः Database कम्प्यूटर प्रणाली में संकलित सूचना।

सूचना के अप्रलेखीय स्रोतः Non-documentry Sources of Information अतिरिक्त सूचना स्रोत जैसे/व्यक्ति, संस्था तथा सरकारी विभाग आदि।

सूचना केन्द्रः Data Centre/Information Centre केन्द्र जहाँ सूचना का संचय, संसाधन कर प्रयोक्ता को उपलब्ध कराया जाय *और देखिए* प्रलेखन केन्द्र।

सूचना कार्यः Information Work

सूचना तकनीकः Information Technology तकनीक जिसके प्रयोग से सूचना प्रयोग में सहयोग प्राप्त किया जाता है।

सूचना तत्वः Data Element/Infor-

mation Element वर्ग विशेष में सूचना की क्रमिक स्थिति अथवा सूचीकरण में प्रयुक्त विभिन्न सूचना अंश।

सूचना देना: Reporting विकास को सार्वजनिक करने की क्रिया।

सूचना नीति: Information Policy सरकार समर्थित संस्था द्वारा सूचना प्रयोग के लिए बनाये गये निर्देश/नियम समूह।

सूचना परिवर्तन: Data Conversion सूचना का एक स्थिति से दूसरी स्थिति में स्थानान्तरण।

सूचनाप्रद सार: Informative Abstract सार जो मूल पाठ अथवा प्रमुख सूचनाओ से अवगत कराता है जिससे कि निर्णय लिया जा सके कि मूल पाठ का पठन आवश्यक है कि नहीं।

सूचना प्राप्ति: Information Retrieval आवश्यकता पढ़ने पर सूचना प्रयोग की क्रिया।

सूचना प्राप्ति प्रणाली: Information Retrieval System निर्देश समूह/प्रणाली जिसकी सहायता से सूचना उपलब्ध की जाती है।

सूचना प्रणाली: Information System निर्देश प्रकार।

सूचना विज्ञान: Information Service सूचना विकास तथा प्रयोग का विज्ञान।

सूचना विज्ञानी: Information Scientist व्यक्ति जो सूचना प्रयोग सम्बन्धी ज्ञान से जुड़ा हो।

सूचना स्थान: Information Field कम्प्यूटर प्रयोग में सूचना के नियमन के लिए निर्धारित स्थान।

सूचना संग्रह प्रशासन प्रणाली: Database Management System (DBMS) सूचना नियन्त्रण के लिए कम्प्यूटर प्रयुक्त निर्देश।

सूचना संचरण: Data Processing/ Information Processing सूचना तत्वों को प्रयोगानुसार व्यवस्थित करने की प्रक्रिया है।

सूचना संचालन: Information Handling *देखिए* सूचना संचरण।

सूचना संचयन: Data Compilation आवश्यकतानुसार सूचना का एकत्रीकरण।

सूचना संग्रह: Data Collection कम्प्यूटर प्रणाली में संकालित सूचना।

सूचना संग्रह तथा प्राप्ति प्रणाली: Data Storage and Retrievel System *देखिए* सूचना केन्द्र।

सूचना सहिता: Data Code सूचना व्यवस्था से सम्बन्धित निर्देश संकलन।

सूचना सम्प्रेषण: Data Communication दो केन्द्रों के बीच सूचना का स्थानान्तरण।

सूचना सम्प्रेषण: Dissemination of Information साधन/सेवा के सहयोग से सूचना प्रयोक्ता को उपलब्ध कराने की क्रिया।

सूचना समाज: Information Society समाज जो अपने परिवेश के विकास से अवगत है।

सूची: Catalogue पुस्तकालय प्रलेखों के प्रयोग के लिए बनी प्रविष्टियों की सूची है।

सूची: List वस्तुओं का आवश्यकतानुसार अंकित विवरण।

सूचीकरण विभाग: Cataloguing Department पुस्तकालय का विभाग जहाँ सूचीकरण का कार्य होता है।

सूचीकरण नियम: Cataloguing Rules *देखिए* सूचीकरण संहिता।

सूचीकरण तकनीक: Cataloguing Technique नियमानुसार सूचीकरण

प्रकार।

सूचीकारः Cataloguer व्यक्ति जो सूचीकरण सिद्धान्तों के अनुसार प्रलेखों की प्रविष्टि उपलब्ध कराता है।

सूची पेटियाः Catalogue Cabinet देखिए पत्र पेटिका।

सूचीकरणः Cataloguing पुस्तकालय सूची बनाने के क्रिया।

सूची इकाई पत्र प्रणालीः Unit Card System of Catalogue मुख्य प्रविष्टि से प्रतिलिपि प्राप्त कर शीर्षक प्रदान कर अतिरिक्त प्रविष्टि आवश्यकतानुसार प्राप्त की जाती है।

सूची-पत्रः Catalogue Card यह मोटे कागज का सफेद लाइनदार अथवा बिना लाइन का 5" X 3" का मानक पत्र होता है जिसको प्रलेख की प्रविशिष्ट अंकित कर सूची में आवद्ध किया जाता है।

सूची प्रकारः Forms of Catalogue सूची को अनेक प्रकारों में उसके आन्तरिक तथा वाह्य गुणों के आधार पर विभक्त किया जा सकता है।

सूची संहिताः Catalogue Code पुस्तकालय सूचीकरण से सम्बन्धित नियम उपनियमों का संकलन।

सुक्ष्म प्रलेखः Micro Document विषय सम्बन्धी विचार जो किसी पत्रिका/पत्र में प्रकाशित होते हैं अथवा विषय से सम्बन्धित छोटी रचना *और देखिए* सूक्ष्म विचार।

सूत्रः Formula निश्चित निर्देश।

सेटेलाइट सम्प्रेषणः Setellite Communication यह मुख्य रूप से उपग्रह विकास कार्यक्रम द्वारा सम्प्रेषण तकनीक विकास का वरदान है।

सेवाः Service क्रिया जिससे पुस्तकालय की सूचना उपलब्ध करायी जाती है।

सेवा निवृत्तिः Superannuation अवधि जिस पर कर्मचारी नियमानुसार कार्य तथा वेतन भुगतान से मुक्त कर दिया जाय।

सेवावधि प्रशिक्षणः In-service Training प्रशिक्षण जिसकी अवधि सामान्य सेवा काल के अर्न्तगत होती है।

संकलनः Assortment विषय को निश्चित गुणों के आधार पर इच्छित क्रम में रखने की क्रिया है।

संकलन अभिलक्षणः Assortment Characteristic अभिलक्षण जिनके आधार पर वर्ग पहचान की जाती है।

संकेतकः Indicator कम्प्यूटर प्रयुक्त उपकरण युक्ति जिससे कार्य स्थान का बोध होता है।

संकेत चिन्हः Inverted Comma चिन्ह जिसके प्रयोग से शब्द/वाक्य की अलग पहचान बन जाती है।

संकाय पुस्तकालयः Faculty Library पुस्तकालय जिसका प्रयोग संकाय करता है।

सांकेतिक अंकः Indicator Digit चिन्ह जिसका प्रयोग अंक की विशेष पहचान के लिए होता है।

संख्या युक्त प्रतिः Numbered Copy प्रति जिसका प्रत्येक पृष्ठ अंकित होता है अथवा विशेष प्रयोजन से संख्या प्रदान कर दी जाय।

संख्यायुक्त प्रविष्टिः Numbered Entry प्रविष्टि को प्रयोग सुविधा के लिए क्रम संख्या प्रदान कर दी जाय।

सांकेतिक सारः Indicative Abstract सार जिससे ग्रन्थ में सम्बन्धित सूचना के होने भर का संकेत मिलता हो तथा पठनीय प्रलेख चुनाव में सहायता मिलती है।

संख्याः Number गणितीय पहचान जिसके मूल्य निश्चित होते है।

संख्यात्मकः Ordinal Name वर्ग की वर्गीकरण प्रणाली के अनुसार वर्ग संख्या।

संख्या शीर्षक: Title in Facet Numbers वर्गीकरण प्रक्रिया में शब्द से अंक में परिवर्तन प्राप्त शीर्षक।

संग्रह: Input/Additions/ Acquisitions पुस्तकालय में प्राप्त सूचना सकंलन।

संकलन: Collection पुस्तकालय संचित प्रलेख/सूचना।

संकलन संख्या: Collection Number संख्या जिसका प्रयोग संग्रह की गणना व्यक्त करता है।

संग्रहालय: Museum दुर्लभ सांस्कृतिक धरोहर को भविष्य तथा वर्तमान की शोध परक आवश्यकताओं के लिए सुरक्षित रखने का स्थान।

संग्रहालय पुस्तकालय: Museum Library पुस्तकालय जो कि संग्रहालय के उद्देश्यों के अनुसार ऐतिहासिक अभिलेख उपलब्ध कराता है/सुरक्षित रखता है।

सग्रंह विकास: Collection Development देखिए संग्रह/संकलन।

संग्रह स्थल: Depository स्थान जहाँ वस्तुओं को संग्रहित/एकत्रित किया जाता है।

संचित अनुक्रमणिका: Cumulative Index अलग-2 उत्पन्न/प्रकाशित अनुक्रमणिकाओं के योग से अवधि विशेष के लिए बनाई जाती है।

संग्रह समाप्त पुस्तक: Out of Stock Book प्रकाशक तथा वितरक के पास अनुउपलब्ध पुस्तक।

संग्रह सूची: List of Additions अवधि विशेष में प्राप्त प्रलेखों की आवश्यकता क्रम में सूची।

संग्रह संख्या का प्रनियम: Canon of Collection Number प्रनियम की व्यवस्था के अनुसार प्रलेख की मौलिक विशेषता जैसे, दुर्लभता, अधिक उपयोगिता, विशेष आकार के आधार पर साथ-2 रखे जा सकें।

संग्रही पुस्तकालय: Depository Library पुस्तकालय जिसका संकलन कम प्रयुक्त पुस्तकों के स्थानान्तरण से उत्पन्न होता है।

संगीत पुस्तकालय: Music Library पुस्तकालय जिसके संकलन संगीत उपकरण होते हैं।

संचयन: Cumulation विभिन्न समयों में प्रकाशित सूचना का सयुंक्त प्रकाशन।

संदर्भ: Reference प्रलेख जिसमें सूचना का संकेत भर होता है अथवा कथन की प्रमाणिकता में उद्धृत कथन जिसका उल्लेख विवरण सहित रचना के अन्त में किया जाता है।

संदर्भ एवम् शोध पुस्तकालय: Reference and Research Library पुस्तकालय जहाँ विशेष विषय की चुनी हुई पुस्तकों का गहन प्रयोग होता है।

संदर्भ अनुक्रमाणिका प्रविष्टि: Cross Reference Index Entry प्रविष्टि जो समान अर्थ आमिव्यति को इगित करती है।

संदर्भ कार्य: Reference Work रचना जिसकी सहायता से संदर्भ सेवा प्रदान की जाती है।

संदर्भ कक्ष: Reference Room *देखिए* पठन कक्ष/अध्ययन कक्ष

संदर्भ संग्रह: Reference Collection प्रलेख जिनका प्रयोग पठन कक्ष में होता है।

संदर्भ विभाग: Reference Department पुस्तकालय विभाग जहाँ संदर्भ ग्रंथ प्रयोग होते हैं।

संदर्भ टिप्पण: Footnote टिप्पण जो विषय के स्पष्टीकरण अथवा पूर्वापर सम्बन्ध के लिए होता है।

संदर्भ प्रविष्टिः Cross Reference Entry प्रविष्टि जो विषय के अन्यत्र भी होने को व्यक्त करती है।

संदर्भ पुस्तकः Reference Book प्रामाणिक सूचना संग्रह जिसका साधारणतः पठन कक्ष में प्रयोग होता है।

संदर्भ पुस्तकालयः Reference Library पुस्तकालय जिसके प्रलेख प्रयोग के लिए बाहर नहीं दिये जाते।

संदर्भ पुस्तकालयाध्यक्षः Reference Librarian पुस्तकालयाध्यक्ष जो तत्काल सूचना प्रदान करता है।

संदर्भ प्रविष्टिः Reference Entry प्रविष्टि जो दूसरी प्रविष्टि की ओर इगित करती है। इस कार्य के लिए *देखिए/और देखिए* जैसे शब्दों का प्रयोग होता है।

संदर्भ स्रोतः Reference Resource सूचना प्राप्ति का माध्यम।

संदर्भ सेवाः Reference Service सेवा जिसमें प्रश्न का प्रतिउत्तर तत्काल प्रदान किया जाय।

संदिग्ध शीर्षकः Ambiguous Title शीर्षक जिसका विषय से सम्बन्ध न हो/भ्रम उत्पन्न करता हो।

संदेशः Message/Communication सूचना समूह जिसका उद्देश्य निश्चित होता है अथवा सूचना का दो केन्द्रों के बीच स्थानान्तरण।

संतुलित संग्रहः Balanced Collection निति परक किसी विषय पर उपलब्ध आवश्यक प्रलेखों का संकलन है।

संभरणः Feedback उपयोगी सूचना उपलब्ध कराने का प्रयास।

सम्पत्ति सूचीः Inventory यथा स्थान उपलब्ध संग्रहों की सूची।

सम्पादक संदर्भः Editor Reference सूची प्रविष्टि में सम्पादक के बारे में अंकित सूचना।

सम्पूर्ण स्थानः Absolute Location देखिए निश्चित स्थान।

सम्पूर्ण आकारः Absolute Size देखिए उचित आकार।

सम्पादकः Editor व्यक्ति जो रचना को प्रकाशन के लिए तैयार करता है तथा रचना उसकी नहीं होती है।

सम्पादनः Editing प्रकाशन पूर्व की प्रक्रिया जिसमें विषय तालिका तथा अन्य प्रयासों से विषय को प्रभावोत्पादक बनाया जाता है।

सम्पूर्ण अंग सिद्धांतः Whole-organ Principle विषय का 'क' भाग यदि 'ख' का अंश है तो 'ख' क से पूर्व रहेगा।

सम्पूर्ण कपडा जिल्दः Full Cloth Binding पुस्तक का सुरक्षा आवरण कपड़े का बनाया जाय।

सम्पूर्ण चमड़ा जिल्दः Full Leather Binding पुस्तक का सुरक्षा आवरण चमड़े से मढ़ा/ठका जाय।

सम्बद्ध महाविद्यालयः Affiliated College विश्वविद्यालय से जुड़े हुए महाविद्यालय जो विश्वविद्यालय के निर्धारित सत्र तथा नियमों का पालन करते हैं।

सम्बद्धक विश्वविद्यालयः Affiliating University विश्वविद्यालय जिनका स्वरूप अनेक विद्यालयों/संकायों के योग से बनता है।

सयंमन का प्रनियमः Canon of Reticence वर्ग अभिव्यक्ति को प्रयुक्त शब्द सरल होने चाहिए।

संयुक्त अनुक्रमाणिका प्रविष्टिः Joint Index Entry सहयोगी लेखक के लिए बनाई गई प्रविष्टि।

संयुक्त लेखकः Joint Author व्यक्ति/समूह/संस्था रचना के लिए इकाई रूप में उत्तरदायी हो तथा अंश के लिए रचनाकार

उत्तरदायी होते हुए भी सम्पूर्ण रचना से अलग नहीं किया जा सके।

संयुक्त लेखक प्रविष्टि: Joint author Entry सहयोगी लेखक का नाम प्रविष्टि की प्रथम पंक्ति में अंकित हो।

संयुक्त प्रविष्टि: Joint Entry जब दो या दो से अधिक प्रविष्टि एक प्रविष्टि में समाहित कर दी जाय।

संयुक्त पुस्तक: Composite Book जब दो या दो से अधिक स्वतन्त्र रचनाओं को एक आवरण में आवद्ध कर दिया जाय।

संयुक्त सूची: Joint Catalogue दो या अधिक पुस्तकालयों की प्रविष्टियों की सामूहिक सूची।

संयुक्त समिति: Joint Committee समिति जिसमें अनेक पुस्तकालयों के प्रतिनिधि होते है।

संयुक्त सलाहाकार समिति: Joint Consultative Committee *देखिए* संयुक्त समिति।

संयुक्त सम्पादक: Joint Editor सम्पादक का समस्तर सहयोगी सम्पादक।

संयुक्त सूची: Union Catalogue एक से अधिक पुस्तकालय संकलनों की सूची जिसकी प्रत्येक प्रविष्टि के साथ ग्रन्थ रखने वाले पुस्तकालय का संकेत होता है।

संयोजक: Compiler व्यक्ति जो विभिन्न स्रोतों से प्राप्त सूचना को उपयोगी क्रम मे रखता है।

संयोजन: Consolidation छोटी इकाई के योग से समूह बनाना।

संयोजी चिन्ह: Connecting Symbol चिन्ह जिनका प्रयोग वर्ग सम्बन्ध बनाने में होता है।

संरक्षक: Patron/Trustee व्यक्ति जो संरक्षक मण्डल का सदस्य हो।

संरक्षक मण्डल: Board of Trustees विश्वस्त व्यक्ति समूह जो पुस्तकालय व्यवस्था सहयोग सम्बन्धी नीति निर्धारण करता है।

संरक्षण: Preservation वस्तुओं को सुरक्षित रखने की व्यवस्था।

संश्लेषित शीर्षक: Synthesised Title सार रूप/मूल विचारों से रचित शीर्षक।

संशोधन: Edit सूचना को नियमित कर व्यवस्था देना।

संशोधित संस्करण: Revised Edition पहले संस्करण का परिस्कृत विकसित प्रकाशन।

संस्था: Agency स्वायत्त निकाय होता है जिस की स्थापना सरकार अथवा व्यक्ति समूह करता है। जिसका उद्देश्य विकास के कार्यक्रम संचालन होता है।

संस्थागत पुस्तकालय: Institutional Library पुस्तकालय जिसके कार्यकलाप का क्षेत्र किसी संस्था की आवश्यकताऐं होता है।

संस्था सदस्यता: Institutional Membership सदस्यता जिससे संस्था के साधनों के प्रयोग में भागीदारी प्राप्त होती है।

संस्करण: Edition पहली बार एक साथ प्रकाशित प्रतियाँ।

संस्करण विवरण: Edition Statement पुस्तकालय सूची पत्र में सस्करण के बारे में स्थान, समय आदि की सूचना अंकित होती है।

संसाधन: Processing पुस्तकालय ग्रन्थ प्राप्ति से प्रयोग तक की तैयारी सम्बन्धी सभी क्रियाएँ।

संसाधन सहयोग: Resource Sharing एक से अधिक पुस्तकालयों द्वारा उपलब्ध संकलन, सेवा तथा तकनीकी ज्ञान का प्रयोग सहयोग से किया जाय।

सांख्यिकी आंकड़ा: Statistical Data संख्यात्मक सूचना।

संहिताः Code निर्देश समूह जो प्रणाली प्रयोग को स्पष्ट करते हैं।

संहिता कोशः Code Dictionary सारांश रूप में प्रायुक्त शब्दों/संकेतों का समूह जो कि सारांश पत्र अथवा रचनाओं में साधारणतः व्यवहृत होते हैं।

संक्षिप्तिकरणः Annotation सूची प्रविष्टि के साथ रचना का सार/मूल्याकंन कारक शब्दों का संकलन मात्र।

संक्षेपित नामः Abbreviated Name उच्चारण सुविधा अथवा भाषा स्वीकृति के अनुसार नाम के किसी भाग/पूर्णनाम को ही संक्षिप्त कर दिया जाता है। जैसे राम किशन शर्मा को रा. कि. शर्मा कहा जाए।

संक्षिप्त संस्करणः Abridged Edition मुख्य संस्करण से सारांश लेकर रचित नया संस्करण।

संक्षेपित सूची पत्रः Abbreviated Catalogue Card सूची पत्र जिसमें मुख्य प्रविष्टि की अपेक्षा चुनी हुई सूचना का समावेश हो।

संक्षेपित सूची प्रविष्टिः Abbreviated Catalogue Card देखिए संक्षेपित सूची पत्र।

संक्षेपणः Abridgement किसी विषय का छोटा रूप जिसमें आवश्यक विचारों को प्रधानता देते हुए कम आवश्यक/अनावश्यक अंशों को छोड़ दिया जाता है।

संक्षेप/सारः Abstract रचना के मूल विचार।

संक्षेपकार/सारकर्त्ताः Abstractor व्यक्ति जो रचना से मूल विचार संकलित कर सार उत्पन्न करता है।

ह

हाशियाः Margin पृष्ठ के लिखित भाग के चारों तरफ का खाली भाग।

हाशिया टिप्पणः Marginal Note पृष्ठ के दाहिनी तथा बायें ओर खाली स्थान पर अंकित टिप्पण।

हस्तलिखित ग्रन्थः Manuscript ग्रन्थ जिसको व्यक्ति द्वारा हाथ से लिखा गया हो।

हस्तलिखित ग्रन्थ सूचीः Manuscript Catalogue सूची जिसमें मात्र हस्तलिखित ग्रन्थों को सूचना को सम्मिलित किया गया हो।

हाई ब्रिड कम्प्यूटरः Hybrid Computer डिजिटल तथा एनोलॉग कम्प्यूटर के योग से बना कम्प्यूटर है।

हार्डवेयरः Hardware कम्प्यूटर प्रणाली प्रयुक्त मशीनी उपकरण।

हास्य नकलः Parody विषय को सादृश्य सहायता से नकल रूप में प्रस्तुत किया जाय।

ह्रासमान विस्तार का प्रनियमः Canon of Decreasing Extension वर्ग शृंखला क्रम में प्रथम पंक्ति से अन्तिम पंक्ति तक विषय विस्तार कम तथा सधनता अधिक होती जाती है।

हीगल वर्गीकरणः Hegel Classification 1872 में हीगल द्वारा उत्पन्न वर्गीकरण प्रणाली।

क्ष

क्षतिग्रस्त-पुस्तकः Damaged Book पुस्तक जो अधिक प्रयोग आदि के कारण फट जाती है और उपयोग योग्य नहीं रहती।

क्षेत्र तालिकाः Area Table तालिका जिसमें क्षेत्र को व्यक्त करने वाले अंकन को सूचीबद्ध किया जाता है।

क्षेत्र अंकनः Sector Notation वर्गीकरण में प्रयुक्त अंकन जब अन्तिम अंक से समानान्तर वर्ग व्यक्त करने को विशेष प्रयोग होता है।

क्षेत्रीय पुस्तकालयः Regional Library पुस्तकालय जिससे क्षेत्रीय आवश्यकता पूरी होती है।

क्षेत्र युक्तिः Sector Device युक्ति जिसमें प्रयुक्त अंक समूह समानान्तर वर्ग को व्यक्त करता है तथा एक अंक के समान जाना जाता है।

त्र

त्रय मासिक पत्रिकाः Quarterly Journal प्रकाशन जिसका अंक तीन माह के अन्तर से अथवा साल में चार अंकों मे प्रकाशित होती है।

ज्ञ

ज्ञात अभिलेख/प्रलेखः Known Document प्रयोक्ता को ग्रन्थ के लेखक प्रकाशक/मूल विचारों के बारे में पूर्व सूचना होती है।

ज्ञानः Knowledge *देखिए* सूचना।

ज्ञान जगतः Universe of Knowledge सम्पूर्ण ज्ञान।

ज्ञानवर्गः Knowledge Class वर्गीकरण प्रणाली में का वर्ग अन्य वर्गों के साथ।

ज्ञान वर्गीकरणः Knowledge Classification सम्पूर्ण ज्ञान जगत को विशेषताओं के आधार पर वर्गों में विभक्त करने की क्रिया।

श्र

श्रेणीः Category वर्गीकरण प्राप्त भाग।

श्रेष्ठ पुस्तकः Best Book विषय की अन्य पुस्तकों से तुलतात्मकता में अधिक गुणों वाली पुस्तक।

शृंखला : Chain वर्ग के कमिक विभाजन से प्राप्त उपवर्गो की सारिणी है।

शृंखला अनुक्रमाणिकरणः Chain Indexing वर्ग संख्या में प्राप्त अंकन के आधार पर प्राप्त विषय-शब्दों से अनुक्रमाणिका बनाने की क्रिया।

शृंखला का क्रमः Order of a Chain कड़ी का शृंखला में क्रम।

शृंखला प्रक्रियाः Chain Procedure विधि जिसमें वर्ग संख्या से क्रमशः विषय व्यंजक शब्द प्राप्त किए जाते हैं।

शृंखला समायोजनः Hospitality in Chain सहयोगी क्रम के वर्गों में अन्य उत्पन्न सहयोगी क्रम वर्ग को स्वीकार करने की व्यवस्था।

शृंखला समायोजन प्रनियमः Canon of Hospitality in Chain सह वर्ग निर्माण प्रक्रिया में अन्त तक उत्पन्न सहवर्ग को वर्गीकरण प्रणाली में स्थान मिलना चाहिए तथा इसके लिए पूर्वक्रम में कोई परिवर्तन न करना पड़े।

श्रव्य-दृश्यः Audio-visual तकनीकी उपादान जिनके द्वारा वास्तविक ध्वनि तथा चित्र एक तथा दोंनो को आवश्यकतानुसार सुना तथा देखा जाता है।

श्रव्य-दृश्य साधनः Audio-Visual Equipment तकनीकी उपकरण जिसकी सहायता से इलैक्ट्रोनिक माध्यम पर उपलब्ध सूचना का प्रयोग होता है।

श्रव्य-दृश्य सम्प्रेषणः Audio-visual Communication दृश्य-श्रव्य संकेत सम्प्रेषण प्रकार।

श्रव्य-दृश्य शिक्षाः Audio-visual Education दृश्य-श्रव्य तकनीक का प्रयोग शिक्षा कार्यक्रम के लिए हो।

श्रव्य-दृश्य यंन्त्रः Audio-visual Apparatus *देखिए* श्रव्य-दृश्य साधन।

ऋण प्रदाय विभागः Lending Library *देखिए* आदान-प्रदान विभाग।